Norton Internet ~~Security~~
For Dumm~~ies~~

MW01014381

Top Internet Security Threats

Home and small business users don't always face the most complex and exotic attack threats. Here are some everyday vulnerabilities you need to watch out for:

1. E-mail attachments containing viruses.
2. E-mail or phone messages that seek to fool you into giving out passwords or other private information.
3. Your children registering for Web services and giving out information you want to keep private.
4. Spyware that advertisers place on your computer without your knowledge in order to track you.
5. Passwords that can be easily cracked, or that are missing.
6. Trojan horses or other malicious code operating system vulnerabilities that you fail to patch.
7. Passersby who notice passwords affixed to monitors or who look over your shoulder while you enter passwords.
8. Disgruntled employees or family members who try steal information
9. Attempts to send you malformed packets to try to bypass your firewall.
10. Malicious code contained in software or other files you download.

Security Tips Checklist

❏ Run Windows Update
❏ Scan for viruses
❏ Designate "private" information that Norton Internet Security will not give out
❏ Change your passwords periodically
❏ Review the event logs
❏ Pay attention to what your children do online
❏ Create strong passwords and store them safely
❏ Opt out of mailings and marketing efforts when you register or make a purchase online
❏ Run LiveUpdate to keep your virus and intrusion information up to date
❏ Use passwords and locks to protect your portable computing devices

Performing Common Security Tasks

Remembering what function each NIS component performs and where to find commands and options can be hard. Here are some suggestions. All steps begin with the main NIS window open.

To Perform This Task	Do This
Create a firewall rule or review existing rules	Double-click Personal Firewall; click Advanced.
Run a security check on your computer	Double-click Security
Add a Web site to your child's list of restricted or permitted sites	Double-click Parental Control, choose the child's account name, click Sites, click Add, type URL.
Instantly stop all network traffic in case you are being attacked	Right-click the System Tray, choose Block Traffic.
Create a new user account	Click User Accounts, click Create Account, type account name and password.
Block or permit content on a per-site basis	Double-click Privacy Control, click Advanced, click the site's name, and change options.

For Dummies: Bestselling Book Series for Beginners

Norton Internet Security For Dummies®

Cheat Sheet

Port numbers you should know

Whether you're reviewing detailed alert messages or log files, you'll see references to ports: virtual channels through which information can pass. Which ports are useful and which should be blocked? Two lists follow. Add your own additions in the blank spaces at the bottom.

Ports to allow: Ports used by common Internet services

Service	Protocol	Port
Web	HTTP	80
Secure Web	S-HTTP	443
E-mail (incoming)	POP3	110
E-mail (outgoing)	SMTP	25
Proxy server	various	8080, 8000, 8100, 8120
News	NNTP	
MSN Messenger	MSNP7	1863
AOL Instant Messenger	OSCAR, TOC	5190
RealAudio	RTSP	7070
Windows Media Player	MMS	1755
_____	_____	_____
_____	_____	_____

Ports to block: Port numbers used by common Trojans and viruses

Trojan	Port
MyDoom.B, F, G, H	1980
Beagle.C through Beagle.K	2745
MyDoom.A	3127
MyDoom.B	3128
Sasser.C through Sasser.F	5554
Beagle.B	8866
MyDoom.B	10080
NetBus	12345
SubSeven	27374
Back Orifice	54321
_____	_____
_____	_____
_____	_____

For Dummies: Bestselling Book Series for Beginners

Norton Internet Security™

FOR

DUMMIES®

by Greg Holden

WILEY

Wiley Publishing, Inc.

Norton Internet Security™ **For Dummies**®

Published by
Wiley Publishing, Inc.
111 River Street
Hoboken, NJ 07030-5774

WILEY

About the Author

A computer geek back in the days when most of his fellow newspaper reporters were still pounding away on typewriters, Holden was excited by the World Wide Web in its early days and has been devoted to it ever since. It was writing about the Internet that allowed him to leave the confining cubicle of his nine-to-five editorial job at the University of Chicago and form his own company called Stylus Media, which is a group of editorial, design, and computer professionals who produce both print and electronic publications. (The company gets its name from a recording stylus that reads the traces left on a disk by voices or instruments and translates those signals into electronic data that can be amplified and enjoyed by many.) But he is aware that power can be used for evil as well as for good, and many of his more than 25 books have focused about security topics that have helped nontechnical users surf the Web and communicate safely. He has also written articles for publications that include *CNET, Forbes, PC World*, and *Computer User.*

Greg balances his technical expertise and his entrepreneurial experience with his love of literature. He received an M.A. in English from the University of Illinois at Chicago and also writes general interest books, short stories, and poetry. Among his editing assignments is the monthly newsletter for his daughters' grade school.

Greg loves to travel, but since his two daughters were born, he hasn't been able to get around much. However, through the Web, he enjoys traveling vicariously and meeting people online. He lives with his family in an old house in Chicago that he has been rehabbing for — well, for many years now. He is a collector of objects such as pens, cameras, radios, and hats. He is always looking for things to take apart so that he can see how they work and fix them up. Many of the same skills prove useful in creating and maintaining Web pages. He is an active member of Jewel Heart, a Tibetan Buddhist meditation and study group based in Ann Arbor, Michigan.

Dedication

To my extended family in my household, my neighborhood, and my spiritual community, all of whom keep me secure and safe and make sure my life runs smoothly.

Author's Acknowledgments

One of the things I like best about this book is that it's a teaching tool that gives me a chance to share my knowledge about security on the Internet, and to explain Norton Internet Security to a wide audience of people who might be intimidated by things like firewalls and intrusion detection software.

I would also like to acknowledge some of my own colleagues who helped me prepare this book and who have supported and encouraged me in other lessons of life. These include Neil Salkind and David and Sherry Rogelberg of Studio B, and Ann Lindner, whose teaching experience proved invaluable in suggesting ways to make the text more clear.

For editing and technical assignments, I was lucky to be in the capable hands of the folks at Wiley Publishing: my acquisitions editor Tom Heine, project editor and copy editor Christine Berman, and technical editor Peter Davis.

Last but certainly not least, the future is in the hands of the generation of my two daughters, Zosia and Lucy, who taught me a lot about the need to use the Internet safely and the wonders it can bring to young lives.

Publisher's Acknowledgments

We're proud of this book; please send us your comments through our online registration form located at www.dummies.com/register/.

Some of the people who helped bring this book to market include the following:

Acquisitions, Editorial, and Media Development

Project Editor: Christine Berman

Acquisitions Editor: Tom Heine

Copy Editor: Christine Berman

Technical Editor: Peter Davis

Editorial Manager: Robyn Siesky

Media Development Supervisor: Richard Graves

Editorial Assistant: Adrienne Porter

Cartoons: Rich Tennant (www.the5thwave.com)

Production

Project Coordinator: Maridee Ennis

Layout and Graphics: Kelly Emkow, Lauren Goddard, Michael Kruzil, Joyce Haughey, Stephanie D. Jumper, Lynsey Osborn, Melanee Prendergast, Jacque Roth

Proofreaders: Susan Moritz, Joe Niesen, Charles Spencer, TECHBOOKS Production Services

Indexer: TECHBOOKS Production Services

Publishing and Editorial for Technology Dummies

Richard Swadley, Vice President and Executive Group Publisher

Andy Cummings, Vice President and Publisher

Mary Bednarek, Executive Editorial Director

Mary C. Corder, Editorial Director

Publishing for Consumer Dummies

Diane Graves Steele, Vice President and Publisher

Joyce Pepple, Acquisitions Director

Composition Services

Gerry Fahey, Vice President of Production Services

Debbie Stailey, Director of Composition Services

Contents at a Glance

Table of Contents

Introduction

· ·

*P*ersonal firewall and anti-virus programs are among the most important applications you can have on your computer. In terms of usefulness, they rank alongside Web browsers and e-mail software. But security programs are often overlooked and maligned. Security programs are overlooked because you tend to take notice of them only when you have a problem. If security programs are doing their job and protecting your computer and the information on it, they go unnoticed. They're like the security guards who stand off to the side in a bank or retail store: They only attract attention when someone tries to break in or take something they shouldn't. Only then do you realize how important they are.

A *firewall* is hardware or software that monitors a computer network, allowing authorized traffic to enter the network and blocking unauthorized connection attempts. When you first install them, firewalls seem to do the opposite of what you want. You want to surf the Web, get e-mail, and exchange instant messages; you want to run animations and let Java applets make Web sites come alive with sound, video, and other interactive features.

But firewalls seem only to be interested in throwing up roadblocks that delay your fun. One alert message after another appears, notifying you of an inbound or outbound connection. The messages you see refer to strange-sounding things like packets, IP addresses, and ports. Instead of surfing at will, you have to make a series of decisions. Firewalls, anti-virus programs, and other applications that control access to and from your computer can be complex to configure and maintain. Luckily, Norton Internet Security (NIS) isn't one of those programs. NIS is easy to use — and it's effective, too.

Yes, Virginia, You Can Find Safety and Privacy Online

If you pay attention to the news, you get the impression that the Internet is plagued by a never-ending series of viruses and other harmful software, plus attacks by hackers who are able to break into the Web sites operated by banks and other prominent commercial entities. For every kind of security threat, Norton Internet Security has a defense. NIS is popular because it isn't just a single program but a suite of security applications. The anti-virus and firewall functions everyone needs are covered in a single package, plus some extras like the ability to block annoying pop-up ads and spam e-mail messages, and control the Web sites your children can and can't visit.

Norton Internet Security is feature-rich and complex enough to require a single book to explain all of its configuration options, and at the same time user-friendly enough to attract an estimated 1.2 million users. This book explains how to get the most out of Norton Internet Security. You find out how to manipulate the program's settings to optimize performance. I also explain how to respond to alerts, make choices about which traffic to block or allow, and how to customize access control for family members or employees who share the same network resources.

How to Use This Book

This book enables you to skip around to the sections that meet your immediate concerns with Norton Internet Security. Feel free to skip back and forth to chapters that interest you. I've made this book into an easy-to-use reference tool that you will be comfortable with, no matter what your level of experience with computers and the Internet. You don't have to scour each chapter methodically from beginning to end to find what you want. The Net doesn't work that way and this book doesn't, either!

Crazy Assumptions This Book Makes About You

Norton Internet Security is the perfect application for home and small business users who have DSL, cable modem, or other high-speed connections to the Internet and who want to protect their networks while not having to purchase special hardware. But that covers a large group of potential readers. Who is this book for, really?

This book is directed at beginning- to intermediate-level computer users. It assumes that you have experience with computers and the Internet, but need help getting connected to the Internet or setting up a small-scale network. You want to figure out how your new firewall, anti-virus, ad blocking, spam stopping, or childproofing set of programs really works. You know how to surf the Web, but aren't up to speed on all its underpinnings, including IP addresses, ports, and protocols. You need simple, easy-to-digest instructions on how to trace attackers and read event logs without feeling overwhelmed. As long as you have a computer and a modem and a little bit of technical know-how, this book will provide you with all the user-friendly instructions you need.

How This Book Is Organized

This book is divided into seven parts. Here are the parts of the book and what they contain:

Part I: Creating Your Own Homeland Security

Part I focuses on one of the fundamental security functions performed by Norton Internet Security: its firewall component, Norton Personal Firewall. You discover how to optimize your computer to run the firewall, how to configure it, and how to optimize it for your needs.

In Chapter 1, you get an introductory overview of what NIS does. You find out about the kinds of attackers and attacks you need to guard against. Chapter 2 gives you instructions on how to install the program, which isn't as easy as it sounds with the addition of an "activation" step. Chapter 3 covers how to interpret the alert messages the firewall sends you, and how to use the messages to create the rules by which the firewall will operate. Chapter 4 helps you take charge of your firewall and use it to trace intrusion attempts.

Part II: Handling Viruses and Malicious Code

Part II of the book addresses the other fundamental security tasks performed by NIS: detecting and removing viruses from your computer. In Chapter 5, you find out about the different types of viruses you need to block. In Chapter 6, you discover that there are other programs you can receive from the Internet that compromise your privacy, such as spyware and keystroke loggers.

A firewall and anti-virus tool is only as good as it is fresh. The software needs to have the latest information about intrusion methods and viruses so it can recognize and block them. Chapter 7 instructs you on the important process of keeping your security software current with LiveUpdate. Chapter 8 tells you how to get control over the malicious files that are stored in the special area known as Quarantine.

Part III: Safeguarding Your Privacy and Your Network

One thing that sets Norton Internet Security apart from other security applications is the attention given to the many privacy intrusions that come from the Internet and that have nothing to do with viruses and hackers. Many originate from advertisers and marketers who want to place products in front of the eyes of as many Internet users as possible, whether or not those users expect to see them or want to know about them. Others come in over wireless networks and make laptops particularly vulnerable.

Chapter 9 examines how NIS helps reduce unsolicited commercial e-mail, otherwise known as spam. The chapter covers not only NIS's own spam blocker, but how to manage your e-mail accounts in a way that reduces spam. Chapter 10 discusses how to configure Ad Blocking, NIS's component for blocking pop-up ads. Chapter 11 looks at privacy invasions from a different angle, examining wireless security weaknesses and suggesting ways to make your cellphone, PDA, or laptop more secure.

Part IV: Access Control

Norton Internet Security has the capability of protecting not only single computers, but all of the computers on a network that shares the same Internet connection. It can also protect not only single users on one computer, but multiple individuals who use the same machine.

In Chapter 12, you find out how to use NIS to protect one user's files from another user — to set up passwords and customized settings that keep someone from reading someone else's e-mail, for example. Chapter 13 looks at Norton Parental Controls, a component of the home edition of Norton Internet Security, which gives parents the ability to set up a list of prohibited Web sites and applications.

Part V: Getting Under the Hood

Part V focuses on troubleshooting, which occurs in connection with startup, network communications, and finding online help. Chapter 14 looks at performance issues that keep NIS from functioning effectively. Chapter 15 suggests ways to keep your computer functioning smoothly in case you lose data or your Internet connection is broken. Chapter 16 delves into the advanced aspects of working with Norton Internet Security, such as the log files accumulated by the firewall.

Part VI: The Part of Tens

Filled with tips, cautions, suggestions, and examples, the Part of Tens presents many kinds of information that will help you improve network security. Chapter 18 identifies a range of common attacks that you need to guard against. Chapter 19 suggests ten other security applications you can use to boost your overall level of security.

Part VII: Appendixes

The book's two appendixes provide supplementary information about security issues and point you to places on the Internet where you can keep abreast of the latest attacks and threats. Appendix A presents you with a set of security terms that help you interpret alert messages, log file entries, and Web site references. Appendix B directs you to locations on the Internet that can help you be smarter about security in general, and can help you trace attacks as well.

Conventions Used in This Book

I've written most of this book with Windows XP users in mind. But, because PCs are so widespread, most of the examples and instructions address Windows 2000, ME, and 98 users, too.

Important bits of information are formatted in special ways in this book to make sure you notice them right away. Here they are:

"In This Chapter" lists: They represent a kind of table of contents in miniature. They tell you the topics covered in that chapter.

Numbered lists: When you see a numbered list, you should follow the steps in a specific order.

Bulleted lists: Bulleted lists, however, indicate things that you can do in any order or include special descriptive information.

Web addresses: When I describe activities or sites of interest on the World Wide Web, I include the address or Uniform Resource Locator (URL) in a special typeface often like this: `http://www.wiley.com/`.

Keep in mind that the newer versions of popular Web browsers, such as Netscape Navigator and Microsoft Internet Explorer, don't require you to enter the entire URL. For example, if you want to connect to the Wiley Publishing site mentioned in the preceding example, you can get there by simply entering the following in your browser's Go To box:

`www.wiley.com`

Don't be surprised if your browser can't find an Internet address you type, or if a Web page that is depicted in the book is no longer where I say it is. Although the sites were current when the book was written, Web addresses (and sites themselves) can be pretty fickle. Try looking for a missing site by using an Internet search engine. Or try shortening the address by deleting everything after the `.com` (or `.org` or `.edu`).

Icons Used in This Book

Norton Internet Security For Dummies also uses special graphical elements to get your attention. These are called icons. Here's what they look like and what they mean:

Points out some technical details that you may find to be of interest. A thorough understanding, however, is not a prerequisite to grasping the underlying concept that is being conveyed. Non-techies are welcome to skip this icon.

Flags practical advice about particular software programs or about issues of importance to e-businesses.

Points out potential pitfalls that can develop into more major problems if you're not careful.

 Alerts you to facts and figures that are important to keep in mind.

 Describes real-world incidents and facts that illustrate the need for security when you go online.

We're In It Together

Improving communication by making it safe for you to share information is the whole point of this book. My goal is to help you express yourself in the exciting new medium of the Internet while maintaining your privacy. So I hope that you'll let me know what you think about this book by contacting me. And remember to check out the *For Dummies* Web site at www.dummies.com.

You're welcome to contact me directly if you have questions or comments. Send e-mail to Greg Holden at greg@gregholden.com.

Part I
Creating Your Own Homeland Security

The 5th Wave
By Rich Tennant

© RICHTENNANT

"Amy surfs the web a lot, so for protection we installed several filtering programs that allow only approved sites through. Which of those nine sites are you looking at now, Amy?"

In this part . . .

Security is on everyone's mind these days, and with good reason. You depend on your government to handle security issues pertaining to what you and your fellow citizens call your homeland. The government monitors who comes into and out of the country and protects sensitive information, among other things.

You install locks on the doors and windows in your home and you have the option of installing an alarm system as well. Such devices take care of your home's physical openings. But what about the other openings into and out of your domain — the wires that connect your computers to the Internet or to one another? Thieves can use these openings to get their hands on your financial information, your files, and even your personal identity.

This part tells you how to install and begin using Norton Internet Security to protect not only your home but your small business network as well. You find out how to prepare your computer, install the software, and configure it to fit the needs of your computers and the people who use them.

Chapter 1

Preparing Your Online Security Blanket

In This Chapter

▶ Uncovering how Norton components work

▶ Understanding who hackers are and what they want

▶ Recognizing common attacks at home and work

▶ Preparing your computer for security applications

▶ Setting up good privacy strategies

*T*he term *security* isn't one that leaps to mind when you think about the Internet. You don't connect to the Internet to be secure, after all. You connect in order to learn, to explore, to be entertained. The first thing you think about when you go online is getting your e-mail or visiting a Web site. Chances are you only think about security when something goes wrong — or when you are made aware of one of the many threats to your privacy and security that you face from the Internet. You may have purchased this book because your computer has been infected with a virus, or because someone has mentioned that, along with your fast new cable modem or Digital Subscriber Line (DSL), you need to have something called a "firewall" or something called "anti-virus software."

No matter what your level of experience with viruses, hackers, and spyware, this book will help you defend yourself against them with the help of a powerful and user-friendly suite of software programs called Norton Internet Security (NIS). This chapter gives you an overview of the program and how to take advantage of its many features. You also find out how to prepare your computer by making use of the resources on the Symantec.com Web site.

To find out more about Norton Internet Security or Norton Internet Security Professional, go to the Symantec Products and Services page (www.symantec.com/product) and select the product you're interested in from the drop-down list near the top of the page. You'll go to a page with more specific details about the package you chose and links to a trial version you can download or a version you can purchase online.

Making the Case for Norton Internet Security

Think about how it easy it is to connect to the Internet through your home network. Whether that network consists of a single computer or two or more machines, after you do the initial setup you have no problem downloading software, reading your e-mail, or even listening to Internet radio. The problem is that it's just as easy for technically adept individuals who like to break into remote systems — hackers — to connect to your computer, too, unless you install software like Norton Internet Security, or other security hardware or software.

Norton Internet Security is a suite of software programs, each of which provides a different kind of protection. It's especially designed for home and small business users who need to access the Internet securely. The following sections give you a quick overview of the various component programs and what they do.

Erecting a firewall

A *firewall* is an application that monitors and filters all the traffic going into and out of your connection to the Internet. That connection is commonly called a *gateway*. In the physical (that is, the real) world, a gateway may be nothing more interesting than a modem with a phone line or cable plugged into it. From the perspective of your computer, a gateway is the point at which information enters and leaves your network.

You may already have heard that a firewall is something you need when you get a high-speed connection to the Internet such as a cable modem or Digital Subscriber Line (DSL) connection. Firewalls *can* be complex to configure and maintain. The firewall that's part of Norton Internet Security, and that is called Norton Personal Firewall, automates many of the administrative tasks, however.

Monitoring and directing traffic with firewalls

Communication on the Internet is always a two-way street. When you connect to the Web site of the auction site eBay, for example, your computer and the Web site's servers communicate by exchanging segments of digital information called packets. First, your browser sends requests to the server in the form of one or more packets. The requests flow in the *outbound* direction from your computer. Then, the server responds by acknowledging the requests, and then sending images and text files from the Web site's servers to your computer so they can be displayed by your browser. Those files flow in the *inbound* direction to your computer. The exchange of messages is illustrated in Figure 1-1.

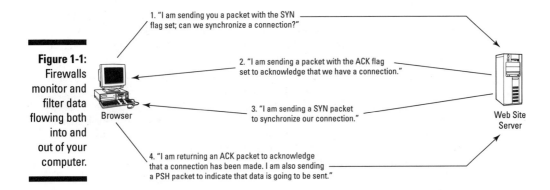

1. "I am sending you a packet with the SYN flag set; can we synchronize a connection?"

2. "I am sending a packet with the ACK flag set to acknowledge that we have a connection."

3. "I am sending a SYN packet to synchronize our connection."

4. "I am returning an ACK packet to acknowledge that a connection has been made. I am also sending a PSH packet to indicate that data is going to be sent."

Browser

Web Site Server

Two elements mentioned in Figure 1-1 bear explaining. A *packet* is a segment of digital information. Each packet can be broken into different sections, including a header and a data payload. Within the header, a number of different bits of information called *flags* signal to another computer on the network what is being requested. The flags are analyzed by programs such as Norton Personal Firewall in order to recognize and block known types of intrusions.

The fact that data packets flow in two directions between your computer and others on the Internet might seem obvious. But it's important to keep this in mind. When you begin to work with Norton Personal Firewall (a process described in Chapter 2), you'll be asked to set up a series of rules. Those rules determine how the firewall will respond to a particular type of data based on the direction in which it is going. Some rules can restrict information flowing in the inbound direction; others can restrict only outbound data going to a specific computer; other rules can block or allow information flowing in both directions.

Your computer's "secret" conversations

Another important thing to remember is that your computer continually carries on a series of packet exchanges with other computers on the Internet whether you're actually using the machine or not. When you have a connection that is always on, such as a DSL line, you can easily leave your computer connected to Web sites and go off and do other things. I, personally, like to listen to Internet radio. Many radio stations have the capability of sending their signal to listeners on the Internet in a process called *streaming*. I frequently leave the computer connected to a station and listen to it while I'm doing chores around the house. While I'm listening, my computer and the server that provides the data stream are in constant communication, checking with one another to make sure they are still there, to make sure the data is available, to verify that it is being received, and so on.

You may think you're doing a single thing on your computer, but in reality, a variety of different connections have been established or are underway. As I write this, my Web browser is connected to the popular Web site Google, and I'm listening to an Internet radio station. Those are only the obvious things going on. In fact, many more connections have been established, and the computer is listening for connections on virtual openings called ports (see the section "Port scans" for a more detailed explanation of these important network communications elements). In reality, my computer might be connected to an e-mail server and waiting for incoming mail, to another Web site, and to other computers on my home network.

Why worry about packets and all the "behind the scenes" communications your computer makes with others on the Internet? The point is this: These communications often occur in the background without your knowledge. Computers can try to connect to your computer while you are on the Internet and you have an Internet application running. Your computer is sending out responses that may or may not provide those remote computers (and their owners) with information about you and your network. Without a firewall, you don't have any control over such communication. *Hackers* — individuals who try to gain access to other computers on the Internet — can and will probe your computer for openings, and then try to exploit any openings they find. (See "Understanding Hackers," later in this chapter, for more information.) A firewall is essential for anyone who has an always-on connection to the Internet for precisely this reason: The firewall polices traffic in a way that you can't. It's like a sentry on duty, day and night.

Combating viruses

You may wonder why hackers try to connect to other computers they find on the Internet. Many reasons exist, but one is that they want to plant a type of virus called a *Trojan horse* (or other harmful program) on someone else's computer. Viruses come in many varieties and perform many different functions. But in general, they function in a way that's similar to the viruses that make you sick:

- ✔ **They contain segments of code that cause problems.** In the case of a human virus, the code is DNA. Computer codes are what make up computer viruses, and what cause those viruses to do harmful things.

- ✔ **They come in many different forms.** According to the Big Picture Book of Viruses (www.tulane.edu/~dmsander/Big_Virology/BVHomePage.html), there are human, fowl, equine, and many other viruses that affect living creatures. In the world of computing, the term "malware" is often used as a catchall term that includes variations such as viruses, worms, Trojan horses, and other harmful software programs.

✓ **They are difficult to detect and infiltrate without your knowledge.** Human viruses can only be seen with the aid of powerful microscopes. If you start sneezing or feeling bad, you can tell you have a virus. Computer viruses can get into your computer as files contained in software you download, or as attachments to e-mail messages that seem harmless. If your computer slows down or stops working, you can tell it has a virus.

✓ **They spread.** All viruses have the ability to move from one place to another and duplicate themselves so as to spread the infection. In one type of harmful program called a worm, this is the only function: Worms continue to multiply, consuming disk space and computing resources. Others duplicate by e-mailing themselves to other users whose addresses they find in Microsoft Outlook Express's address book, for example.

Viruses are among the most harmful security threats on the Internet, and anyone who goes online should have some form of virus protection. For whatever reason, a lot of people all over the world seem to take pleasure in phishing: sending e-mail messages to other people with attachments that contain viruses or other malicious programs. I regularly receive several such e-mail messages each week. The body of the message might say, "Your document is attached," "Look at this," or perhaps nothing at all. Anyone who clicks on the attachment to open it will unleash a virus or other program. And people unknowingly cause their own computers to be infected all the time by such means.

Norton AntiVirus takes the uncertainty out of receiving messages with suspicious attachments. It has the capability of recognizing attachments that are likely to contain harmful code; it can even scan the attachments and detect the viruses. It sends up alert messages, such as the one shown in Figure 1-2, before you even open up a message.

Figure 1-2:
Norton
AntiVirus
displays
alert
messages
the moment
a virus is
detected.

After identifying the virus, Norton AntiVirus takes steps to repair it (in other words, to change the code so that it doesn't cause any damage to your files or perform any unauthorized actions). If the file cannot be repaired, AntiVirus stores it in a special file called a quarantine area, where it cannot cause harm to your computer or the files within it.

Norton AntiVirus can protect your computer from viruses and other harmful programs such as worms, macros, and Trojan horses. But the program has to be periodically updated with new information about these programs so it can recognize new ones as hackers develop them. See Chapter 5 for more about how to use Norton AntiVirus.

Blocking unwanted content

Anything that consumes time, disk space, processing power, and browser "energy" detracts from your experience of the Internet. This isn't the way businesses that provide content and services on the Web think, however. They send you e-mail messages you didn't ask for, advertising products you don't necessarily want. They want to advertise other products and services, and frequently, they do so by causing browser windows to pop up (or under) the Web page you really want to see.

Popping Web page pop-ups

One of Norton Internet Security's most welcome features is its capability of preventing pop-up pages from appearing by means of a component called Ad Blocking. Ad Blocking not only stops banner ads and new browser windows from appearing, but stops Flash presentations and other intrusive content, too. It illustrates the fact that Norton Internet Security exists not only to block security but to improve your overall experience of the Internet, which includes giving you more control over what you see online.

See Chapter 6 to find out more about how to use Norton Internet Security to block ads as well as "spyware" and other programs that erode your privacy.

Throwing out spam

Norton Internet Security exists not only to make your experience on the Internet more secure, but more pleasant as well. One of the things that makes cyberspace unpleasant is the amount of unsolicited e-mail messages you receive. The number of messages circulated online appears to be steadily rising, despite legislation in the United States (specifically, the CAN-SPAM Act that's supposed to regulate it). One of Norton Internet Security's component programs, Norton AntiSpam, is designed to cut down on spam before it ever gets to your e-mail inbox. See Chapter 9 for more on AntiSpam, and "Adopting Effective Privacy Strategies," later in this chapter, for details about how you can provide extra control yourself.

Keeping your business secure

A survey conducted by the Business Software Alliance in 2003 found that two-thirds of corporate security professionals surveyed believe that they are likely to experience a major cyber-attack on their organization. However, only 78 percent of those security professionals believe their own organization is prepared to defend against such an attack.

Attacks can come from outside the corporate network. But in many cases, the real threat comes from within. Employees who have been fired or who have an axe to grind against the organization can cause substantially more harm than hackers on the other side of the world. The former employees know what resources the company holds, such as customers' credit card numbers or personal information, or proprietary information about products under development that their competitors might pay to own. They also know which computers hold the information. If the company has neglected to change passwords after the employees have left, they may be able to break in to those computers with virtually no technical expertise.

The 2003 Computer Crime and Security Survey conducted by the Computer Security Institute and the FBI reported that 56 percent of respondents experienced unauthorized use of their network computing resources. The total annual losses resulting from such intrusions amounted to more than $201 million. You can read more about the 2003 Computer Crime and Security Survey at www.gocsi.com/forms/fbi/pdf.jhtml.

Protecting your children

If you have kids, you already know how they love the Internet. It's an endless playground full of games, amusements, information, and ways to make friends. They take to it quickly and, before long, they know more about cyberspace than you do. The same ease of use and wealth of information can cause problems for both parents and children. Without your knowledge, your children may be exposed to violence, improper images, and other content that they shouldn't know about.

Through a Norton Internet Security component called Parental Control, you gain a measure of control over what your children can see and do online (at least, while they are in your house and using a computer on which Norton Internet Security has been installed). You can block Web sites that seem unsuitable, develop a list of "acceptable" Web sites, and get information about the sites your kids have visited while they are at the computer keyboard. Find out more in Chapter 13.

Understanding Hackers

Sometimes, protection begins with understanding — in the case of security on the Internet, that means understanding what the threat is, what those who threaten you want, and how they work. With some general knowledge at hand, you can take steps to anticipate trouble.

In general, the threats that come to you from the Internet are from hackers. A hacker is someone who is good with computers (though not necessarily a programmer). Such an individual uses any of a number of different ways to gain unauthorized access to computers. Reasons vary widely as to why hackers try to break in to remote systems, the way they attempt such break-ins, and what they hope to find. But with a little general knowledge about who is out there and what they might be after, you can be that much more effective in securing your computer.

"White Hat" hackers

The classic hacker, known as a "white hat," isn't necessarily out to do harm or even to steal files. He or she is primarily interested in breaking into systems under controlled conditions with the goal of improving security. (Another type of hacker, called a gray hat, does break-ins in order to discover how things work and open up any sources of knowledge that they can find — and claim credit for it.)

Some hackers (such as the ones who run the Hackers.com Web site (www. hackers.com) claim to be interested in instructing the public on the ethics of hacking. Unfortunately, such hackers make up only a small number of those who break into other people's computers. Some less benign variations on the hacker theme are explored below.

Script kiddies

As the name implies, script kiddies tend to be young, but that's not always the case; they're beginning hackers. Often, they are looking for a thrill in their spare time, and they use their knowledge of computers (or knowledge they have gleaned from various Web sites devoted to hacking) in order to gain control of remote systems. Some are computer programmers who spread viruses and other malicious scripts and use other techniques to exploit weaknesses in computer systems. Others are primarily interested in breaking into as many computer systems as possible, then claiming credit for it in order to gain attention. They may claim credit by defacing Web sites — in other words leaving messages that can be read by their fellow script kiddies.

Script kiddies, who are sometimes called packet monkeys, can hardly be called harmless. They are known for carrying out Denial of Service attacks in which as many as several hundred computers are infiltrated by a hacker and used to overload a Web site simply by connecting to it so many times that the site's server becomes overloaded and ceases to respond to legitimate requests.

A 14-year-old Canadian script kiddie known as MafiaBoy carried out one of the most notorious attacks ever in February 2000. The attack, called a Denial of Service, prevented visitors from accessing many of the biggest Web sites, including those of Amazon.com, eBay, and Yahoo. The boy was arrested in April 2000. In January 2001, he pleaded guilty to 58 charges related to the attacks. He was eventually sentenced to eight months in a juvenile detention center. As I was writing this book, an 18-year-old German student and computer programmer confessed to creating a virus called Sasser that affected millions of computers around the world. The virus exploited a flaw in the Microsoft Windows operating system and caused computers to repeatedly shut down and reboot.

Thieves

Many hackers can be called "black hats." Their goal is to steal someone's identity, money, or other goods and services. In Chicago, where I live, hackers recently gained access to the state's database of temporary license plate numbers, apparently hoping to be able to generate fake licenses for autos.

Some very competent hackers attempt to break into banks and military facilities, hoping to steal money, maps, or information. Others try to break into e-commerce Web sites that use encryption to secure data, but these are for the most part difficult targets. These days, the most frequently stolen item on the Internet is personal identity, which is fast becoming an epidemic. If people can get their hands on legitimate Social Security numbers, credit card numbers, and other data, they can make fraudulent purchases that can cost the victim time, energy, and money.

Crackers

Passwords are among the most widespread security measures on the Internet. Everyone who goes online has a password of some sort. Because passwords are so widespread and protect resources that are often highly valuable (such as bank accounts, Internet access accounts, or software programs), they are frequently a target. Crackers are primarily interested in obtaining passwords in order to go online and gain access to systems and data, and to assume your identity.

All too often, a cracker's job is made easy by the fact that an individual user has chosen a ridiculously simple password — or no password at all. Here are examples of passwords you shouldn't use:

- 123abc
- MaryJones
- password
- administrator

Even if one of these easily-guessed passwords is not used, crackers can still uncover passwords that aren't secure enough. They can use a special pass-word-cracking application that can guess it in one of three ways. It might perform a *dictionary crack,* which runs through all the words contained in the dictionary in rapid succession. It might conduct a brute force crack, which runs through a series of random characters and submits huge numbers of possible passwords to the server very quickly. Finally, it might do a *rule-based crack,* which is performed if the cracker has knowledge about the rule used to create the password.

In the early days of the war with Iraq, it was reported that U.S. intelligence broke into an e-mail account used by Uday Hussein, one of the sons of former Iraqi dictator Saddam Hussein. The password used on the account was reported to be a simple word in the dictionary that was easily cracked.

Demon dialers

Some of the earliest hackers were individuals who tried to abuse not computer networks, but phone systems. They developed and used special devices called black boxes in an effort to make free phone calls. They had a number of goals: They wanted to get something for nothing, they wanted to feel like they were putting one over on "Ma Bell," and they wanted to have a way to connect to bulletin board services by dialing the same number over and over again until a connection was made.

Today, hackers use software that dials phone numbers in rapid succession. But rather than trying to connect to a bulletin board service, such software is used for less benign purposes. Sometimes, software applications called dialers infiltrate computer systems without the owner's permission. They then dial out through the Internet to a 900 number or FTP site, typically to accrue charges. These programs, which are known as "demon dialers," "war dialers," or simply "dialers," can also be used to launch a Denial of Service attack against a remote system.

Computers that have direct connections to the Internet are able to make phone calls online using a technology called Voice Over IP. You might be able to use the technology to save some long-distance phone charges (as long as you are willing to accept some compromises with the quality of the audio).

What intruders want

You might well ask what all these nefarious individuals are looking for, and why they would go through the trouble of breaking into your computer. Some are only looking for valid e-mail addresses: these are the marketers, or the businesses that sell e-mail addresses to bulk mailers who are going to be sending you spam e-mail. (You might even get junk "snail mail," if your mailing address falls into a marketer's hands.) That's the least of your problems, however. Here are some more serious potential pitfalls:

- ✔ Access to your children
- ✔ Your credit card information, so they can make purchases
- ✔ Your e-mail program, so they can distribute viruses or other harmful software as widely as possible
- ✔ Access to your Web browser and those of as many other individuals as possible, so they can launch a coordinated attack on a high-profile Web site (such as Microsoft's). This is called a Denial of Service attack.
- ✔ Access to your computer system so they can place programs on it, glean information from it, and generally disrupt it.

As this quick survey of hacking's "cast of characters" indicates, if you want to be really secure you need to be prepared for a variety of attempts to gain access to your computer. The section that follows suggests what to look out for when an attack is underway, and how Norton Internet Security can help you detect it.

Recognizing Garden-Variety Attacks

If you are a home user with a handful of computers on the Internet, you can count yourself lucky. You aren't likely to run into the most dangerous hackers, who save their talents for breaking into defense systems, universities, and e-commerce Web sites. You're more likely to experience one of the more common incidents mentioned in the sections that follow.

It's true that Norton Internet Security should, if all of its components are installed correctly and the product is updated on a regular basis, thwart such events before damage occurs. But it's still good to know what to look for. You may be able to take further steps that make your computer even safer. If Norton Personal Firewall notifies you that someone is doing a port scan on your computer, you may want to make sure that vulnerable ports are closed. If Norton AntiVirus detects a virus, you may want to download a new set of virus definitions and do a manual virus scan as described in Chapter 5.

Norton Internet Security can perform a wide range of security functions. But no security application is a cure-all. Like any security program, it can be undone by new attacks, new viruses, unsafe passwords, employee break-ins, or other weaknesses. The descriptions in the following sections will alert you to some potential weak spots you might want to strengthen.

Port scans

Your home has a variety of openings to the outside world. Each opening is set aside so that a different kind of object can pass through. Air and light flow through windows. Mail goes through the mail slot. Gas flows through one set of pipes, and water through another. Information of different sorts flows into and out of your computer.

Depending on the software you have installed, you can send and receive that information using preassigned ports. Chances are you have a Web browser, an e-mail application, and an application that enables you to send and receive instant messages. Data from each of those sources enters and leaves your computer via a virtual opening called a *port*. Don't look on the back of your computer for this sort of port. It isn't a physical opening but an abstract designation that software programs use to communicate with one another over a network.

Problems occur when a computer is "listening" on a port — in other words, waiting to receive a connection on that port — but the port isn't actually being used. Such open, unused ports are vulnerable openings that hackers can exploit. In order to identify open ports, hackers use software that attempts to connect to each port, one after another. This series of connection attempts is called a *port scan*. A port scan isn't an attack in itself, but it can lead to one if the hacker finds an open port.

Ports are especially important because they frequently turn up in the alert messages that Norton Internet Security displays. Certain ports, such as 137 or 53, show up frequently in attack attempts. If you know the port the hacker is trying to access, you can make a reasonable guess what attack is being tried and take steps to protect your computer from further damage.

Some common ports, the Internet communications services that use them, and the kinds of attacks that can occur on those ports are listed in Table 1-1.

Table 1-1		Ports and Attacks	
Port Number	*Type of Service*	*Protocol Used*	*Attack*
20, 21	File transfers	File Transfer Protocol (FTP)	FTP "bounce" attack
25	Outgoing e-mail	Simple Mail Transfer Protocol	The "cancel" attack or other e-mail attack
53	Domain name lookups	Domain Name Service (DNS)	Buffer over flow attack
80	Web browsing	HyperText Transfer Protocol	NIMDA virus
137	NetBIOS	Name Service	Worms or viruses, or attempts to access shared files

A *protocol* is a set of standard instructions or rules that computers must use when they communicate over a network. Having a standardized set of rules and instructions enables computers from different manufacturers, using different operating systems, to share information and connect to one another. When it comes to firewalls and security, you need to know about two protocols: Transmission Control Protocol (TCP) and User Datagram Protocol (UDP). Along with Internet Protocol (IP), TCP is the fundamental, underlying protocol that makes it possible for computers to exchange information securely by breaking it into uniform and manageable sets of data called *packets*. UDP is a less secure, simpler protocol that is more vulnerable and that is frequently exploited by hackers.

IP address attacks

In order to send a package from one place to another, you need to label it with an address. That way, the delivery person can find the correct destination. Computers on a network need to be able to find one another as well. The "street address" used by computers is called an IP address. Many hackers operate by attempting to locate IP addresses that they can then scan for points of entry.

The IP stands for Internet Protocol, a set of standards that enables computers to locate one another on the Internet or a private network. The version currently in use on the Net is Internet Protocol Version 4 (IPv4). But the available IPv4 numbers are dwindling, and a more complex and number-rich version, IPv6, had just been instituted as I was writing this book. In IPv4, each computer on a network is assigned an IP address, a set of four numbers separated by dots, such as 192.168.34.1. Each of the four numbers in an IP address can have a value of between 0 and 255.

Hackers use (or rather, misuse) IP addresses in two general ways. First, they try to locate as many static and legitimate IP addresses as possible. A computer's IP address is static when it does not change from session to session. It is legitimate when it can be traced to a real computer that is connected to the Internet, as opposed to a "private" IP address that can only be used on an internal network such as that operated by a corporation or other organization. Hackers sometimes try to locate as many IP addresses as possible; they then attempt to break into each of the computers associated with each address in order to launch a coordinated attack against another Web site.

Problems with "always on" connections

Every computer that is connected to the Internet has an IP address. But some IP addresses are temporary or dynamic, while others are constant or static. If you dial in to a Web server and connect to the Internet using a modem, your IP address is temporary. It is assigned to you by your Internet Service Provider (ISP), and it only lasts for the length of the phone call. When you disconnect, the address is assigned to another customer of the ISP. When you want to reconnect, you get a new, temporary IP address that is assigned to you from the ISP's pool of available addresses.

IP addresses of computers that are connected to the Internet are one of the things that hackers try to determine in order to break in to computers. But because of their transitory nature, temporary IP addresses are not only difficult to detect, but they are useless to hackers.

The problem comes when you upgrade to an Internet connection that is always on — as long as the computer is on or your cable modem or DSL router is on (all of these devices can be switched off when you do not need to go online, for greater security). Rather than dialing in to a server with your modem, you are connected all the time thanks to a cable modem or Digital Subscriber Line (DSL) connection. When you connect to the Internet using one of these two kinds of systems, you get high-speed access. But you also get an IP address that seldom, if ever, changes.

Most ISPs that provide cable modem and DSL access offer their subscribers temporary IP addresses. But if the user is online for days or even weeks at a time, that temporary address remains the same during that time. A few users (such as me) pay extra to have static IP addresses, which never change. Obviously, they are even easier for hackers to find and exploit. It's great to have a direct connection to the Internet, but keep in mind that such a connection makes it even more important that you install and configure Norton Internet Security to provide the protection you need.

The second way in which hackers misuse IP addresses is by "spoofing" them. A spoofed IP address is one that has been deliberately falsified in order to conceal the identity of the person operating the computer — in other words, the hacker himself, who does not wish to be traced so as to continue probing and breaking into remote computer systems.

Back doors

As I mention earlier in the section "Port scans," computers have a variety of both physical and virtual openings through which information can pass. The "front doors," or the approved openings, are the plugs that you use to connect peripheral devices such as hard drives, or the ports that are assigned to let certain software programs communicate.

But computers have "back doors" as well. A back door is a hidden opening, often unknown to the end-user, through which hackers can infiltrate remote systems. A back door may be a port that is left open. But it can also be a password stolen or misused by an employee, or a way of accessing a network from a remote computer. It can also be an opening that is created by a computer program the user downloads. Unknown to the user, the program's author has planted code in the program that establishes communication with the author through the Internet.

Some back doors are caused by flaws in system software or other applications. Microsoft Windows is occasionally the culprit. In April 2004, hackers believed to be from Brazil, Germany, and the Netherlands attempted to take advantage of a security flaw in a particular version of Windows in order to gain back-door access to major financial institutions in Australia. The security flaw was repaired by a patch issued by Microsoft, but all the banks' servers may not have installed it. However, the global security monitoring service, Internet Security Systems (www.iss.net), issued alerts to the banks, and the attacks were thwarted. The lesson: Always install security patches issued by Microsoft or other software vendors as they become available.

Trojan horses

After hackers discover the presence of a "back door" on a remote system, they can send software through that back door into the system. Often, the software appears to be harmless. But inside, it has a potentially harmful payload. Such software is called a Trojan horse. Perhaps the worst kind of Trojan horse is one that comes disguised as a program designed to get rid of viruses or other malicious software. Instead of performing anti-virus functions, the program injects viruses into the system.

In early 2004, a security company called Intego announced that it had discovered what was believed to be the first Trojan horse designed to attack Macintosh computers. The program — which was described as harmless — came inside an MP3 file that could be downloaded from the Internet. Although this Trojan horse was harmless, the company said it pointed the way for other, more harmful programs that might be planted in the future.

Social engineering: Ha, fooled ya!

The term *social engineering,* invented by hackers, is a complicated-sounding term for fooling a person into giving out sensitive information that a hacker can then use to gain access to a system, use someone else's credit card account, and so on. Even companies that have teams of security professionals in place, as well as firewalls and other intrusion detection systems, can have their work undone by such methods.

The most famous hacker to date, Kevin Mitnick, was an expert at social engineering. He gave a speech to a group of hackers in 2000 where he boasted that he was able to "obtain any number, listed or unlisted," as well as network access passwords and other information. You can read a report of the talk at `http://zdnet.com.com/2100-11-522261.html`. Being aware of social engineering attempts is one of the best ways to improve computer security. If someone sends an e-mail message that induces you to give out your credit card or bank account information, they will bypass all the safeguards provided by Norton Internet Security and any other security devices you have installed on your computer.

Viruses in downloaded software

Sometimes, it seems like you can find, download, and enjoy just about anything online. Whether you're looking for a piece of music, a trial version of a software program, an installer file that helps you install a larger program, or something else, be very careful and make sure you have Norton AntiVirus running before you click the Download button or link.

The file sharing sites that enable users around the world to share and download music and other files often give users more than they bargain for. In order to use sites such as KaZaA, Gnutella, or Morpheus, you need to download software that enables you to connect to the sites, search for shared files, and download. Over the years, such software has been known to have the capability of keeping tabs on what you do. These programs aren't exactly viruses, but they fall under a different category of software known as *spyware*. The manufacturers of spyware pay a small fee to the file sharing companies to distribute the utilities. The utilities, which are often installed and run without the user's knowledge, can cause ads to pop up automatically on the user's machine and keep track of the Web sites the user visits so that ads can be tailored to his or her personal preferences. Here are a few examples of software "extras" that you don't ask for, but might get anyway:

- ✔ **cydoor.** Early versions of this program installed themselves in a part of Windows systems called the Registry, and were configured to start up automatically whenever your system was rebooted (whether you knew the program was there or not). The program downloads ads onto your computer. You can install the application, but you don't always have a choice about whether it's installed in the first place.

- ✔ **SaveNow.** A program that takes up processing resources, collects information on what Web sites you visit, and that automatically launches pop-up ads.

- ✔ **b3d.** A program distributed by a company called Brilliant Digital. At one time, this software turned your computer into a part of the company's worldwide network, giving Brilliant the ability to use your system for itself and its clients.

The last program mentioned on the list is no longer bundled with KaZaA. But because it used to be part of the program, would you really trust these people now?

You can read a review of KaZaA that mentions these bundled files and others at www.dooyoo.co.uk/computers/applications/kazaa.

Infected files

People can do an ever-increasing amount of work on computers and also on the Internet. People who write or edit for a living, as I do, know that entire books can be written and edited online. In the days when floppy disks used to be exchanged on a regular basis, viruses could (and did) spread from one person's computer to another. They can be spread when infected files are downloaded, opened, or copied.

The Internet has dramatically reduced the instance of floppy disk infection, but individual files can still be infected by macros and other harmful substances. A *macro* virus is a type of virus that infects a specific type of file. Commonly, Microsoft Word has been infected by macros, as has Microsoft Excel. Macro viruses aren't as prevalent as they once were. A major macro virus outbreak accompanied the release of the Windows 95 operating system in 1995; another occurred in the year 2000. But viruses you download from file sharing networks or from CDs you receive from untrustworthy people can contain infected files as well. The moral: Keep Norton AntiVirus installed, don't open any file you don't recognize, and only download files from trusted sources.

Visiting Symantec Security Response

Symantec Security Response has a variety of resources besides the virus scanner that you should check on a regular basis. It's an especially good idea to visit the site if you manage the network for a small business; you can notify co-workers of any serious virus attacks and download any removal tools, for one thing. Here are some other reasons why you would want to visit the site:

- ✔ **Find out about updates.** The home page displays the most recent set of virus definitions included with Live Update, the component included with Norton Internet Security that automatically updates the program. A definition is a set of characteristics that identifies a virus or other intrusion; a firewall or anti-virus program uses the definitions to recognize security threats and handle them appropriately.

- ✔ **Learn about the latest security advisories.** Some threats can be handled by Norton Internet Security alone, but some (such as those that affect Microsoft Windows) require you to install patches to prevent intrusions.

- ✔ **Download an analyzer.** An analysis tool called DeepSight prepares reports of any intrusion attempts or virus attacks you have faced. It's designed to work with Norton Internet Security and is available for free. (Find out more in Chapter 4.)

- ✔ **Get background information.** The links presented under the heading "reference area" on the Symantec Security Response home page provide you with a wealth of general data about computer security.

If you use Norton Internet Security in a business environment and you need to inform your colleagues about security issues, the resources listed earlier can help you prepare well-researched reports and make sensible recommendations based on current security conditions.

Adopting Effective Privacy Strategies

If you use Norton Internet Security and do nothing else to protect your computer, you haven't really created a secure environment for yourself, your family, or your office. You also need to adopt some sensible strategies when you sign up for online services or communicate via e-mail or instant messaging. It's a matter of changing the way you approach the Internet. If you are aware of privacy dangers and you adopt the approaches mentioned in the sections that follow, you'll help NIS protect your computer that much more effectively — because there will be fewer intrusions to fend off.

Don't believe everything you read

Some people will do anything to get your attention on the Internet. When they approach you online, they can't always use images or sounds to reach you. Instead, they try to entice you and tempt you using a variety of possible strategies:

- ✔ **They try to generate fear.** You might receive e-mail or Web-based messages such as, "There has been a security breach and your account has been compromised. You need to verify your personal information right away."

- ✔ **They arouse curiosity.** You connect to a Web page, and you see a warning informing you about a new search utility that you can install. Or, a dialog box appears, asking if you want to make the current page your browser's start page.

- ✔ **They offer you something too good to be true.** You see a copy of an expensive and complex program on a file sharing site, absolutely free. When you download the compressed file that supposedly contains the program, you get shortcuts that are automatically added to your Start menu, and that point to "adult" Web sites.

Be suspicious of everything you see online, only subscribe for services you really need, and never offer to sign up, subscribe, download, or install something for nothing. As they used to say at the University of Chicago, "There ain't no such thing as a free lunch." That applies to free downloads, too.

Recognize suspicious e-mail warning signs

It doesn't take long before you'll be able to recognize e-mail scams that can cause you harm. Bad spelling and grammar are an obvious , as are outlandish claims. I, personally, have received e-mail messages in recent weeks that said the following:

- ✔ "something is fool"
- ✔ "Would you like to become a successful real estate investor just like Donald Trump?"

✔ "Need to lose weight?"

✔ "This is the best way to control spam."

✔ "Did you ask me for that?"

Almost all of these messages had an attachment just waiting for me to click on it. I didn't, of course, knowing that it probably contained a virus or other malicious program. Norton Internet Security not only has the capability of blocking much spam, but also for detecting suspicious e-mail attachments the moment they reach your inbox: You get an alert about a possible virus before you get to open it. But you still need to recognize e-mail spams just in case a new one manages to get past Norton Internet Security and into your computer.

Give out as little as possible

The Internet is a remarkably open place. It's a perfect medium for chatting, making online friends, sharing information, and learning about current events. But be selective about what you share and who you share it with.

One of the best ways to give out information that enables marketers to "attack" you with unwanted e-mail messages is by filling out forms. When you sign up for something, you typically provide your name, address, phone number, and e-mail address (if not more). Do you know what the online service you register with is going to do with that information?

One of the best ways to protect your privacy is to give out as little as possible. Do you have to provide a business with your real address and phone number? Why do they *need* such information, if they are only planning to contact you by e-mail? Don't fill out any fields on forms that are not required; when you do provide an e-mail address, make it an address that you have reserved for such registrations. That way, your "registration only" e-mail address will get all the special offers, confirmations, notices, and other messages you didn't ask for when you signed up. Your primary e-mail address will stay relatively free of spam if you just don't use it to sign up for anything, and if you give it out only to personal acquaintances you trust.

A sense of "minimalism" applies to running computer programs as well as filling out registration forms. Throw out or disable applications you don't use or don't need so they cannot be misused. Sometimes, system software runs programs that you don't need and that represent a security risk. Some versions of Microsoft Windows automatically started up Internet Information Server, a built-in Web server, which became a well-known vulnerable spot that hackers could breach.

Managing Your Passwords

One of the best things you can do, when you are preparing to install Norton Internet Security, is to tighten up your existing passwords and adopt a more secure policy toward any passwords you plan to set in the future. As you already know, a password is a set of characters you enter on your keyboard and submit to an application, a Web page, or a Web site server in order to go online, gather your e-mail, or use a software program or online service. When you send the password to the program or server, it is checked against a database of approved passwords. If a match is made, you gain access.

Norton Internet Security does not protect your passwords. It doesn't keep unscrupulous individuals from guessing them or stealing them, which can open up your whole computer to intrusion. Poor password security (or lack of passwords) can undo everything NIS tries to protect, so passwords are examined in some detail in the sections that follow.

Picking a good password

The most effective passwords are ones that are created randomly, by a software program that generates them for you, and that have a one-time use. After that single use, they are discarded. Such passwords are virtually impossible to crack, but they are also very impractical. You want to be able to quickly enter your own password (one that you can easily remember) whenever you go online, place a bid on eBay, or view the status or your checking account. You don't want to wait for a program to devise the password for you.

The best passwords are at least six to eight characters long. They use both numerals and alphabetic characters. A good password looks like this:

```
w3Ju@!39Gxv$
```

This would be a very hard password to crack, even for someone using a special software program. But could you possibly remember such a password? It can be helpful to use a recognizable slogan or phrase to create a password that sticks in your mind. Think about a slogan or phrase you can recall easily, such as You Ain't Nothin But a Hound Dog. The initials can be used to create a password:

```
YANBAHD
```

To make this password even more secure, add the date the song was a big hit, 1956:

```
YANBAHD56
```

For *really* good security, mix the upper and lower case, like this:

```
yAnBaHd56
```

The result is a highly secure password. Because anyone who uses the Internet needs more than one password, you can create a set of passwords that follows the same formula — in this case, the titles of Elvis Presley songs, such as ILYRSG, WTARM, and WMRAYN.

Encrypting your passwords

Coming up with a password that proves difficult for "cracking" software to uncover is only half the battle. The other half is storing your passwords in a secure place. You can't be expected to memorize all of your passwords. I, personally, think I have at least 25 combinations of usernames and passwords. It's also insecure to use the same password for every service you use — if someone obtains one password, they can gain access to all of those accounts.

Encryption provides a foolproof way to store your passwords. Encryption is the process of manipulating information so that it cannot be read by unauthorized individuals. Information is manipulated by means of a mathematical formula. Only authorized individuals who have the formula can decrypt the information in order to read it. On the Internet, some Web sites can encrypt sensitive information that passes between a browser and a server. Such encryption needs to be highly secure, and is accomplished by means of complex formulas called algorithms. The algorithms process large prime numbers to create long sets of alphanumeric characters called keys. The keys are then used to encrypt information and ensure that the individuals who possess the keys are who they say they are.

One way in which you can use encryption is to encrypt your passwords and store them using a specially designed software program. Several programs are available to help you conceal your passwords; two examples are described below.

Norton password protection

Symantec markets a password encryption tool with the Norton brand, but it's a product that's separate from Norton Internet Security. Norton Password Manager protects much of the data that Internet users give out when they fill out forms. It has the capability of creating and storing multiple user profiles, so all of the people who use your computer can store their passwords there. Each user creates a profile that contains his or her address, phone number, and other contact information (see Figure 1-3). Password Manager enters the information for you automatically whenever you fill out a form. It also enters passwords automatically when applications prompt you for them.

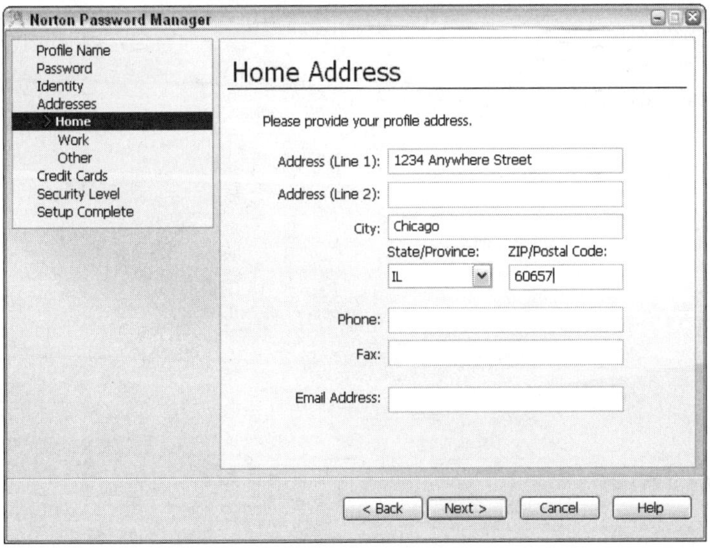

Figure 1-3:
Norton
Password
Manager
takes the
work out
of filling out
forms and
remember-
ing pass-
words.

The trick, of course, is that you need to create a password in order to create a secure user profile. When you have the profile in place, you can store all of your credit card and bank account numbers, as well as passwords. The program then fills out forms for you automatically using your securely stored information. But you need to remember one password — your account password — in order to get access to your passwords. (Luckily, Password Manager lets you record a "hint" so you can remember this password more easily.) After you enter your personal information and credit card data, you can begin to store passwords as you visit Web sites and are prompted to enter them. The program's interface (see Figure 1-4) closely resembles that of Norton Internet Security, as you'll see in Chapter 2.

You don't necessarily need to install a software program in order to securely store your passwords. You can also store them online using a service that protects your sensitive information. Obviously, you place a great deal of trust in such services. Consider PasswordSafe (www.passwordsafe.com) or one of the password safety services listed by an organization you really can trust, the Electronic Privacy Information Center, at www.epic.org/privacy/tools.html.

Password Officer

This program by Compelson Laboratories (www.compelson.com) comes in four different versions. You can't beat the price of Password Officer Lite: It lets you store ten passwords or other items for free. A Standard version lets you store 40 items and costs $29; the DeLuxe version has unlimited storage capacity and costs $59.

Figure 1-4: Norton Password Manager complements the features provided by Norton Internet Security.

The program not only stores passwords but also creates them for you. You assign each password a number or other code or a short account name that is easy to remember (see Figure 1-5). You only need to enter the code or name when you want to enter a password; Password Officer enters the actual password for you automatically.

Figure 1-5: Password Officer not only stores encrypted passwords but generates them for you.

Leaving passwords in place after you have memorized them is tempting. But you'll achieve an even greater level of security if you make an effort to change your passwords every few weeks or months. That way, if someone has cracked a password without your knowledge, the access they gain will last only until you change the password.

If you're looking for just the right password management application, read PC Magazine's review of password managers at `www.pcmag.com/article2/0,1759,1587793,00.asp`. (Password Officer is not included, however.)

Chapter 2

Getting Started with Norton Internet Security

● ●

In This Chapter

▶ Installing Norton Internet Security

▶ Deleting files that can interfere with installation

▶ Activating the software and configuring component programs

▶ Beginning to use the software and setting program options

● ●

*Y*ou shouldn't have to read an entire chapter (or almost an entire chapter) devoted to installing and beginning to configure Norton Internet Security (NIS). In an ideal world, you would just insert the CD into your computer's CD-ROM drive and setup would practically take care of itself. In a fantasy world, you wouldn't need Norton Internet Security at all; the Internet would be perfectly secure.

This is the real world, of course. Installing NIS will hopefully be a smooth process. But you have a number of configuration decisions to make, and there is the potential for trouble when you either try to install the program or operate it. When you get the software up and running, you see events that you may not have expected, such as alert messages and notices informing you that e-mail messages are being scanned for viruses and e-mail programs are being "configured." This chapter explains how to make the right choices when installing Norton Internet Security, how to overcome any problems that occur, and how to understand program events when you see them.

Preparing Your Computer for Norton Internet Security

Norton Internet Security operates most effectively if you prepare your computer beforehand. Some measures are mandatory: You need to uninstall or disable other firewall or anti-virus applications so they won't interfere, for example. Having two or more firewall programs on your computer can confuse your operating system — especially if those competing firewall programs are configured to run automatically when the system starts up. Other measures are optional and will improve the speed and efficiency of your computer so NIS can run more efficiently. Over the years, the package has grown in file size as well as memory and processor requirements.

Cleaning up your file system

A good first step in preparing your computer for Norton Internet Security is to clean out any programs that are consuming hard drive space and that are no longer needed, or any other firewall or anti-virus programs you already have that might conflict with NIS and prevent it from operating correctly. In the sections that follow, I give you some suggestions of the types of files you might clean out.

Deleting files you don't need

Cleaning up your hard drive to conserve unused space won't improve your security directly, but it will help Norton Internet Security run more smoothly. Follow these steps to clean out files you don't need and that can accumulate during the course of surfing the Web and using the Internet:

1. **Choose Start⇨All Programs⇨Accessories⇨System Tools⇨ Disk Cleanup.**

   A dialog box appears notifying you that Disk Cleanup is calculating how much space you will save by performing this action. Then the Disk Cleanup dialog box appears (see Figure 2-1).

Figure 2-1:
Clean up files you don't need to maximize available disk space for NIS's application and log files.

2. **Check the boxes next to the items you want to delete.**

   The ones you mark will be thrown out; those you don't mark will be saved.

   If you need more detailed information about one of the groups of files shown, click it and read the description in the Description part of the dialog box. If you need even *more* detail, select one of the groups of files and click View Files.

3. **Click OK.**

   The files you selected are deleted.

The savings in disk space can be substantial: In Figure 2-1, you can see that you can save 15M by using Disk Cleanup. Cleaning out files you don't need on a periodic basis is a good idea not only for NIS but also for other applications. NIS generates log files as it operates, so disk space can be used up if you have limited storage space. But cleaning up is also good when you have plenty of storage space.

Another popular Symantec application, Norton SystemWorks, provides you with a One-Touch Cleanup button to clean up your hard drive in a flash, as well as an application called Norton CleanSweep, which clears out applications you don't use or don't need. Find out more at www.symantec.com/sabu/sysworks/basic.

Uninstalling applications you don't need

I don't want to say that NIS is a memory hog, but it is fair to say that, as the number of applications in the suite has grown, it has developed a healthy appetite for both Random Access Memory (RAM) and hard drive storage space. To free up more space, you can delete any applications you don't need. How do you know what you don't need? Add/Remove Programs includes a utility that indicates how often you've used the program and when it was last used. (This information appears when you click on a program's name.) If you haven't used an application in two or three years, for example, you can probably delete it without losing anything. Otherwise, it's a matter of common sense: If you think you might need a program, keep it; if you're sure you'll never use an application again, delete it by following these steps:

1. **Choose Start⊏▷Control Panel on Windows XP. (On other versions of Windows, choose Start⊏▷Settings⊏▷Control Panel.)**

   The Control Panel window opens.

2. **Double-click Add or Remove Programs.**

   You'll probably have to wait a few seconds as your computer gathers the list of available programs.

3. **When the list of programs appears, scroll down and select one you no longer use or need.**

   A button labeled Change/Remove appears next to the program's name (see Figure 2-2).

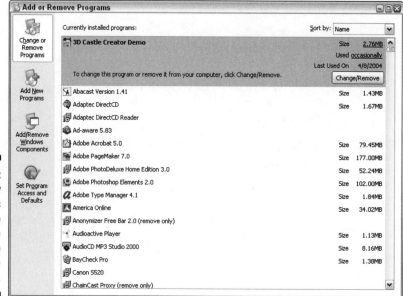

Figure 2-2: Remove any programs you no longer use to free up disk space for NIS.

4. **Click Change/Remove.**

   A dialog box appears asking you to confirm that you want to delete the program.

5. **Click OK.**

   The program is deleted.

6. **Repeat Steps 3 through 5 for any other programs you want to delete.**

   Pay special attention to those applications that consume many megabytes of disk space as listed in the right-hand column in Add/Remove Programs. If you can delete such programs, you'll free up a lot of space for other programs, including NIS, to operate.

RAM is the type of memory your computer uses to run applications. NIS requires between 64 and 128MB of RAM, depending on the version of Windows you use. NIS 2004 requires 64MB of RAM for Windows 98, 96MB of RAM for Windows Me and Windows 2000 Professional, and 128MB of RAM for Windows XP Home or Professional. Find out more about the program's system requirements at www.symantec.com/region/reg_eu/product/

`nis_requirements.html`. (The NIS Professional requirements are at `www.symantec.com/region/reg_eu/product/nispro_requirements.html` but they are the same as the ones for the Home version of NIS.)

Defragmenting your drive

In order to operate smoothly, NIS's component applications need to work together. Those applications, in turn, will operate more smoothly if they can access the files they need (such as log files, which contain records of the traffic that attempts to pass through your network gateway) as quickly as possible.

Files are stored in locations that are not contiguous, but that are scattered in fragments throughout your hard drive. Over time, as you create and delete files and applications, your computer's hard drive can become fragmented. The term *defragmenting* describes the process of reorganizing the information on a hard drive so that files in a single application are located next to one another, and unused areas of the drive are grouped into their own sections rather than being scattered throughout the drive.

You may improve NIS's performance if you defragment your hard drive, and doing it before you install NIS can save you some time. Windows comes with a built-in defragmenting utility. To access it, follow these steps:

1. **Choose Start⇨All Programs⇨Accessories⇨System Tools⇨ Disk Defragmenter.**

    The Disk Defragmenter dialog box opens.

2. **Select a hard drive, and click Analyze.**

    In the upper part of the dialog box, the message under the Session Status column will read Analyzing . . . as your drive is scanned. Scanning may take several minutes or as much as a half hour or more, depending on the amount of information contained on the drive. Analysis and defragmentation can take a long time (even up to several hours) and they can slow down other work you're doing. Consider starting before going to bed. That way, the process will be be done when you get up in the morning.

    A dialog box appears, telling you your drive has been fully analyzed.

3. **Click Close.**

    The dialog box closes and you return to the Disk Defragmenter dialog box.

4. **Inspect the visual indicators when they appear.**

    A set of colored bands appears in the lower part of the Disk Defragmenter dialog box (see Figure 2-3). The white bands represent empty space. The more fragmented the drive is, the farther apart the white bands will be.

Figure 2-3:
Defrag-
menting
helps NIS
and your
applications
run more
efficiently.

5. Click Defragment.

The process of defragmentation starts. You can follow the progress in the lower part of the dialog box (in the box under Estimated Disk Usage After Defragmentation) as the empty areas are rearranged.

Note: Defragmenting your drive before installing NIS (or even after you install it) isn't mandatory. If your computer is newly installed or if Disk Defragmenter's analysis indicates that only a small part of your hard drive is defragmented, you can skip this step. But if you have, for example, 50 percent or more fragmentation, defragmenting is a good idea. You probably will see some improvement in performance, though it may not be dramatic.

Uninstalling previous versions of NIS

You don't need to uninstall previous versions of Norton Internet Security or Norton Personal Firewall before you install Norton Internet Security 2004. In fact, keeping the previous edition is generally a good idea because any rules and settings you may have created with those versions can be adopted by NIS 2004. As a result, you don't need to recreate all the rules from scratch.

Of course, you may want to start from scratch. You may be installing a whole new operating system or a whole new computer. Or you may want to recreate all the rules one by one so you can make sure they are the ones you want. In that case, you do need to uninstall any previous versions of the program you may have. If one of the programs is not operating (for example, if you have a version of NIS that has expired), it might start up and quit, thus preventing the new version from starting up at all.

Removing previous versions of NIS itself (or of Norton Personal Firewall, if you have that application installed by itself) is usually straightforward. The key word, though, is "usually." In my own experience, I've generally been able to remove NIS by one of the two "official" methods:

- Choose Start➪All Programs➪Norton Internet Security➪Uninstall Norton Internet Security.

- Choose Start➪Control Panel, double-click Add/Remove Programs, choose Norton Internet Security, and then click Uninstall.

Sometimes neither of those options removes the applications, however. Sometimes, only some of the application files are removed. Other times, the application files are removed, but references to the original application remain in the Windows registry. Symantec itself acknowledges this because it makes a special removal utility, a file named RnisUPG.exe, available for free on its Web site. You'll find it at `http://service1.symantec.com/SUPPORT/nip.nsf/docid/2001090510510636`. Follow the instructions on this page to download and run the software.

The registry is an area within the Windows operating system where critical information is stored about users, applications, and hardware. Its database of information is used to run applications and determine what device should run them. It's a complex and extensive set of information that should only be edited by experienced users. Be sure to back up the contents of your system before you start working with the registry; in case you damage your system, you can return to the backed-up version. Symantec's removal utility deletes the references to NIS within the system so you don't have to access the registry directly.

Doing a security check

Symantec doesn't assume that you currently have any anti-virus program on your computer before you install and start to use NIS. You may never have scanned your hard drives for viruses. It's even possible that you're installing NIS because your computer has been infected by a virus and won't start at all. If you want to do a virus scan before you install Norton Internet Security, you can do so from the CD or from the Symantec Web site.

Scanning for viruses from the CD

If your computer doesn't start up, or it starts up but you suspect that you have a virus, you can do an immediate virus scan from the program CD before you actually do the installation. Follow these steps:

1. **Insert the Norton Internet Security 2004 CD into your computer's CD-ROM drive.**

2. **Choose Start⇨Turn Off Computer, then click Restart.**

   Any open applications or files close, and your computer restarts. After restart, a dialog box appears asking if you want to boot from your hard drive or from the CD-ROM.

3. **Click Boot from CD-ROM.**

   Your computer restarts from the CD, and the emergency virus scan program automatically begins to scan for viruses. Any viruses that are found are removed — but be aware that the process of completely scanning your computer can take several hours.

4. **When the scan is complete, remove the CD.**

   You can then resume working with your system normally; you don't have to restart.

In order to perform a virus scan from the Norton Internet Security CD, your system needs to be configured to boot up from the CD-ROM drive. Determining whether yours is configured correctly is easy — just insert the NIS CD. If the CD starts up and the virus scan begins automatically, you don't need to change a thing. If it doesn't, you need to change your computer's BIOS settings so that it boots up from the CD-ROM drive. Follow the instructions that came with your computer to change the BIOS settings.

Scanning for viruses from Symantec's Web site

Symantec Corporation, the company that makes Norton Internet Security and a variety of other applications, has a useful Web site that you should make a point to visit in order to keep up with security issues. The part of the site that reports on the latest virus attacks and provides tools to remove viruses is called Symantec Security Response. This part of Symantec's Web "empire" has become so well known that, when you connect to the home page at www.symantec.com, you see a prominent heading for Symantec Security Response rather than advertisements for the company's software products.

One of the things you can do on the Symantec Security Response site (http://securityresponse.symantec.com) is conduct a virus scan. It's true that you can scan for viruses when you install Norton Internet Security, and even when you first insert the program's CD into your CD-ROM drive. But you might still consider doing a manual scan on the Web site. For example, suppose you have a home network with two or three computers. You need to be aware that, as part of the license agreement, Norton Internet Security can be installed on only one of those computers (see the section "Activating and Configuring NIS," later in this chapter, for more on this subject). The others can be scanned over the network after you install NIS. However, you might scan them before you install NIS for an even greater level of security. Just follow these steps:

1. **Point your browser to** http://securityresponse.symantec.com.

   The Symantec Security Response home page appears.

2. **Scroll down the page, and click the link labeled Check for Security Risks.**

   A new Web page entitled Symantec Security Check opens (see Figure 2-4).

3. **Click the Start button under the heading Virus Detection.**

   A Security Warning dialog box appears (see Figure 2-5) asking you to confirm that you want to install and run a program called Virus Detection distributed by Symantec Corporation.

4. **Click Yes.**

   The Security Warning dialog box closes. A progress bar is displayed on the Symantec Security Check Web page, indicating the number of files on your computer that have been scanned for viruses.

Figure 2-4: You can scan your computer for security vulnerabilities or viruses using the controls on this page.

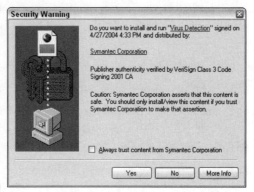

Figure 2-5:
This down-
loaded
software is
harmless,
but you
should
generally
be wary
of such
warnings.

Hopefully, you'll see the number zero next to Files Infected. If you see a different number, install Norton Internet Security right away and have the Emergency program on the CD automatically remove the virus for you. (The scanner only detects the viruses, but doesn't remove them; rather, you are encouraged to purchase Norton AntiVirus or Norton Internet Security.)

If you want, you can also go on to test your computer for vulnerable spots (such as open ports) that can be compromised by a hacker, but installing Norton Internet Security and configuring the program as described in Chapters 3 and 4 should close the vulnerabilities for you.

If your copy of Microsoft Internet Explorer is earlier than version 5.0 or does not have the capability of running ActiveX controls or other scripts enabled, the test may not work. If it doesn't, choose Tools⇨Internet Options from the Internet Explorer menu bar to open the Internet Options dialog box. Click the Security tab, and move the security slider to Low or Medium-Low for the length of the virus scan, if needed. Then click OK to close the Internet Options dialog box, and click Start to restart the scan. You can move the slider back to a more secure setting after the test is complete.

Performing an Initial Virus Scan

When you are ready to install Norton Internet Security, follow these steps:

1. **Close any other applications you have running.**

   The program buttons are removed from your taskbar.

2. **Uninstall any anti-virus programs you have on your computer.**

   Use Add or Remove Programs as described in Chapter 1.

3. **Disable any other firewall programs you have running.**

   This includes Windows' built-in program Internet Connection Firewall. If you need to disable this firewall or verify that it is running, follow these steps:

   a. **Choose Start➪Control Panel.**

   The Control Panel window opens.

   b. **Double-click the Network Connections icon or click the Network Connections link.**

   The Network Connections window opens.

   c. **Right-click the icon that represents your current network connection.**

   (If you have a direct connection to the Internet, right-click Local Area Connection.) The shortcut menu appears.

   d. **Choose Properties.**

   The Properties dialog box for your selected connection appears.

   e. **Click Advanced.**

   The Advanced tab comes to the front.

   f. **Make sure the box next to "Protect my computer and network by limiting or preventing access to this computer from the Internet" is not checked (see Figure 2-6).**

   If it is, uncheck the box to disable Internet Connection Firewall.

   g. **Click OK.**

   The Properties dialog box closes.

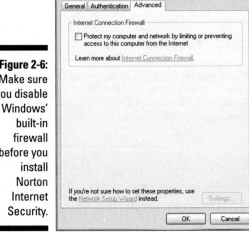

Figure 2-6:
Make sure you disable Windows' built-in firewall before you install Norton Internet Security.

4. **Insert the NIS CD in your CD-ROM drive.**

   If your computer is configured to run from the CD-ROM drive, the program starts and the Welcome to Norton Internet Security window appears. (If it doesn't, open the CD from My Computer or Windows Explorer and double-click the file SYMSETUP.EXE.)

5. **Click Install Norton Internet Security.**

   A window appears asking whether or not to perform a virus scan.

6. **Unless you have done a comprehensive virus scan recently (chances are you haven't), click the option for doing the pre-install scan.**

   The Pre-Install Scanner opens (see Figure 2-7).

Be aware that you don't necessarily have to run the pre-install scan application if you already did a manual virus scan as described in Chapter 1. In that situation, you can click the Stop Scan button to close Pre-Install Scan and proceed with setup.

Figure 2-7:
If you haven't done a virus scan yet, the Pre-Install Scan application will do it for you.

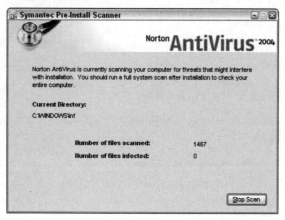

Preparing for installation

When the scan is complete, a text file opens, reporting on the number of files scanned, the number of viruses found (if any), and the number of files that were repaired. Close this file, and close the Pre-Install Scan window, and the first Norton Internet Security Setup window appears. Follow these steps to proceed with setup:

1. **Click Next.**

   The License Agreement appears.

2. **Click I Accept the License Agreement, and then click Next.**

3. **Enter your 24-digit product key, which is on the back of the envelope that held your CD.**

   Keep in mind that the characters in the key are case-sensitive.

4. **Click Next.**

   The Select the Installation Type screen appears.

You have two options for the type of installation: default and custom installation. Choosing custom installation enables you to select the programs you want to install. Choose this option if you don't want to install one of Norton Internet Security's components. If you don't have children, you may not want to install Parental Control; there's no harm in installing the program if you don't need it, other than the disk space consumed.

If you choose Custom and click Next, you see a screen that asks if you want to install Norton AntiVirus. Deselect the "Install anti-virus on your computer if you don't want to install the program" check box; otherwise, leave it as is. Then click Next.

The Install Accounts and Parental Control screen appears (see Figure 2-8). Both of these components are intended for computers with multiple users. If only one person is using the computer you're installing Norton Internet Security on, you may want to click No and then click Next. Otherwise, leave Yes selected and click Next. You then choose your installation location and proceed with actually installing the files.

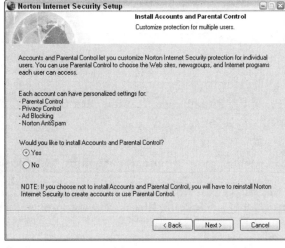

Figure 2-8:
You can choose not to install the multiuser components of Norton Internet Security.

Choosing an installation location

After you choose your installation type and customize the components to be installed (if needed), you decide where to install the program. By default, the installation program seeks to install the software in the same directory where your other software programs are installed: the Program Files directory, which is located within your primary disk drive (the one where your operating system files are also located).

You can change the install location by clicking Browse and choosing a new location: You may want to choose a different hard drive if you have more space available there, or you might want to choose another computer on your network if you want to install NIS on it and you have purchased the license to do so.

After the program files have been installed, a window appears with general information about the program. After you read the information in this window, you can choose to restart your computer either immediately or at a later time. You need to restart in order to start using NIS.

Deleting previous installation files

Suppose your computer doesn't start at all, even to do a pre-install scan. You attempt to install from the NIS CD, and the installation doesn't work. You need to start your computer using an Emergency Rescue Disc. Before you re-insert the CD and proceed with the installation, you need to remove any files that were placed on your computer by the original, aborted installation. To remove the files, follow these steps:

1. **Click Start.**

   The Start menu appears.

2. **Choose Run.**

   The Run dialog box opens.

3. **Type** %TEMP% **in the Run dialog box, then click OK.**

   A Windows Explorer window opens, displaying the contents of the Temp folder.

4. **Select all the files that were created as part of the failed installation.**

   Use Ctrl+Click to select the files one by one.

5. **Choose File⇨Delete to delete the files so you can proceed with the installation.**

How, exactly, do you know which files are system-related or which ones were created by trying to install Norton Internet Security? This can be difficult. Often, the files in the Temp folder have names that say nothing about their purpose. Try selecting the Date Created column to sort the files in the Temp folder by date. Delete any that were created at the same time when you attempted the installation. If you attempted the installation, say, an hour ago, delete all files that were created in the last hour.

Deleting other Symantec products

When I first attempted to install Norton Internet Security, I experienced problems. Even after running several virus scans and deleting temporary installation files, I received the following message shortly after beginning the installation:

```
The installation encountered an error and was unable to
               complete the installation
```

After doing some research on the support area of Symantec's Web site, I discovered that this message can appear when other Symantec products are present. I had a copy of Norton Password Manager installed, and apparently the other software was causing a conflict. I had to uninstall Password Manager and then restart my computer before Norton Internet Security would install. I also had to remove several keys from the Windows registry, and then perform a clean reboot of Windows.

The problem can also occur when you attempt to install NIS 2004 over a previous version of either NIS or Norton AntiVirus. In that case, you need to uninstall the other versions along with registry keys created by the installations. In that case, you may have to use special removal software provided by Symantec. Go to the Symantec support area (`www.symantec.com/techsupp`) and search the knowledge base for the support document with the ID number 2003100708194336. Click the link under Enterprise, click Knowledge Base, enter the number in the search box, and then click Go.

Opening Norton Internet Security

After you install Norton Internet Security, you are prompted to restart your computer. As the computer restarts, notice that the process takes longer than it did before. You may also notice in your system tray a Norton AntiVirus icon, a Norton Internet Security icon (with a red X on it to indicate it's currently disabled), and the following:

- ✓ **A desktop shortcut.** You can double-click this shortcut to start up the program in the future to do configuration (you can also start up the program by double-clicking the system tray icon, however, so you may want to delete the desktop shortcut if you want to save desktop space).

- ✓ **A welcome screen.** The yellow screen shown in Figure 2-9 appears to let you know installation is complete.

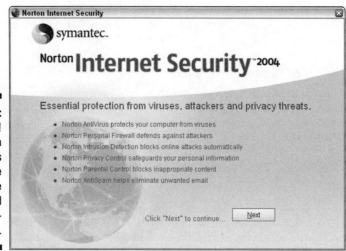

Figure 2-9:
Success!
This screen
appears
when the
software
has installed
success-
fully.

✔ **A LiveUpdate message.** After the Welcome screen appears, you see a message prompting you to update your virus protection. You may wonder why updating is a good idea, especially if you just installed the program. The reason is that new virus definitions have probably come out since the version of the program you have was first made available. You should choose to download any new information that is available. After the update, you'll need to restart your computer — again.

✔ **Configuration messages.** When you first start up Microsoft Internet Explorer after installing NIS, you see a message stating that the program is being configured. After configuration is complete, the program window opens normally.

✔ **Outgoing e-mail messages.** When you first send an outgoing e-mail message, you'll see a window pop up just above your system tray, informing you that the message is being scanned by Norton AntiVirus.

Activating and Configuring NIS

I say it earlier, but it bears repeating: Unless you purchase a special license that specifically enables you to install Norton Internet Security on more than one computer, you can only place it on a *single* computer. This policy is enforced by a process called product activation.

If you have installed recent versions of Microsoft Office or Microsoft Windows, you should be familiar with product activation. Activation is the process of submitting your CD key to Symantec so the product cannot be copied to another computer after you install it. You must activate Norton Internet Security within 15 days after you install it; if not, the program will cease to function.

You probably thought that when you entered your license key during installation you were activating the software. Actually, you do that now; when you leave the Welcome screen the first Activation screen appears (see Figure 2-10).

Figure 2-10: Activate NIS immediately and you won't have to worry about it again — at least for a year.

As the screen indicates, you can activate and register now, activate now, or activate later. I suggest that you leave the first option (activate and register) selected, and click Next. Follow the instructions on subsequent screens to complete activation. For me, the process took less than a minute.

Be aware that you have purchased a license to use Norton Internet Security for one year. Near the end of that year, you will receive repeated reminders that you need to purchase an updated version so you can continue using the software. Otherwise, the software will cease to function.

Handling post-installation tasks

After activation is complete, you see a screen with the unexciting title Post Install Tasks. The title is misleading: These aren't just tasks you are going to undertake, but this is where you really begin to work with Norton Internet Security.

One security consideration is determining who gets access, either from the Internet to your computer network or from your network to the Internet. Another is keeping your security software up to date to keep up with a constantly changing set of viruses and intrusions. If you leave the four options shown on the Post Install Tasks screen checked and then click Next, Norton Internet Security automatically initiates each process. The following sections discuss these essential steps in setting up your security perimeter.

Creating an allowed list

The first post-installation configuration task is reducing spam. Norton AntiSpam, the Norton Internet Security component designed to reduce the amount of unsolicited commercial e-mail you receive, imports all of the names in your Microsoft Outlook Express address book (see Figure 2-11).

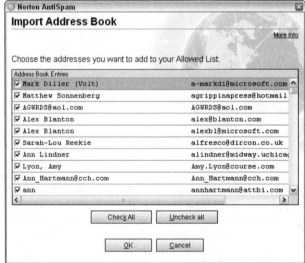

Figure 2-11: Include only the minimum number of names on your "approved" list.

Go through the list, deselecting the names of people you don't correspond with and leaving the others selected. If you use another e-mail program (such as Netscape Messenger or Eudora) as well as Outlook Express, the names included in those programs' respective Address Books will not automatically be added to your AntiSpam list of "approved" individuals. You'll have to add the names manually as described in Chapter 9.

When you're done selecting and deselecting names, click OK. When the import has been completed, a dialog box appears with the message "Address book(s) import successful. You have added __ addresses to your Allowed List." Click OK to close the dialog box, quit Norton AntiSpam, and move on to the next configuration task.

Protecting your private information

How secure is the information that moves between your computer and another across the Internet? Only as secure as the computer that holds the information and the network that transfers it. In the case of the Internet, information is notoriously insecure. Sensitive personal information such as bank account holdings and credit card information needs to be encrypted when it moves along the Internet. But even then, hackers can intercept it, and the server that holds the information can be compromised.

Norton Internet Security's Private Information feature protects the information you send out either by e-mail or by filling out forms with data you submit to Web sites. The Private Information dialog box (see Figure 2-12) pops up as soon as you close Norton AntiSpam as described in the preceding section.

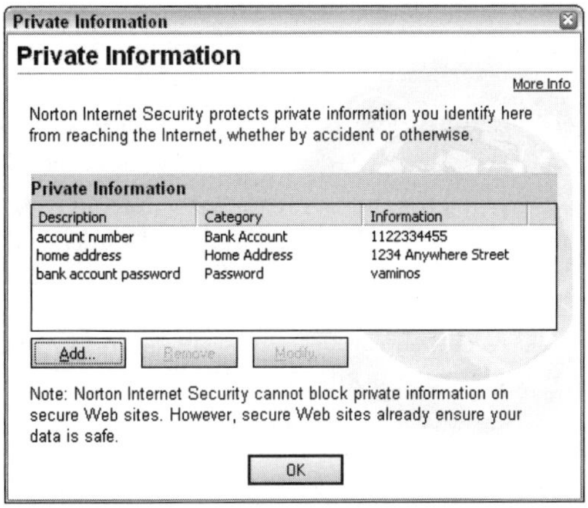

Figure 2-12:
The Private Information feature prevents you from accidentally transmitting sensitive information online.

Private Information performs a very complex security task: It is able to scan the content of e-mail messages and the attachments to those messages, and block sensitive information from being sent. Paradoxically, to keep yourself from submitting your sensitive data by accident, you have to submit it on purpose to Norton Internet Security. To add information, follow these steps:

1. **Click Add in the Private Information dialog box.**

   The Add Private Information dialog box appears (see Figure 2-13).

2. **Select the type of information you want to protect from the drop-down list at the top of the Add Private Information dialog box.**

3. **Enter the name of the information you are protecting, and type the information.**

   The form fields within the dialog box are filled out. You can also deselect the check boxes at the bottom of the dialog box, which tell you what communication methods are covered by the protection, such as e-mail and instant messaging.

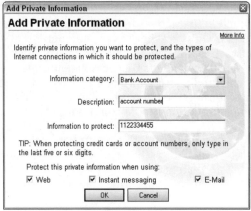

Figure 2-13:
The Add
Private
Information
dialog box
lets you
specify how
you want to
protect your
information.

4. **Click OK.**

   You return to the Private Information dialog box, where the information has been added.

   Any information you type in the Add Private Information dialog box, including account passwords, is displayed in Private Information in clear text — in other words, the text is perfectly readable on-screen. Password characters are not replaced by dots as they are in other applications. Make sure no co-workers or others are watching as you type the information on-screen, or it could be compromised.

5. **Repeat Steps 1 through 4 for any other bits of sensitive information you want to add.**

6. **Click OK.**

   The dialog box closes and the next dialog box, Parental Control Wizard, appears.

Because e-mail, instant messaging, and communications on the Web are all protected by Private Information, you can use the tool to keep your children from giving out their address, phone number, or other information to strangers, at least using those Internet services. (Chat rooms are not supported.)

Creating user accounts

Chances are you're not the only one who uses your computer. If you have children, you probably let them go online once in a while, if only to do homework. You may also have friends or co-workers who use the machine to access the Internet. If you do, you should have separate user accounts established, one for each individual. That way, you can access your e-mail separately, and other settings remain separate as well.

If you have multiple user accounts on a computer, you can set up Norton Internet Security to recognize those accounts. If you ensure that each other person who uses your computer accesses his or her individual account by logging out before they log on, you begin to exercise access control. Norton Internet Security can provide an even greater level of control.

The dialog box that appears after Private Information, the Parental Control Wizard, is intended to protect any children who use the computer to access the Internet. The first step in being able to control the Web sites your kids visit and the services they use is to establish accounts for each one. After Norton Parental Control "knows" who your children are through their respective accounts, it can monitor what they do online and make sure they don't visit locations you have specifically restricted.

If you want to skip this step and don't need to set up user accounts, click Close. To set up user accounts, follow these steps:

1. **Choose Windows accounts or Norton Internet Security accounts.**

   If you already have usernames and passwords set up for each of your family members or co-workers, leave the Use Existing Windows Accounts option selected. Otherwise, choose Create Norton Internet Security Accounts. (This example assumes you will choose the latter option.)

2. **Click Next.**

   The Supervisor dialog box appears. You need to create a supervisor account here for yourself, and create a password for it.

3. **Type your password twice, and then click Next.**

   The Create Accounts dialog box appears (see Figure 2-14).

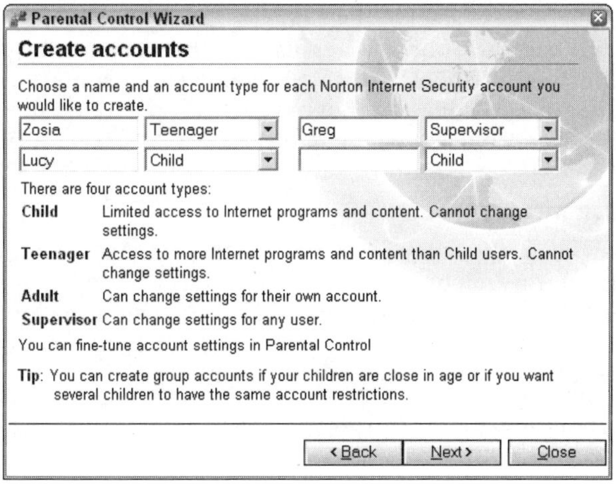

Figure 2-14: Use this dialog box to create separate accounts for each user.

4. **Choose a username and type of account (child, teenager, or adult) for each person you want to have an account, and then click Next.**

   The Choose Passwords dialog box appears.

5. **Type a password for one of the accounts you created.**

   (Keep in mind that, if your children need to enter the passwords, the passwords need to be relatively simple.) Then click Next and create a password for the next account, and so on, until all accounts have passwords.

6. **Click Next.**

   The passwords are recorded, and the Set Startup Account dialog box appears. This is the account that is used first when the computer starts up.

7. **Select the account you want to use when the computer starts up, then click Next.**

   (If you have a Windows user account that you use normally, this Norton Internet Security account appears instead when you restart.)

8. **Click Finish.**

   The Parental Control Wizard closes and the Norton Internet Security window closes.

If this is the first time you're connecting to the Internet with Norton Internet Security, you may see a Network Detector window appear. You have to choose the type of network you're using (Home, Office, or Away, which is used for a coffeeshop, bookstore, or other public venue). See "Detecting (or Redetecting) the Internet," later in this chapter, for more information.

The Set Startup Account dialog box suggests you set the startup account to one of the child accounts you created for maximum protection because these accounts have the highest level of restrictions. But if you use the computer 90 percent of the time and your children use it only occasionally, you should set it to the Supervisor account for your convenience. Just make sure you log off when you are done so your children have to log on with their own passwords when they want to use the machine.

Confronting the latest threats

An essential part of any security program, whether you use Norton Internet Security or another firewall or anti-virus program, is keeping your software up to date. Every day, new virus threats and new intrusion signatures emerge. Checking regularly for new virus and attack definitions so security software can recognize and handle them is essential.

A *signature* (also sometimes called a *definition*) is a set of characteristics that defines a computer event. In terms of security, an intrusion attempt signature can be a series of probes from a single source, a flood of connection attempts from multiple sources, or packets that are sent to a network gateway with improper or forged information in an attempt to cause a server to crash, thus opening access to the network.

Norton Internet Security's LiveUpdate component automatically checks for updated definitions on a regular basis. After you have configured user accounts for parental control, the LiveUpdate dialog box shown in Figure 2-15 appears. Click Next to have the application check for updates from the Symantec Web site; any updates that are available will be downloaded and automatically added to Norton Internet Security's database of security threats.

Figure 2-15:
LiveUpdate
checks for
updates
immediately
after you
install
Norton
Internet
Security.

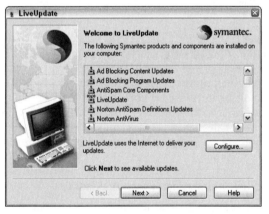

You may ask why LiveUpdate is operating at all, given that you only installed Norton Internet Security a matter of minutes ago. The answer is that the product may have been sitting on the shelf of the computer store where you purchased it for weeks or months. In the intervening period, dozens or even hundreds of new viruses may have emerged. LiveUpdate checks Symantec's Web site for any current threats you have and downloads them, in the background, so you can continue with other work while the information is installed.

Click Next to have the program check for updates, so you can see what's available. Because the program needs to check for updates to several applications, including Norton AntiSpam, Norton AntiVirus, and Norton Internet Security, the process can take a few minutes. When the list appears, scan it to make sure you have available disk space. Then click Next to download the new information. A series of progress bars appears to keep you aware of the progress of each installation. When the installations are all completed, a list of the updates appears along with a message stating that the products are now up to date.

Click Finish to close LiveUpdate. You may see a dialog box informing you that some of the updates require you to restart your computer. Be sure to close any applications you have running and save any work you have underway before clicking OK, which will initiate the restart process.

You don't have to install the updates shown. You can deselect any updates you don't need to save disk space. For example, when I did a check I was presented with updates to Norton Password Manager, even though I had already uninstalled the application as described earlier in this chapter.

ICSA Labs, in its 2003 Virus Prevalence Survey, found that the number of virus threats facing corporations continues to grow. In fact, the likelihood that a company will be hit with a computer virus or worm approximately doubled for each of the survey years through 1999 and is growing at a rate of about 15 percent per year. Find out more at `www.trusecure.com/company/press/pr_20040322.shtml`.

Detecting (or redetecting) the Internet

When you finish the post-installation configuration tasks described in the preceding sections, don't be surprised if you are suddenly disconnected from the Internet. It's part of Norton Internet Security's access control approach. When you set up a security perimeter, either for a home network or for a large-scale business enterprise, you can take one of several approaches:

- ✔ **Deny-All.** This approach blocks all traffic in and out of the network to begin with. You allow traffic gradually as needed.

- ✔ **In Order.** The network administrator or security administrator establishes a set of rules for network communication, and those rules are applied in order.

- ✔ **Best Fit.** The firewall determines which rules are to be followed.

Norton Internet Security follows the first approach, one that can also be called the approach of "least privilege." The computers in the network are given a minimal amount of system privileges to begin with. Least privilege reduces the chances that someone with a high level of control, such as a supervisor or someone with a "superuser" account, can cause a security breach.

When you connect to the Internet from a new location or after you configure access control as described in the previous section, a dialog box appears telling you that your previous network connection has been broken and a new one needs to be created (see Figure 2-16).

Figure 2-16:
You identify
your net-
work so you
can create
different
network
settings
later if
needed.

Select a network location from the What Location Do You Want to Use drop-down list. The options shown each come with their own level of security:

- ✔ **Office.** This setting gives you a minimal amount of protection. It assumes you are using Norton Internet Security in a corporate environment and that a separate, hardware-based firewall is already in place on the network. Choose this setting only if these conditions apply.

- ✔ **Home.** This setting provides an average level of security. You can browse the Web and get your e-mail freely; Norton AntiVirus scans incoming and outgoing e-mail messages for virus infections.

- ✔ **Away.** You should use this setting if you have installed Norton Internet Security on a laptop and you are connecting to the Internet through a wireless network or from a remote location. Wireless "hot spots" of the sort provided in coffee shops are highly insecure, so Norton Internet security provides extra protection.

- ✔ **Default.** This level uses the security settings already in place on your computer.

- ✔ **Use custom settings.** Choose this setting if you want to create a custom set of security settings. You might want to create a special Hotels setting for hotels, which sometimes have wireless networks, for example.

If you are in doubt about which settings to choose, choose Home. Then click OK. Your connection to the Internet should be restored.

You can change the settings later if you need to change locations and are operating with a different network or different security setup. Find out more in Chapter 11.

Using Norton Internet Security

You've installed the program; you've activated the software; you've configured access control; you've updated signatures and definitions. Perhaps you even had to restart your computer after the update was complete. At this point, you can begin to use Norton Internet Security.

At first, "using" the set of security programs may mean nothing more than watching alert messages pop up from your system tray. As you start your e-mail application, Norton AntiVirus informs you that it is scanning an application; Norton Personal Firewall will present you with a message stating that rules are being created for an application. You'll gain much greater control by getting to know the main program window and the options within it.

Touring the main window

One of the first things you notice about NIS is that you don't have to start it up. The program launches when you start up your computer, and it runs in the background unless you specifically stop it.

You can configure NIS to start up manually, too: Click Options, choose Norton Internet Security, and click Manual under the heading Start Norton Internet Security. You can stop Norton Personal Firewall by clicking the Turn Off button in the main program window or by right-clicking the Norton Internet Security icon in the system tray and choosing Disable from the shortcut menu that appears. This doesn't stop Norton AntiVirus, however. You can stop that application separately by right-clicking the Norton AntiVirus icon in the system tray and choosing Disable Auto-Protect from the shortcut menu.

Even though NIS is running in the background, it's not advisable to ignore the program for long periods of time. You may want to change firewall or anti-virus settings, or customize access control options, as described in subsequent chapters. You can change such settings in the main program window. You launch the window by doing one of the following:

- Right-click the system tray icon and choose Norton Internet Security from the shortcut menu. See "Using the system tray," later in this chapter, for more information.
- Double-click the NIS shortcut on your desktop.
- Choose Start➪All Programs➪Norton Internet Security.

When you do any of these things, the window shown in Figure 2-17 opens. Take a minute or two to acquaint yourself with its main features.

Click to block all network traffic

Click to update virus information

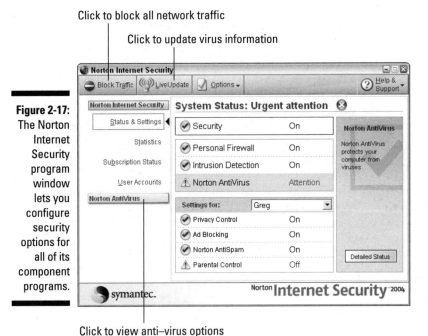

Figure 2-17:
The Norton
Internet
Security
program
window
lets you
configure
security
options for
all of its
component
programs.

Click to view anti–virus options

By default, the program window launches with Norton Internet Security's general options on top. If you want to view options specific to Norton AntiVirus, you can either click on the silver bar on the left side of the window or double-click the Norton AntiVirus link in the middle of the window.

The Options button at the top of the window lets you view detailed configuration settings for Norton Internet Security and Norton AntiVirus. I discuss these options in Chapters 4 and 5, respectively.

Notice that in Figure 2-17, the message Urgent Attention appears at the top of the Norton Internet Security window. The message is displayed because you have not yet scanned your computer for viruses using Norton AntiVirus. Symantec suggests that you scan your hard drive for viruses at least once a week, and this message is intended to remind you to do so. In order to make the message "go away," you need to double-click Norton AntiVirus to open the AntiVirus options, then click the Scan Now button on the right side of the window. Because you already scanned your hard drive for viruses either before or during installation, I suggest that this step is optional, and you can wait a few days before conducting your first virus scan.

Starting or stopping components

The main Norton Internet Security window provides you with an easy way to turn components on or off: Click the <u>On</u> or <u>Off</u> link in the center column of the window, while the Norton Internet Security options are displayed. That, at least, works for Privacy Control, Ad Blocking, Norton AntiSpam, and Parental Control. But if you want to turn Norton Internet Security or Norton AntiVirus on or off, you also have two other options: the system tray and Windows Explorer.

Using the system tray

The system tray is an area at one end of the Windows taskbar (the opposite end from the Start button) where the current time is displayed. The system tray also holds program icons for applications that are configured to have them in that location. Double-clicking one of the icons opens the program's application window. Right-clicking one of the icons opens a shortcut menu that lets you control the application. The shortcut menu for Norton Internet Security is shown in Figure 2-18.

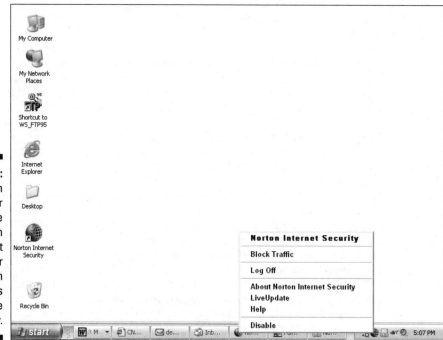

Figure 2-18: You can enable or disable Norton Internet Security or Norton AntiVirus from the system tray.

The shortcut menu gives you a quick way to perform tasks such as logging off so someone else can use his or her account, blocking all traffic, or disabling Norton Internet Security altogether. Norton AntiVirus has its own system tray icon, which allows you to enable or disable virus protection or configure the application.

Using Web Assistant

Web Assistant is a toolbar you can add to Microsoft Internet Explorer's regular set of toolbars. It enables you to combat some of the marketing tools that commercial Web sites try to put before your eyes, and that slow down your Web surfing experience. If you see a pop-up ad or other ad on a Web page, you can click it and drag it into Norton Internet Security's Ad Trashcan. You can also configure the program to automatically block pop-up ads from appearing on the current Web site. Click the down arrow on the Web Assistant toolbar and choose either Block Ads from This Site or Block Popups from This Site from the menu that appears (see Figure 2-19).

You can also use Web Assistant to keep remote Web sites from placing small bits of digital information called cookies on your hard drive. A cookie is data that identifies you either during a visit, or so that the site can provide you with personalized content when you revisit it in the future. Many Web surfers regard any information placed on their computer without their knowledge as an invasion of privacy. You can find out more about how Norton Internet Security blocks ads and cookies in Chapter 10.

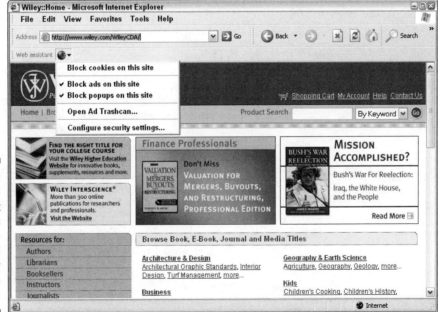

Figure 2-19: Web Assistant helps improve your level of privacy while you surf.

Using Windows Explorer

Norton AntiVirus has its own toolbar that is added to your copy of Windows Explorer, the built-in software for browsing files and folders in your computer's file system. To display the toolbar, choose View⇨Toolbars⇨Norton AntiVirus. Click the down arrow in the toolbar to launch a system scan, view files that are in quarantine, or look up virus definitions on the Symantec Web site.

Setting options

Each of the components listed in the main NIS program window has its own configuration options. For example, if you click Intrusion Detection or Ad Blocking and then click the Configure button, a window appears that enables you to turn on or off this particular feature. You can also change how the component works. Such options can be highly technical, however, and they will be discussed in subsequent chapters.

Selecting a default security level

When you use Network Detector to identify your current network, Norton Internet Security automatically adopts a set of built-in security settings. The default settings should be adequate, but you can change them if you're using a laptop or moving to a new location. Follow these steps:

1. **Double-click the desktop shortcut or the system tray icon for Norton Internet Security.**

   The main program window opens.

2. **Double-click Personal Firewall.**

   The Personal Firewall options appear (see Figure 2-20).

3. **Move the slider up or down to change the current setting, and read the description of the setting that appears just to the right of the slider.**

4. **Click OK.**

   The security level changes (if you moved the slider) and Norton Internet Security closes; you return to the main program window. At the very least, verifying your current security level is a good idea. You may want to change the settings if you are attacked, if you change locations, or if you are especially concerned about a virus or intrusion you hear about in the news media.

Dealing with performance slowdowns

Suppose you have just started using Norton Internet Security and you notice slowdowns in how the computer performs various tasks. It takes you longer to connect to Web sites, longer to get your e-mail, longer to launch programs, and so on. Such complaints have been voiced by NIS users occasionally. Even if you have cleaned up unnecessary files and applications as described in Chapter 1, you still have some options for improving your performance:

✔ Install more memory. If you can install more RAM (in other words, if you have not yet reached your computer's maximum capacity) or hard drive space, do so. Installing more RAM should bring you immediate benefits. If you can install a new hard drive, move as many files there as possible. Consider keeping your program files on one drive and all your working files on the other.

✔ Stop unnecessary services. Windows may have a variety of services running in the background that you don't need and that are taking processing capability away from NIS. Open the Control Panel, double-click Administrative tools, double-click Services, and scan the list of running services. (Under the Status column, the message Started denotes that a service is running. Right-click the word Started and choose Stop to stop the service.)

✔ Install the latest service pack. Service packs issued by Microsoft can improve performance.

✔ Check your Internet connection. Even if you have a broadband connection, it may not be running as fast as your ISP advertises. You can test your connection on the DSL Reports Web site (`www.dslreports.com/stest`).

You can also install Norton SystemWorks if you need to clean up your computer to improve performance. If all else fails, you may need to upgrade your computer to make sure you have a fast enough processor and enough processor capability to run NIS efficiently.

Setting LiveUpdate options

As I say earlier in this chapter, LiveUpdate is a component of Norton Internet Security that periodically reminds you to install updates so the software remains up to date. It probably won't take long for you to become acquainted with LiveUpdate: A window pops up soon after you have installed the software, immediately asking if you want to update it. You can either click OK or specify when you next want LiveUpdate to check for available downloads.

Unless you want to put up with repeated LiveUpdate messages, you have to click OK to perform the check. The fact that the check happens behind the scenes so you can continue to work, plus the fact that new updates are almost always available when LiveUpdate checks the Symantec Web site, should assure you that the updating is necessary. See Chapter 7 for more about configuring LiveUpdate.

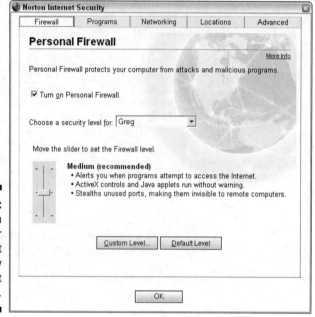

Figure 2-20:
You can
change your
default
security
level at
any time.

Chapter 3

Setting Rules for Your Firewall

In This Chapter

- Getting a handle on firewall basics
- Interpreting alerts and viewing details
- Making access choices
- Scanning your file system
- Unblocking applications

One of the most important functions any security program can perform is to provide you with notification when a "situation" has occurred. You want to know if someone has sent you an e-mail with a virus attached, or is attempting to connect to an application without your knowledge. Being aware of such potential problems gives you the chance to "teach" your firewall how to react in the future. You establish rules that the firewall can use when it encounters similar security threats.

Nevertheless, it can be disconcerting and a little nerve-wracking when you see your first security alert. You're sitting at your computer, working away on your favorite applications, when it happens: Norton Internet Security presents you with an alert message, such as the one shown in Figure 3-1.

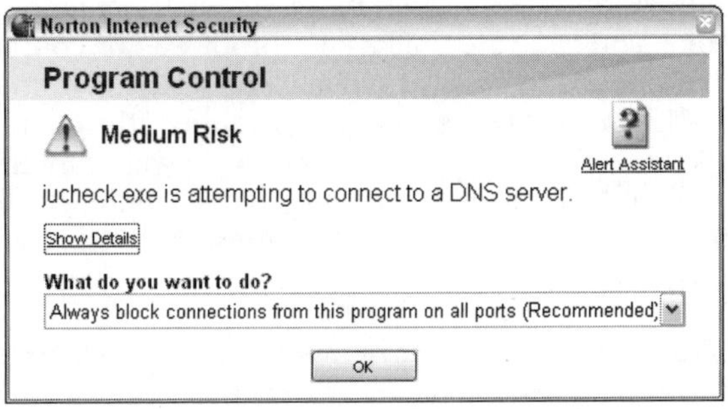

Figure 3-1: Alert messages can appear without warning and leave you wondering what to do.

As you can see, the alert message in this example indicates that an application named jucheck.exe is attempting to make a connection to something called a "DNS server." While you are scratching your head wondering what jucheck.exe and a DNS server are, you are asked to make a decision from the drop-down list in the bottom half of the dialog box. You can:

- ✓ Always allow connections from this program on all ports
- ✓ Always block connections from this program on all ports
- ✓ Manually configure access for this program

The thing you don't want to do is panic: The fact that the alert message appears at all means that Norton Internet Security is doing its job. It may have prevented a real attack; the event may also be a harmless connection attempt caused by a program that was performing a legitimate task.

In this example, the options indicate that jucheck.exe is a computer program (the file extension .exe, which is used for executable programs, should be another tip-off), so the options are useful from an educational standpoint. But there's that word "port" again. What does it mean to enable the program to use all of your computer's ports? Should you use all ports or just allow some? And which option should you choose?

These sorts of questions naturally arise when NIS presents you with alert dialog boxes and asks you to make decisions. This chapter explains what the messages mean and how to make informed choices that set up sensible rules by which your firewall will be able to protect your computer.

Understanding Your Firewall

Firewalls have quickly become a required rather than an optional part of virtually every network, whether at home or in a business environment. When they are maintained and upgraded on a regular basis, firewalls are among the most effective security tools you can use. Unlike a fireproof wall or container, a network firewall is not supposed to prevent *all* hackers, viruses, or unauthorized traffic from entering the protected area — in this context, the computer or network on which it is installed. Rather, a computer firewall is intended to monitor traffic in and out of a network gateway, allowing authorized traffic to pass through and blocking unauthorized traffic. Firewalls act as two general categories of security devices:

- ✓ **Packet filter.** NIS uses rules that have been developed either automatically or as a result of decisions made by the computer user (that's you) in order to allow or deny the passage of packets of digital information.

- ✓ **Application gateway.** An application gateway decides whether or not applications should have access to the wider network (usually, the Internet).

Some firewalls are incorporated into hardware devices such as routers; others combine both software and hardware. Norton Internet Security is a software firewall, which means it monitors traffic into and out of a single computer. If the computer is set up to function as a server that enables files (or an Internet connection) to be shared among several machines on a network, NIS can provide some protection for those other networked computers as well.

Firewall Basics

You can understand firewalls more easily if you consider the function of a security guard at the entrance to a major movie studio. On any given day, hundreds or even thousands of cars as well as pedestrians pass through the guard's security station. How does the guard (we'll call him Ray) know who can be allowed admittance and who should be barred? Ray's decisions can be made based on a set of security rules like these:

- ✔ All authorized personnel should wear an ID card.
- ✔ All authorized personnel should pass through Gate A.
- ✔ All delivery trucks should come through Gate B.
- ✔ All individuals should pass through a metal detector.
- ✔ The security gate can be shut completely in case of emergency.

A firewall performs similar functions for applications that attempt to send packets through the security checkpoint it provides. On a firewall, approved entry and exit points called interfaces are designated for specific types of data, but not others. Firewalls inspect the data within a packet that identifies it, such as its source IP address; they use such criteria to allow some packets to pass and others to be blocked. If an intruder gets through, the firewall notifies the user with an alert message, just as security guard Ray would do.

Positioning the firewall

Another fundamental aspect about firewalls that directly affects their effectiveness is their location on a network. Firewalls are designed to provide "perimeter security" — they are most effective when positioned on the perimeter of a network. Norton Internet Security is intended to be installed on one computer, unless you have a multicomputer license.

NIS ideally should be installed on a computer that is dedicated solely to network security and that has only a minimal number of services installed on it (called a *bastion host*). In home and small office applications, a bastion host is impractical; NIS should then be installed on the computer that serves as the network file server or domain controller, as shown in Figure 3-2.

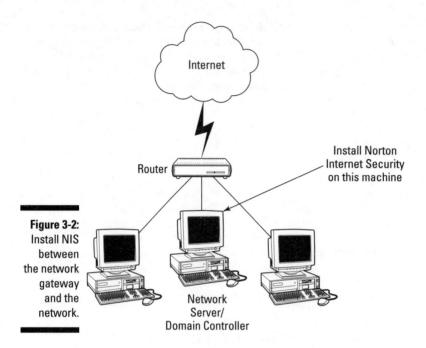

Figure 3-2:
Install NIS
between
the network
gateway
and the
network.

On large networks, firewalls are located on computers in a mini network called a Demilitarized Zone (DMZ). The computers on the DMZ hold the Web server, e-mail server, and other resources that might need to be accessed by computers outside the main network. The computers on the main network are protected from direct contact with computers on the Internet.

Guarding data transfer

All firewalls, at the most basic level, provide protection by filtering packets. As described in Chapter 1, a packet is a unit of digital information that enables data to be transferred between computers on a network. A packet contains two types of information:

- ✔ **Header.** The header part of a packet contains general information about what protocol was used to send it and the IP address of the source computer and the computer that is being contacted.

- ✔ **Data.** The data part of a packet is the actual information you see and work with — the contents of an e-mail message, for example.

A firewall selectively forwards packets from one network to another if the header or data in the packet are allowed to pass. The data might cause the packet to be blocked if Norton AntiVirus detects a virus or other suspicious program contained in it. The header might cause the packet to be blocked if the IP address, port, or protocol information in the header matches one of the "block" rules established by the firewall. Although NIS does have the ability to establish rules automatically, some basic knowledge of those criteria (ports, protocols, and IP addresses) can help you understand the firewall better and make decisions about how to set up effective rules.

IP addressing for success

Internet Protocol (IP) is one of the fundamental protocols that enables computers to "talk" to one another on the Internet. IP provides for an addressing system that computers use to locate one another. The version of Internet Protocol that is most widely used on the Internet, Internet Protocol Version 4 (IPv4), calls for addresses that contain 32 bits of data. The 32 bits are grouped into four numbers that have a value of 0 to 255. Each number is separated by dots (for example, 192.168.3.1). IP addressing can become very complicated, but the most important aspects you need to know are these:

- ✔ **The IP address corresponds to the domain of the organization or individual that owns it.** Exactly how much of the address corresponds to the domain depends on whether the IP address is Class A, Class B, or Class C (see below). For example, the domain name wiley.com corresponds to the IP address 208.215.179.146. The first part of the address, 208.215.179, can be said to be wiley.com's network address — though you need to know another number, the network mask, to know this for sure. If you know the network mask, the IP address can help you determine where someone else (such as an attacker) is located — or at least, what organization their IP address corresponds to.

- ✔ **The second part of an IP address is the station address.** This part of the IP address corresponds to an individual computer (or station, or host) on the network. The last part of the IP address (in this example, 146) can be used (along with the network mask) to calculate the station address — the number that corresponds to an individual computer on the network.

A *data bit* is a unit of digital information — literally, one or more zeros or ones (0 or 1) that, in combination, constitute a computer file or instruction. Those who are familiar with IP addressing will note that a network address is more complicated than I have described above: The actual network address and station address require you to know the subnet mask of the network and to perform calculations that are well beyond the scope of this book. A newer version of IP, IPv6, has been developed because the number of available addresses in IPv4 has begun to run out due to the widespread use of the Internet. IPv6 calls for much larger and more complex IP addresses than those currently seen. This book will focus on IPv4, however, because these are the types of IP addresses you are likely to see when working with NIS alert messages.

The other important thing to know about IPv4 addresses is that they come in five classes: Classes A through E. The IP addresses you see in alert messages and in NIS log files will be from Classes A through C because these are the three classes used on the Internet. The class of an IP address is described by the first of the four numbers. Within each class, a range of addresses has been designated for use on private networks rather than the public Internet:

- **Class A:** These addresses have first numbers ranging from 1 to 126. Within this class, addresses from 10.0.0.1 to 10.255.255.254 are private.

- **Class B:** These addresses have first numbers ranging from 128 to 191. Within this class, addresses from 172.16.0.1 to 172.31.255.254 are private.

- **Class C:** These addresses have first numbers ranging from 192 to 223. Within this class, addresses ranging from 192.168.0.1 to 192.168.255.254 are private.

In addition, Microsoft uses a system called Automatic Private IP Addressing (APIPA) to dynamically assign IP addresses in the range 169.254.0.1 to 169.254.255.254 to computers on a network when a more common addressing system called Dynamic Host Control Protocol (DHCP) isn't available.

Why, you ask, do you need to know about public versus private messages? So you aren't confused (or are less confused) when you read alert messages or try to scan NIS log files, as described in Chapter 16. If you see an alert message that reads:

```
The computer at 204.131.255.10 is attempting to connect to
          172.16.1.2 on port 80. What do you want to do?
```

You know that the computer attempting to make the connection is a remote one on the Internet, while the destination computer is on a private network — undoubtedly, your own home network. When you set up a home network, using Microsoft Windows, AppleShare, or another system, your computers are probably assigned dynamic IP addresses. These are private IP addresses: They are used only for communications between the machines on the network.

If you want to know your computer's current IP address, start up your Web browser and connect to the Convert Host Name to IP address Web site (www.hcidata.co.uk/host2ip.htm). Enter a host name (any host name, such as microsoft.com or dummies.com) in the Domain Name box and click Find IP Address. A page appears that displays the IP address corresponding to the domain name. In addition, if NIS's Browser Privacy component is not completely blocking your browser information, you will also see the IP address of your own computer.

You can also determine the IP address of your computer by choosing Start⇨ All Programs⇨Accessories⇨Command Prompt to open a command prompt window on Windows XP systems. Then type **ipconfig** and press Enter. (On Windows XP, 2000, Me, or 98 systems, choose Start⇨Run, type **winipcfg**, and press Enter. You'll see the IP address for your own computer as well as your network gateway.

Checking ports in a storm

As you found out in Chapter 1, any computer can listen on multiple ports, each of which can be a vulnerable point. You also found out you might have one or more services listening on ports that you don't even use. If you decide to establish packet filtering and application access rules with NIS manually rather than automatically, you'll be asked to decide whether a rule should apply on all of your computer's available ports, or on a specific port.

You can't always adjust what ports your applications use when they attempt to access the Internet. But because Web browsers are so popular and central to any Internet security effort, Norton Personal Firewall does let you check and adjust the port or ports that your browser uses when it connects to Web sites.

The official list of ports and the applications that use them is maintained by the Internet Assigned Numbers Authority and is available at www.iana.org/ assignments/port-numbers.

Filtering network traffic

Along with restricting unauthorized traffic from entering the network from the outside, firewalls can selectively permit traffic to go from inside the net-work to the Internet or other network.

Packet filtering depends on the establishment of rules. Many of those rules depend on the protocol being used to make the connection and transfer the desired information. Many different protocols can be used on the Internet, but the three that turn up most frequently in firewall alert messages and the rules that are established as a result of those alerts are ICMP, UDP, and TCP.

ICMP rules

IP, by itself, has no way of letting the host that originated a request know whether or not a packet was received at its destination in its entirety. It can, however, use Internet Control Message Protocol (ICMP) to report any errors that occurred in the transmission.

There's a significant difference between the way ICMP is *supposed* to be used and the way it is frequently misused. ICMP is supposed to let one computer on a network know that another computer is present and reachable on the network. Computers send simple "ping messages" to one another to verify such connectivity. Ping messages are only one kind of communication that can be sent using ICMP; others include messages that notify the network administrator of trouble, such as Destination Unreachable or Destination Host Unknown messages.

The danger is that ICMP packets can be filled with false information that can trick your hosts into redirecting or stopping communications.

UDP rules

User Datagram Protocol is not used on the Internet quite as often as TCP, but it's very important from a security standpoint. That's because it is a very insecure protocol and one that is frequently exploited by hackers. UDP is regarded as highly suspect because it is connectionless: Packets can be exchanged by computers using UDP even if they have not established a formal connection. This makes it relatively easy for a hacker to send a mal-formed or dangerous packet to another computer using UDP.

This protocol is similar to TCP in that it handles the addressing of a message. UDP breaks a message into numbered segments so it can be transmitted, then reassembles it when it reaches the destination computer. Unlike TCP, UDP is connectionless: It simply sends segments of messages without per-forming error checking or waiting for an acknowledgement that the message has been received. Such a protocol is useful for video and audio broadcasts on the Internet. TCP and UDP are often mentioned together in discussions of firewalls because both transmit data through a combination of a port and an IP address (which is called a *socket*) and thus open up vulnerabilities. It's useful to set up rules to block UDP traffic on ports 21 and below, and to block traffic on ports that control hardware such as keyboards, hubs, and routers; see Chapter 2 for more information.

TCP filtering rules

Transmission Control Protocol (TCP) is one of the fundamental protocols used on the Internet. TCP is a more secure way of creating a connection between computers because it provides for acknowledgement and verification of a con-nection. It ensures that data sent from one computer will reach its intended destination completely and in the correct sequence. The TCP protocol makes use of six control flags that can be included in the header part of a packet. You may occasionally see references to such packets when researching what an alert message means or how a particular type of attack works:

- SYN (Synchronize sequence numbers, used to initiate a connection)
- ACK (Acknowledgement)
- PSH (Push function, used to move data from one computer to another)

✔ URG (Urgent)

✔ RST (Reset, used to reset a connection)

✔ FIN (Used to indicate that all data has been sent)

You don't have to know how all of these flags are used to make TCP secure. You just need to know that, in some kinds of attacks, flags are forged so they are sent in mixed-up or illegal sequences. If the destination computer does not know how to handle such information, it may let the connection be established so that the hacker can infiltrate the targeted computer.

Decoding All Those Alert Messages

You've always got the option of simply following what NIS presents as the recommended course of action when you are trying to decide how to respond to an alert message. When one action seems better than the others, NIS will present as the preferred one, as in this example:

```
Block this connection on all ports (Recommended)
```

In my experience, what NIS presents as the "preferred" one isn't really preferable. It often suggests that you block a connection to a Web site when you are simply trying to view a Web page, for example. Always use your judgment when deciding whether to block or permit.

If you are trying to do something that involves connecting to a Web site or another Internet-based location, don't be surprised if you see a succession of alert messages appear. If you have Internet Explorer, Outlook Express, and Netscape Communicator all open and connected to Web sites, you might see alert messages for each of these applications, including Microsoft Messenger, which works with Outlook Express. You may have to click Permit for each of these alert messages, one after another. If you're tired of receiving alert messages for a particular application, skip ahead to the section, "Running a program scan," later in this chapter. Select the application from the list in the Program Control window (see Figure 3-3), click on the setting in the Internet Access column, and choose Permit All from the shortcut menu that appears.

You'll generally be better off if you take some time to research what is happening and to evaluate the potential threat so you can minimize possible damage. The following sections examine ways to research an alert to take away the sense of alarm and gain control over your computer security through better understanding of the issues underlying the threats you face.

No instant action is necessary when you're responding to an alert message. You can leave it on your screen for minutes or even hours while you research the event and determine the best course of action. While the message is on-screen, NIS is preventing the connection attempt and protecting your computer from intrusion. If a message asks the question "What do you want to do?" you must make a decision; otherwise, the alert is primarily informational and you don't have to choose an option.

Categorizing alert messages

Most of the alert messages you'll see from Norton Internet Security are probably in the form of Internet Access Control Alerts. But you'll probably see some others once in a while and, if they don't appear often, they can confuse you. If you know what kind of alert message you are faced with at a given time, you can handle it better. The four types of alerts are described in the following sections.

Internet Access Control alerts

Norton Internet Security is all about monitoring traffic to and from the Internet. Accordingly, most of the alerts you see from the program are Internet Access Control Alerts. These appear when an application on your computer attempts to make a connection with a remote computer on the Internet. The obvious ones occur when Internet Explorer or Outlook Express attempt to connect to a server. But other, more obscure applications, such as Microsoft Generic host Process for Windows 32 Services, need to make connections as well (see Figure 3-4).

Figure 3-3:
You can
always
allow an
application
unrestricted
access if
you want to
keep alert
messages
from
appearing.

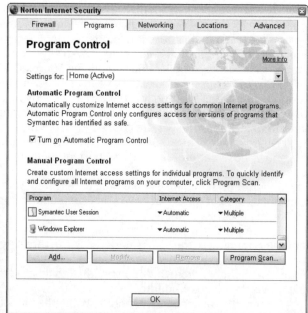

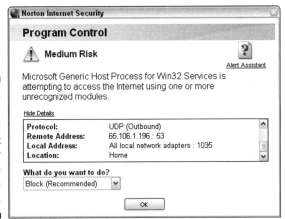

Figure 3-4:
Some
applications
you may not
be familiar
with need to
access the
Internet.

Often, the alert messages that NIS displays have Block as the default option. You don't have to automatically choose this option. If the application is one that you know should access the Internet (such as a Web browser), you should choose Permit instead. If you make a choice and want to change it, you can always do so at a later time, as described in "Customizing Internet access," later in this chapter.

Security alerts

Security Alerts may look scary, but they're actually reassuring: They inform you if a possible attack against your computer was detected by NIS and that the program stopped the attack from occurring. The attack may have been from an external computer, or from a program on your computer such as a Trojan horse that was prevented from making a connection to another computer on the Internet.

You don't have to make a decision or actually do anything when you see a Security alert. Just click OK to close the window, or select Yes and then click OK if you want more information on the attack.

Settings alerts

Every application installed on a Windows-based computer stores operating information in the part of Windows called the registry. If hackers want to bypass the protection provided by Norton Internet Security, Norton AntiVirus, or Norton Personal Firewall, they may attempt to make changes to the registry settings of either of these programs. (Yes, they are able to access someone else's registry over the Internet using specially designed applications.)

NIS, NAV, and NPF are both configured so that, if any changes are made to their registry settings, a Settings Alert message is displayed. (The registry settings for these programs are actually encrypted.) You must immediately click OK when the alert message appears. Another dialog box appears informing you that your computer needs to be restarted. You must click OK in order to protect your original registry settings and keep the hacker from getting around your firewall and anti-virus programs. After the computer restarts, the default registry settings will replace the previous ones.

Cookie alerts

These alerts appear when you have configured Cookie Blocking (in the Privacy Control window; see Chapter 10) to Medium. At the Medium setting, Privacy Control alerts you whenever a Web site is either attempting to place a cookie on your hard drive or is trying to connect to a cookie that was placed there earlier.

Usually, NIS presents Permit as the "Recommended" action for cookies, because most cookies aren't a security threat by themselves. I talk more about cookies in Chapter 10.

Many Web sites don't let you access content unless you have cookies enabled. Don't block access to all cookies unless you are sure the site will still be usable after you prevent them from being placed.

Confidential information or private information alerts

You see one of these alert messages when NIS detects that one of the pieces of information you have identified as private is about to be submitted to a remote Web site. They aren't alerts exactly; think of them as notifications that are sent to you — after NIS has already quarantined a virus, blocked an intrusion, or otherwise neutralized a possible security breach.

Most informational alerts give you the option of getting more information about what occurred. In some occasions, you may be prompted to restart your computer. Other than that, you don't have an option; NIS decides whether to block or allow the connection attempt, whether it was from a Trojan horse or from a relatively benign cookie.

Viewing alert details

When you click Show Details in the Program Control dialog box, a set of new information appears that tells you when this program attempted to access the Internet, where it is located on your computer, and what computer it is trying to reach. Here's an example from an alert message I received:

- ✔ **Time:** 5:31 PM
- ✔ **Date:** 5/14/2004
- ✔ **Program:** jucheck.exe
- ✔ **Path:** C:\Program Files\Java\j2re1.4.2_03\bin\

✔ **Protocol:** UDP (Outbound)

✔ **Remote Address:** 65.106.1.196:53

✔ **Local Address:** 208.177.178.150:0

This set of information is worth understanding, because it tells you a great deal about this connection attempt. Here's my explanation for each of the bits of information presented:

✔ The time and date are significant because I was not working at my computer at the time; the application was attempting to make a connection automatically, without any activity by me.

✔ The .exe filename extension indicates that this is an executable program — in other words, a computer program. I don't recognize the name of this application, so it makes me suspicious.

✔ The path pointing to the program's location indicates that it has something to do with my copy of the Java application that lets my browser process Java applets on Web pages.

✔ The UDP protocol is a notorious security risk and one that is frequently exploited by hackers, so this makes me even more suspicious.

✔ The remote address is the IP address of my own Domain Name Service server, which operates on port 53. The local address is my network gateway's IP address.

So far, I don't feel I have enough information to decide whether to block or permit this access attempt. In such a case, you can use another utility that appears in all of NIS's alert messages: the Alert Assistant, which I describe in the following section.

Investigating alerts with the Alert Assistant

If you want to find out more about a particular alert message, or any alert presented by NIS, click the Alert Assistant link. The Alert Assistant window opens with the heading Internet Access Control Alert (see Figure 3-5).

Most of the information provided in this window is no different than what I have explained already. But there is one thing of interest: The IP address that the program is attempting to connect to, 65.106.1.196, is a clickable hyperlink. Click it, and the Visual Tracking window appears (see Figure 3-6).

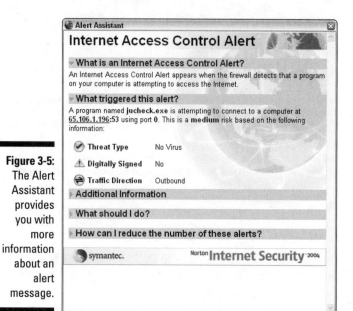

Figure 3-5:
The Alert
Assistant
provides
you with
more
information
about an
alert
message.

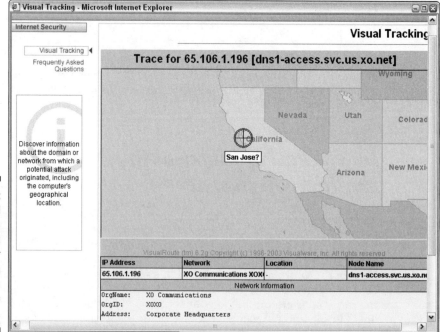

Figure 3-6:
Visual
Tracking
shows you
the origin or
destination
of a
connection
attempt.

The Visual Tracking map gives you a geographic location for the IP address that you clicked. Just above the map, the domain for the IP address is given: In this case, it's the author's own ISP, XO Communications. So, the application `jucheck.exe` is trying to connect to my DNS server. The question remains: Why?

I turn to Google. I find out that the program `jucheck.exe` stands for Sun Java Update Checker. It's probably a legitimate program that wants to check for a new version of its own software. But do I want it to do this? Other listings on Google are from individuals who complain that `jucheck.exe` consumes a large amount of processing capacity. And do you really need this program to be making connections without your knowledge? Whenever it does so, a port is opened on your computer, and your IP address is transmitted to a remote computer whose purpose is unknown to you. Based on this information, I choose the option recommended by Norton Internet Security in the first place: Always block all connections from this program on all ports.

Disabling alert messages

When I did a test on enabling cookies, I set up NIS to send me an alert message whenever a Web site attempted to place a cookie on my computer. I soon came to regret this. A flood of alert messages resulted — a never-ending flood, in fact. Many of them came from a site that, I thought, was supposed to provide me with services without being intrusive: Windowsmedia.com.

If you ever want to turn off alert messages for this specific sort of event, you can do so by following these steps:

1. **Open NIS or NPF.**

2. **Double-click Personal Firewall.**

3. **On the Advanced tab, click Trojan Horse.**

4. **Locate the rule generating the alerts, and click the rule to highlight it.**

5. **Click Modify.**

6. **On the Tracking tab, deselect "Notify me with a security alert."**

7. **Click OK in any open windows.**

   The windows close and you return to the main NIS window. From now on, when the rule is triggered by a connection attempt, you won't see a security alert window.

The steps also work for general programs. You might want to let a potentially harmful application into your network in a controlled situation just to see how it functions so that you can block such applications more effectively in the future. A good setting in which to do this would be a work environment where the computer can be isolated from other machines, however.

Making Access Choices

When you decide whether to block or allow an event, you balance access versus risk. The entire experience of going online is such a balance: If you never connected to the Internet, you would never be in danger of electronic intrusions — but you wouldn't have any access, either. Dial in with a modem connection, and your risk is less than you'd have with an always-on connection, but so is your level of access. You can't block all traffic all the time, or you won't have any connection with the Internet at all.

For most Internet access alerts and security alerts, the alert window that appears presents you with four choices from the drop-down list:

- ✔ Permit the connection on a one-time basis.
- ✔ Permit the connection every time it is attempted.
- ✔ Block the connection on a one-time basis.
- ✔ Block the connection every time it is attempted.

If you check the Always Use This Action box, you set up a rule that will govern all future connection attempts of this sort — from the same computer, using the same port.

Which applications should you allow, and which should you block? Table 3-1 gives you some guidelines.

Table 3-1	Blocking versus Allowing Applications	
Application	*Suggested Action*	*Comments*
Microsoft Generic host Process for Windows 32 Services (Svchost.exe)	Permit	Enables Windows to run network-related services; okay to permit in most cases, though some Trojan horses use it
Internet Information Server (Inetinfo.exe)	Block	Vulnerable to attack; not needed unless you are running a Web server
Local Security Authority Service (lsass.exe)	Block	Verifies logons from other computers, so is not required for most single-user PCs; was exploited by the Sasser virus

Application	Suggested Action	Comments
Microsoft Printer Spooler Service	Permit	Needed for network printing
Microsoft TCP/IP Con-figuration Utility	Permit	Needed for TCP/IP network communications
Microsoft Windows Messenger	Permit	Even if you don't do instant messag ing, it is needed by Outlook Express and Internet Explorer
Simple Network Management Protocol (snmp.exe)	Block	Only useful for home or business networks
Symantec Event Manager Service messages	Permit	Needed to provide you with alert
Symantec LiveUpdate	Permit	Needs to access Symantec's Web site to see if updates are available to NIS

What Do You Mean, That Program Is Trying to Access the Internet?

After you install Norton Internet Security, you may see a series of alert messages when you restart your computer. Alternatively, you may see the Security Assistant Wizard. The Security Assistant Wizard only appears the first time that you restart the computer after installing Norton Internet Security or Norton Personal Firewall. After you close the Security Assistant Wizard, you cannot use it again. If you never see the Security Assistant Wizard, you can run a program scan.

Running a Program Scan

Running a program scan can reduce the number of alert messages you see and decisions you have to make. In a program scan, Norton Internet Security and Norton Personal Firewall scan your hard drive for any applications that are capable of connecting to the Internet. When the scan is complete, Norton displays the applications in a list. You can then decide whether to have NIS automatically configure rules by which the programs can access the Internet, or you can manually create the rules. If you do not run the Program Scan Wizard, each time an Internet-enabled program attempts to access the Internet, a security alert appears. To run the Program Scan, follow these steps:

1. **Start Norton Internet Security.**

   The main program window opens.

2. **Double-click Personal Firewall.**

   Another window labeled Norton Internet Security appears, with the Personal Firewall tab in front.

3. **Click the Programs tab.**

   The Program Control set of options appears.

4. **Click Program Scan.**

   The Program Scan set of options appears (see Figure 3-7).

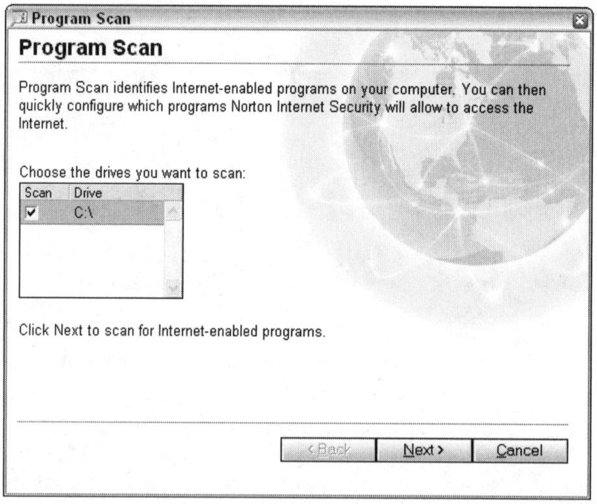

Figure 3-7: This dialog box lets you select a disk drive to scan for Internet-enabled applications.

5. **Select the box next to the drive you want to scan, and then click Next.**

   (If you only have one drive available, the check box next to it will be pre-selected and you don't have to do anything.) A new window labeled Program Scan appears, with a progress bar (see Figure 3-8) indicating the progress of scanning all the applications on your computer that can potentially access the Internet.

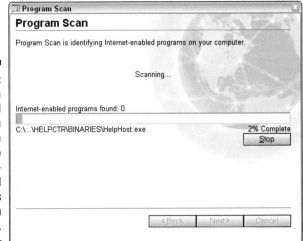

6. **Watch the progress.**

   The scan can take several minutes to complete, as Program Scan evaluates the access settings for each of the applications. When the scan is complete, a box labeled Internet-enabled programs appears. The message at the top of the Program Scan window changes to "Click a program's check box to configure its Internet access settings."

7. **Make one of three choices:**

   - Click Check All if you want to have Norton Internet Security configure settings automatically for each of the applications.

   - Click Uncheck All if you want Norton Internet Security to set access settings for none of the applications. You'll see plenty of alert messages if you choose this option.

   - Click Add if you want to manually configure access options for a specific application. If you choose this option, follow the steps described in "Customizing Internet access," later in this chapter.

8. **Click Next.**

   The options Automatic Program Control and Manual Program Control appear.

At this point, you can choose whether you want Norton Internet Security to configure access control to all of your Internet applications, or whether you want to select certain applications and configure manual access yourself. I discuss those two options in the following sections.

Automatic configuration

If you want NIS to decide how and when your applications are to access the Internet, select the Turn on Automatic Program Control box, then click OK. Norton Internet Security will automatically set up rules for your applications. This means the number of alert messages will be reduced. But they won't go away altogether. You'll still see such messages when an external Web site tries to connect to you, or when a new application you have installed tries to connect to a Web site or other resource on the Internet.

Even if you have Norton Internet Security automatically control your programs, you can still do manual configuration by following the steps presented in the preceding section to display the Program Control dialog box, and then choosing an application from the list. Then, follow the steps in the section that follows.

Customizing Internet access

Sometimes, you need to configure access options manually for a particular application, even if Norton Internet Security has automatically set access options as a result of a program scan. For example, I let NIS do automatic configuration for Internet Explorer. But when I attempted to listen to audio on a Web site, Internet Explorer attempted to make the connection with the aid of a variety of programs called "modules" that enable it to view Shockwave animations, Windows Media audio files, and the like. Access was prevented, so I had to configure Internet Explorer manually. To perform your own manual access configuration, follow these steps:

1. **Open the Program Control dialog box as described in the previous section.**

   The Program Control window opens.

2. **Click Add.**

   The Select a Program dialog box appears.

3. **Click the Look In drop-down list and browse your file system to select an executable program to configure.**

   Such a program will have an .exe file extension.

4. **Select the application, and then click Open.**

   The Program Control dialog box opens (see Figure 3-9).

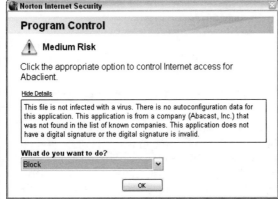

Figure 3-9:
You can
select an
application
and
configure
Internet
access
yourself.

5. **Click the down arrow under the heading "What do you want to do?", select one of the options (Block, Permit, or Manually Configure Internet Access) from the drop-down list, and then click Next.**

   If you select Block or Permit, the dialog box closes and the rule is accepted. If you select Manually Configure Internet Access, the Add Rule dialog box appears (see Figure 3-10). You might want to manually configure a rule if you want an application to make only outbound rather than inbound connections — for example, you can send "ping" messages to other computers on an outbound basis, but they cannot send inbound ping messages to you. Manual access means the traffic is allowed through the firewall so it can be logged.

Figure 3-10:
By estab-
lishing
a manual
access rule,
you can
log access
attempts
by an
application.

6. Select the type of connection you want this application to make, and then click Next.

You can choose Outbound (connections to other computers), Inbound (connections from other computers) or both (connections to and from other computers).

7. Decide which computers or Web sites you want to be included in the rule you have chosen.

Choose Any Computer if you don't want to pick a specific destination machine. If you chose Permit, you can use this dialog box to monitor connections to a specific Web site or a computer that you identify by its IP address, for instance. If you chose Block, you can use this dialog box to restrict the rule to a specific computer. If you want to choose a computer, click Only the Computers and Sites Listed Below, click Add, and Enter the IP address(es) of the machines you want to monitor.

Note: A network adapter is a router or network card that enables you to connect to the Internet or another corporate network. Only click Adapters if you are sure you have more than one adapter; chances are you only have one.

8. Click Next.

The next dialog box gives you the chance to restrict communications to TCP or UDP, or to choose specific ports you want to restrict. This can come in handy if you suspect that an application is being used to connect to a hacker's computer on a port such as 135; you can then click "Only the types of communication or ports listed below," click Add, and choose a port from the Specify Ports dialog box (see Figure 3-11). You can specify a range of ports (such as 135–137) by entering the starting and ending ports in the appropriate boxes. Then click OK.

Figure 3-11:
The Specify
Ports dialog
box lets you
restrict an
application
or rule to
a specific
port.

9. **Specify how you want to be notified.**

   If you want to minimize the number of alert messages you see, leave Create an Event Log Entry checked. Otherwise, check Notify Me with a Security Alert.

10. **Click Next.**

    In this screen, you name your rule (delete the default name Firewall Rule and type a new name) and select a category under which the rule will be included.

11. **Click Next.**

    Select a location where you want the rule to apply: Home, Away, Default, or Office. Choose the location you use most often, or click Check All if you want the rule to apply to all possible locations.

12. **Click Next.**

    A summary of all the settings you have created appears. Review the list; if you want to make any corrections, click Back repeatedly until you reach the screen where you can make the change. Otherwise, click Finish.

When you consider that all of your computer applications can be customized to restrict access to inbound or outbound direction, to specific ports, or to specific computers, you begin to understand just how much control you can have over how your computer interacts with the Internet.

Unblocking Applications You Blocked

The list of programs you worked with in the preceding sections can be used with a variety of configuration tasks. Suppose you decided to block an application in response to an alert message and you selected the "Always use this action" box. This doesn't mean the application is permanently blocked, however.

To unblock the application, open the main NIS window, double-click Personal Firewall, and click the Programs tab. Select the program you want to block, and then click the Remove button. If a warning message appears, click OK. Click OK to close the Program Control window. The application will now be able to operate without being blocked by NIS; if NIS displays an alert message when you try to use the application, be sure to choose Permit rather than Block as the access option.

Turning Program Control On or Off

As you have probably figured out by now, Program Control is the component of NIS that automatically determines whether or not applications should be allowed to access the resources to which they are trying to connect. Suppose you don't want NIS to perform control at all. You can turn off this function by opening the main Norton Internet Security window, double-clicking Personal Firewall, clicking Programs, and deselecting the Turn on Automatic Program Control box.

Chapter 4

Strengthening and Customizing Your Firewall

Many of Norton Personal Firewall's rules and options are configured automatically, and for good reason: Casual users are often intimidated by the technical jargon and the many choices they are asked to make when they try to set things up manually. However, you and your network will be better off if you take a little initiative and work directly with the firewall: The computers on your network will be able to connect with one another, and you can perform useful and satisfying tasks like tracking down computers that try to do reconnaissance or even launch attacks against you. NIS makes it easy to perform advanced configuration tasks and take control of your own computer security, as you'll discover in this chapter.

Working with Intrusion Detection

Most firewalls primarily monitor and filter network traffic. But Norton Personal Firewall also performs Intrusion Detection — detecting and alerting the user to attacks based on patterns of behavior and well-known characteristics called *signatures*.

In Intrusion Detection, your computer scans traffic that enters and leaves and performs actions based on whether or not the traffic matches a set of known attack signatures. If it finds a match with an attack signature within a packet that arrives at your computer or network gateway, NIS's Intrusion Detection component automatically discards the packet and breaks the connection with the computer that sent the data. Intrusion Detection can thus block an attempt by a hacker to exploit a known operating system or program vulnerability.

Intrusion Detection is important because most hackers don't invent a new type of attack — they merely try to reproduce one that has already worked successfully. Intrusion Detection protects your computer against most common Internet attacks. Many such attacks have been given strange sounding names, but they can cause a system to crash or enable a hacker to gain a control of that system. They include

- ✔ **Bonk.** The Bonk application takes advantage of a problem with older versions of Windows. It attacks the part of the computer that enables TCP/IP communications to take place and it can crash your machine.

- ✔ **Nimda_Propagation.** The Nimda worm was one of the most widespread and severe ever. Nimda is sent by e-mail. Once installed on a computer, it attempts to copy itself to network shared resources or Internet Information Server. Worse yet, it creates a guest account that gives a hacker administrator privileges to a computer.

- ✔ **RDS_Shell.** This attack uses (or rather, misuses) a Remote Data Services (RDS) interface to Microsoft's Internet Information Server. It can potentially enable a hacker to execute commands on your computer — something you definitely don't want to happen.

You'll find a lengthy list of attack signatures that Norton Personal Firewall can detect at `http://securityresponse.symantec.com/avcenter/nis_ids`.

Intrusion Detection does not scan for intrusions by computers in your Trusted Zone: your own network. However, Intrusion Detection does monitor the information that you send to trusted computers for signs of zombies and other remote control attacks. See the section, "Configuring Your Network," later in this chapter, for more information on how to identify the "friendly" computers you don't need NIS to scan.

Reducing intrusion alerts

In my experience, Norton Internet Security doesn't display intrusion alerts as frequently as it does program control alerts or virus detection messages. When an alert does come, it can be quite alarming. It's upsetting to think that someone you don't know is trying to connect to your computer without your permission for reasons you don't understand.

Again, you need to keep in mind that, when an alert does appear, it means the program has done its job and protected you from what *might* be an authorized access. I emphasize the word *might* because intrusion alerts can result mistakenly from normal network communications that only resemble an attack signature.

If you receive repeated warnings about possible attacks, and you know that these warnings are being triggered by safe behavior, you can create an exclusion for the attack signature that matches the benign activity. To exclude an attack signature from monitoring, just follow these steps:

1. **Open the main Norton Internet Security window and double-click Intrusion Detection.**

   The Intrusion Detection window opens (see Figure 4-1).

2. **Click Advanced.**

   The Intrusion Detection Signature Exclusions window opens. In a few seconds, an extensive list of the attack signatures that NIS monitors by default and blocks if necessary appears.

3. **In the Signatures list, select the attack signature that you want to exclude, and then click Exclude.**

   The signature moves to the Excluded Signatures box on the right side of the window.

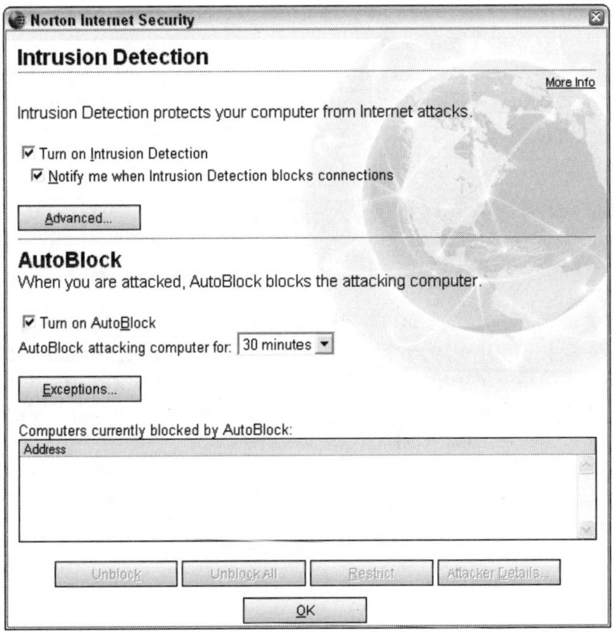

Figure 4-1: This window lets you configure NIS's Intrusion Detection controls.

4. **When you are done excluding signatures, click OK twice.**

   The Intrusion Detection Signature Exclusions window and the Intrusion Detection window both close.

You can always move a signature from the list of excluded ones back into the list of included ones. To do this, open the Intrusion Detection Signature Exclusions dialog box, click the signature you want NIS to watch out for, and click Include.

Each exclusion that you create leaves your computer more vulnerable to attacks. Be selective about choosing an attack to exclude. Make sure that, when you create an exclusion, you choose behavior that is always benign.

Deactivating intrusion detection

The other control in the upper half of the Intrusion Detection window enables you to turn Intrusion Detection on or off. You may want to turn off this function if you are testing the network for vulnerabilities and you are running a controlled test. For example, you may be allowing a malformed packet into the network to see if other protections, such as hardware firewalls, are functioning correctly.

Completely deactivating Intrusion Detection is an extreme measure, of course. If you want to maintain protection against break-ins but don't want to look at notifications that NIS sends you after a connection has been blocked, you can keep Intrusion Detection "on" while turning notifications "off." Just open the Intrusion Detection window and deselect Notify Me When Intrusion Detection Blocks Connections, while leaving Turn On Intrusion Detection selected.

Keeping a remote computer out of your network

Not long ago, I was plagued by a series of port scans. The scans went on for days and were originating from a single computer which turned out to be on the West Coast of the United States. The computer was included in the database of the security site DSheild (see "Tracking hackers with DShield," later in this chapter) as one that had attempted to connect to hundreds of other sites. It was good to know that I wasn't the only one singled out for such "attention," but it made me want to block all connection attempts from that suspect machine.

Identifying a computer to block

To block a computer, you need to identify the machine in some way. After you discover how to interpret NIS's alert messages, you can configure a rule that keeps the machine from connecting to yours. You can identify three different groups of computers:

- ✔ **A single IP address.** You get the IP address from NIS's log files.

- ✔ **A range of IP addresses.** If you notice that a group of IP addresses is trying to intrude on your network, you can describe it as 201.35.66.2–201.35.66.10, for example.

- ✔ **An entire subnet.** A subnet is a network within a network — a group of interconnected computers that uses a range of IP addresses. You need to specify the IP address of one of the computers in the subnet, and then also include the second part of the network address, which is called a subnet mask. In most cases, public IP addresses have a subnet mask of 255.255.255.0, but this can vary depending on the size of the subnet.

After you get the computer's IP address, you can use it to block the machine. You enter the IP address or addresses you want to block in the AutoBlock section of the Intrusion Detection window.

Blocking a computer

Although the Intrusion Detection window has a section called AutoBlock, it doesn't enable you to manually block one or more computers. As the name implies, AutoBlock works automatically. To manually block a computer, you use Norton Personal Firewall to set up an advanced rule especially for that machine. Follow these steps:

1. **Open the main Norton Internet Security window and double-click Personal Firewall.**

   The Personal Firewall window opens.

2. **Click Advanced.**

   The Advanced tab comes to the front.

3. **Click General.**

   The General Rules window appears.

4. **Click Add.**

   The Add Rule dialog box appears.

5. **Click Block, and then click Next.**

   The next Add Rule dialog box appears.

6. **Check the option you want — Connections from Other Computers, Connections to Other Computers, or Connections to and from Other Computers — and click Next.**

   The next Add Rule set of options, entitled "What computers or sites do you want to block?", appears.

7. **Click Only the Computers and Sites Listed Below, then click Add.**

   The Networking dialog box appears. This is where you identify the computer(s) you want to block.

8. **Click the button next to Individually, Using a Range, or Using a Network Address.**

   Type the IP address or addresses in the box provided (see Figure 4-2) and click OK. The Networking dialog box closes and you return to the Add Rule dialog box, where the IP address you entered is displayed.

9. **Click Next.**

   The next set of options, entitled "What protocols do you want to block?", appears.

10. **Click the button next to the protocols you want to block.**

    Your choice depends on the type of attack attempt you experienced. If a computer at IP address 192.168.101.22 tried to connect on port 1234 TCP, you should block connections on TCP, for example. When in doubt, click TCP and UDP. If you want to specify a port, fill in the bottom portion of this dialog box. When you are done, click Next.

11. **In the next dialog box, click the box that signifies whether you want to create an event log entry or create an intrusion alert when a connection attempt occurs that matches this rule.**

    You may want to choose the alert option if you are very concerned about a hacker and don't often scan the log files.

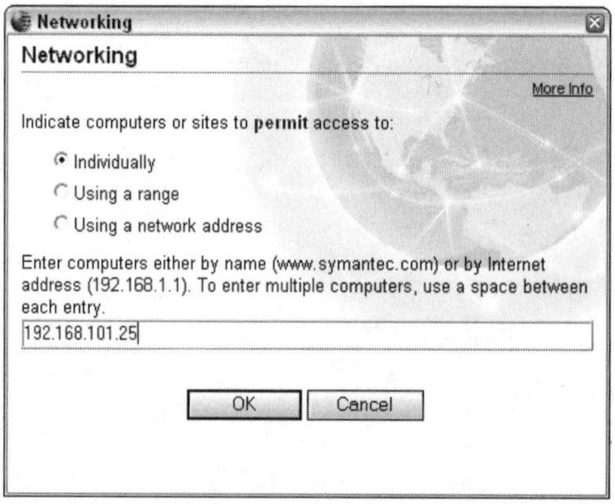

Figure 4-2:
Use this
dialog
box to
specify the
computer(s)
you want to
block.

12. **Click Next.**

   The next set of options appears, which asks you to create a name for the rule.

13. **Enter a rule name and click Next.**

14. **Choose the location where you want the rule to apply, and click Next.**

   A summary of all your rule settings appears.

15. **Click Finish.**

   The rule is created.

If you receive persistent port scans from particular computers, you may want to create rules to block all traffic from those machines on all ports, for example. But be aware that the traffic may be from unauthorized users working at the domains of friends or business associates; don't block all traffic from those sites just because of the actions of one individual.

Restricting a computer

Computers you add to the AutoBlock list are automatically blocked for a period of thirty minutes after an intrusion is detected. Norton Internet Security lets you go a step further and block a computer from gaining access to one of your trusted machines by adding that computer to your Restricted Zone. Computers in the Restricted Zone don't appear on the blocked list because all communication with restricted computers is blocked. To restrict a computer, follow these steps:

1. **Open the Norton Internet Security main window and double-click Intrusion Detection.**

   The Intrusion Detection window opens.

2. **In the AutoBlock list, select the name of the computer you want to restrict.**

   The name is highlighted.

3. **Click Restrict.**

4. **Click OK to close the Intrusion Detection window.**

Adjusting AutoBlock settings

Intrusion Detection, like many features offered by Norton Internet Security, has an automatic component. When AutoBlock detects an attack, it automatically breaks the connection to the external computer for a length of time you can control (by default, 30 minutes).

AutoBlock may prevent communications with one of the computers in your own network. If you have received an intrusion alert message stating that one of your own computers is being blocked, or if you can't view any of the shared files on the computer and you suspect AutoBlock is the culprit, you may want to turn off AutoBlock as a test to see if this is the problem. To turn off the program, follow these steps:

1. **Open the main NIS window, and double-click Intrusion Detection.**

   The Intrusion Detection window opens.

2. **Deselect the option Turn on AutoBlock, then click OK.**

If you can now communicate with your local computer, you need to remove it from the AutoBlock list.

By default, AutoBlock blocks each computer for 30 minutes. Use the drop-down list to customize how long you want to block attacking computers. Make sure to turn AutoBlock back on when you are done.

Note: AutoBlock stops all inbound communications with a specific computer. If you receive an alert stating that you are being attacked and you need to immediately stop all inbound and outbound communication with all computers, use Block Traffic.

If a computer that you need to access appears on the list of computers currently blocked by AutoBlock, select that computer and click Unblock to unblock it. If you have changed your protection settings and want to reset your AutoBlock list, you can unblock all of the computers on the AutoBlock list at once.

If the computer you need to reach does not appear on the AutoBlock list, you can exclude it from being automatically blocked. To exclude a specific computer from AutoBlock, follow these steps:

1. **Open the main NIS window and double-click Intrusion Detection.**

   The Intrusion Detection window opens.

2. **Click Exceptions.**

   The Exclusions dialog box opens (see Figure 4-3).

3. **Click Add.**

   The Networking dialog box appears.

4. **Type the computer's individual IP address or its computer name.**

5. **Click OK three times.**

   The Networking, Exclusions, and Intrusion Detection windows close.

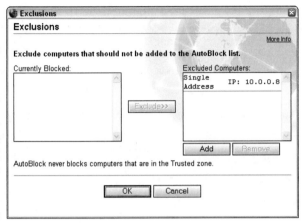

Figure 4-3:
Use this
dialog box
to keep one
of your
trusted
network
computers
from being
blocked.

Because the computer is on your local network, you may already know the
name, or you can get it by going to the computer, right-clicking My Computer,
choosing Properties, and clicking Computer Name.

Configuring Your Network

One of the ways to customize Norton Personal Firewall is by controlling the
number and type of alerts you receive. Another is by identifying computers
on your network that are "friendly" machines. By telling NPF which computers are friendly, the firewall won't send you alert messages about them.
Instead, you'll receive messages about the computers that are outside your
network and that are potentially "unfriendly."

Hello, computer! Identifying trusted machines

Chances are you use more than one computer to go on the Internet. One of
the most frustrating things that can happen after you install NIS is the loss of
a connection: either you can't get on the Internet, or you lose your ability to
"see" and share files with computers on your own home network. This is
where you can choose one of two approaches to solve the problem: the
Network Wizard or manual network configuration.

The Network Wizard

You have installed Norton Internet Security, and you suddenly lose all connection with shared files and printers on your network. The probable cause

is that Personal Firewall is blocking the computers on your network that have the shared resources you need. What do you do? You need to identify those trusted network computers so Personal Firewall doesn't block them. This isn't a task you have to perform manually. NIS comes with a Network Wizard that let's you access your own network machines while protecting you from computers outside the network. Follow these steps to run the wizard:

1. **Open the main NIS window and double-click Personal Firewall.**

   The Personal Firewall window opens.

2. **Click Networking.**

   The Networking tab jumps to the front.

3. **Click Wizard.**

   The first screen of the Home Network Wizard appears. Read the instructions and click Next. Follow the instructions on subsequent screens to identify your networked computers.

If you see the heading No Changes Made and a message stating that Norton Internet Security could not find any network adapters, click Finish to return to the Home Networking screen. You may see this screen even though you know that you are part of a network and you share files with one or more computers in your home or office (I did). If that's the case, you need to manually configure your network, which I describe in the next section.

Manual configuration

In order to identify your trusted network computers so Personal Firewall can refrain from blocking them, you need to know the names or IP addresses of those computers. Normally, you could get the names from Network Neighborhood, the icon on your Windows desktop that keeps track of your own local computers. But if those computers are being blocked, they may not show up in Network Neighborhood. (Even if they do appear, you still may not be able to connect to those machines when you double-click their icons.) You need to manually configure the network for NIS. Follow these steps:

1. **Click the Networking tab of Personal Firewall as described in the preceding set of steps.**

   The Home Networking options appear.

2. **Click Add.**

   The Networking dialog box appears.

3. **Type the names or IP addresses of any computers you want to permit access to, then click OK.**

   The Networking dialog box closes, and you return to the Home Networking options with the IP address or name you just entered.

4. Click OK.

The Home Networking options close and you return to the main NIS window.

Reviewing your firewall's default rules

If you need to manually create a rule to block a computer, as described earlier in this chapter, you get a look at Norton Personal Firewall's default rules. These are rules that come with the NIS software. They permit routine types of network communication with the other trusted computers on your network and between your computer and itself. Chances are you won't need to change these rules. But knowing they exist and understanding what they do is a good idea.

To view the default rules, open the main NIS window, double-click Personal Firewall, and click Advanced. When the Advanced Firewall options appear, click General to view Personal Firewall's existing rules (see Figure 4-4).

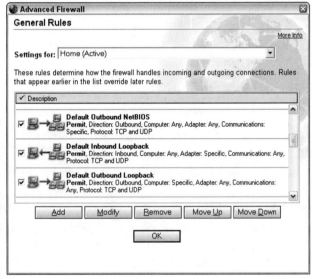

Figure 4-4:
Personal
Firewall
comes with
default
rules that
connect
your local
computers.

What, exactly, do these default rules accomplish? Here are some brief explanations:

- **ICMP rules.** Enable your computers to send messages to one another and other computers on the Internet to verify that they are present. All outbound messages are permitted, but most inbound messages are restricted to certain types that are considered "safe" because they don't give potential attackers information about your computer or your network.

✔ **DNS rules.** Enable your computer to connect to your Internet Service Provider's Domain Name Service server so you can stay connected to the Net.

✔ **NetBIOS rules.** Control the NetBIOS communications that take place between computers on a Windows-based network. By default, outbound messages are permitted but inbound ones are blocked for additional security.

✔ **Loopback rules.** If you ever want to run server software on your computer or test scripts, you'll probably need to send a loopback message to yourself at some point. A loopback IP address is a default address, 127.0.0.1, that a computer reserves for its own use.

Other default rules block well-known attacks that use the Bootstrap (Bootp) protocol or that attempt to connect using port 1900 or 5000. You can modify any of these rules if you need to. For example, my default set of rules included one that blocked both inbound and outbound Windows File Sharing and was probably preventing me from connecting to shared resources on another computer. To change this sort of default rule, you can do the following:

1. **Click the rule in the General Rules window.**

   The rule is highlighted.

2. **Click Modify.**

   The Modify Rule dialog box appears.

3. **Click one of the options in the dialog box that you want to modify.**

   In this case, I want to permit file sharing with one other computer on my network but no others. On the Action tab of Modify Rule, I click Permit.

4. **Click Connections, and choose Connections to and from Other Computers.**

5. **Click Computers and click Add.**

   Enter the IP address of the computer with which you want to share files.

6. **Click Communications.**

   Click the button next to the type of protocol you want to permit (TCP or UDP) or the number of ports you want to permit (you may want to choose All Types of Communication (all ports, local and remote).

7. **Optionally, click Tracking or Description if you want to change either of those settings for this rule, then click OK three times.**

   All open dialog boxes close and you return to the main NIS window.

It's tempting to choose all types of communication when you're trying to permit a connection to one of the computers on your own trusted network. But there's a chance of a security risk: If a hacker has gained control of the computer on your network to which you want to connect, you could be giving that hacker access to your other networked computer as well.

If you consider one of your default rules more important than the others (for example, if you have been attacked and specifically want to block communications with a single computer), select the rule you created to block that computer, then click Move Up to move it higher on Personal Firewall's list of rules. This means the blocking rule will be processed before the others on the list. Similarly, you can click Move Down to move other rules down on the list.

Tracking Down Hackers

Detecting intrusions is only one part of Internet security. You can let Intrusion Detection do its work automatically and not think about it very much. Or, you can go a step further and perform incident response — actions the computer takes after an incident occurs. Incident response consists of a determination of what occurred and countermeasures that ensure the network remains secure.

If you work in a business environment and a hacker actually steals files or other resources, you can try to track the hacker down and pursue legal action. But this is a time-consuming project that may or may not be successful: Identifying hackers by name is extremely difficult because they are proficient at concealing their identity. Proving what they did by providing sufficient evidence in court can also be time-consuming and expensive.

For most home users, it's more practical to identify the attacker by IP address and then report that address to a Web site that tracks attackers, as described in the sections that follow.

Finding out about your attackers

When someone attempts to attack one of your computers, you naturally want to find out more about the individual's location, habits, and whether other computers have been attacked as well. As mentioned earlier, it can be difficult to identify an attacker with precision because hackers often intentionally falsify the IP address listed as the origin of the attack. Not only that, attackers may have gained control of someone else's computer and used it to launch an attack against you.

Although you may not be able to get the individual's name or even a precise IP address, you may be able to at least locate the domain from which the attacker operates. To see if any attacks have occurred and, if so, to find out about the perpetrators, open the main NIS window and click Statistics under the heading Norton Internet Security. The Statistics for Personal Firewall and other NIS components appear (see Figure 4-5).

As you can see in Figure 4-5, I found I was attacked a few days ago, and eight intrusion attempts were made against my computer. Personal Firewall handled all these incidents in the background and I never even received an alert message about them.

If you see such information in your own firewall statistics, click Attacker Details. A new browser window opens with Visual Tracking information about the individual. The computer attempting to make a connection to me was located in North Korea (see Figure 4-6).

So far, I know that the computer attempting to connect to mine is located in North Korea and has an IP address of 61.77.116.98. Unfortunately, this does not mean the attacker actually resides in North Korea: Someone in another part of the world may have gained control of this computer and be using it to try an unauthorized connection.

I can, however, find out one more useful detail about the attacker by clicking the tiny Details link at the bottom of the Visual Tracking screen. Clicking Details produces a separate window with more detailed information about the computer's location — not geographic, but on the Internet. The report, shown in Figure 4-7, is a little difficult to understand and not as complete as it should be. A search should tell you what domain the IP address belongs to, and provide you with an e-mail address or Web page where abuses can be reported. If you can't find what you are looking for using Visual Tracking, you can search for more information on the Internet.

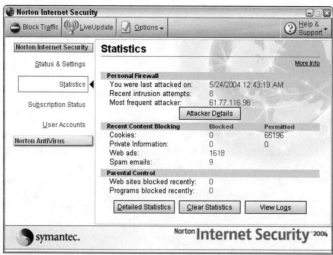

Figure 4-5:
Your firewall statistics can be startling: You may find that you have been attacked without even realizing it.

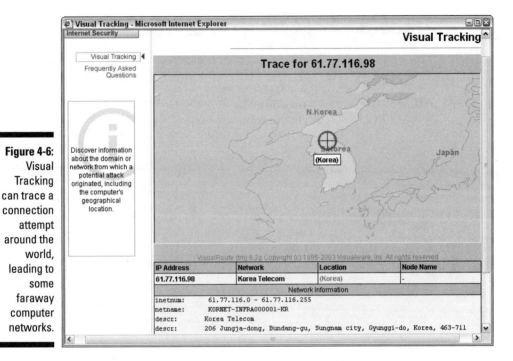

Figure 4-6:
Visual
Tracking
can trace a
connection
attempt
around the
world,
leading to
some
faraway
computer
networks.

Figure 4-6:
Visual
Tracking
can trace a
connection
attempt
around the
world,
leading to
some
faraway
computer
networks.

I discuss the Detailed Statistics and View Logs options in the Statistics window in Chapter 16.

```
NETWORK: 61.77.116.98 [256]

inetnum:     61.77.116.0 - 61.77.116.255
netname:     KORNET-INFRA000001-KR
descr:           Korea Telecom
descr:           206 Jungja-dong, Bundang-gu, Sungnam city, Gyunggi-do, Korea, 463-71
descr:           GYUNGGI
descr:           463-711
country:     KR
admin-c:     IA4643-KR
tech-c:      IM4603-KR
remarks:     This IP address space has been allocated to KRNIC.
remarks:     For more information, using KRNIC Whois Database
remarks:     whois -h whois.nic.or.kr
mnt-by:      MNT-KRNIC-AP
remarks:     This information has been partially mirrored by APNIC from
remarks:     KRNIC. To obtain more specific information, please use the
remarks:     KRNIC whois server at whois.krnic.net.
changed:     hostmaster@nic.or.kr 20040426
source:      KRNIC

Java Applet Window
```

Figure 4-7:
Details
about an
attack
should lead
you to the
attacker's
ISP.

Tracking hackers with WHOIS

After you know the IP address of a possible attacker, you can track it using a variety of resources other than NIS's own Visual Tracking. For example, you can do a WHOIS search using one of many databases around the world. A WHOIS database holds registration information for domain names around the world. When I did a WHOIS search on the ARIN.NET database www.apnic.net/apnic-bin/whois.pl for example, I came up with the following information:

```
OrgName:    Asia Pacific Network Information Centre
OrgID:      APNIC
Address:    PO Box 2131
City:       Milton
StateProv:  QLD
PostalCode: 4064
Country:    AU

ReferralServer: whois://whois.apnic.net

NetRange:   61.0.0.0 - 61.255.255.255
CIDR:       61.0.0.0/8
NetName:    APNIC3
NetHandle:  NET-61-0-0-0-1
Parent:
NetType:    Allocated to APNIC
NameServer: NS1.APNIC.NET
NameServer: NS3.APNIC.NET
NameServer: NS4.APNIC.NET
NameServer: NS.RIPE.NET
NameServer: TINNIE.ARIN.NET
Comment:    This IP address range is not registered in the
            ARIN database.
Comment:    For details, refer to the APNIC Whois Database
            via
Comment:    WHOIS.APNIC.NET or http://www.apnic.net/apnic-
            bin/whois2.pl
Comment:    ** IMPORTANT NOTE: APNIC is the Regional Internet
            Registry
Comment:    for the Asia Pacific region. APNIC does not
            operate networks
Comment:    using this IP address range and is not able to
            investigate
Comment:    spam or abuse reports relating to these
            addresses. For more
Comment:    help, refer to
            http://www.apnic.net/info/faq/abuse
Comment:
RegDate:    1997-04-25
Updated:    2004-03-30
```

This set of information might look intimidating, but it's easier to understand than it seems. The WHOIS database tells you that this IP address falls within a range that is tracked by the Asia Pacific Network Information Centre, located in Milton, Australia. It also gives you a Web page you can visit to report abuse: www.apnic.net/info/faq/abuse. When you go to this page, you find a set of FAQs about spammers and hackers. The FAQ page informs you that APNIC will not be able to investigate your complaint. However, there is a link to the APNIC WHOIS database, which can lead you to the Internet Service Provider associated with the IP address 61.77.116.98. A search of this database provides me with the names of several individuals at Korea Telecom, along with e-mail addresses I can use to report abuse: ip@ns.kornet.net, for example.

While I was attempting to research this IP address, Norton Internet Security presented me with an alert message, stating that it had blocked an attempt to send the well-known Trojan horse program NetBus to my computer. This attack was later reported, in Statistics, as coming from the same IP address I was researching.

Tracking hackers with DShield

An organization called DShield helps provide up-to-date security information by gathering firewall log file reports from computers around the world. The log files provided by volunteers give evidence of who's doing the hacking, and what kinds of attacks are attempted at a given time. The extensive records compiled by DShield over the years provide you with another resource where you can track hackers. Go to the DShield Reports page (www.dshield.org/reports.php) and you'll find links to the Top 10 ports, attackers, and attack patterns currently being reported.

Click IP Info, and your browser displays a simple form into which you can enter the IP address you are trying to research. Click Submit, and you'll get any information about the address that DShield already has. In the example IP address I have been writing about, DShield did not have any records. Other searches I've performed on DShield have turned up IP addresses that were responsible for hundreds of attack attempts against various Web sites. Such data gives you an indication of whether the IP address is being operated by an actual hacker (in this case, the number of attacks is likely to be high) or whether it has been hijacked by someone else (in this case, the number may be low).

Another useful resource contained on the DShield Web site is the ability to gather data from your log files and send it to the site's database. You need to download a special piece of software called DShield Universal Firewall Client to do this. The software periodically checks your log files and sends data from the log files to DShield. Go to the page entitled How to Submit Your Firewall Logs to DShield (www.dshield.org/howto.php) and click Norton Personal Firewall to find out what you need to download, if you want to participate.

Filing a report on your attacker

Following up on attacks by filing reports is a part of incident response that is often overlooked by security administrators and home users alike. It may or may not do any good to report the incident. However, virtually all ISPs prevent their customers from using the ISP's resources to launch spam e-mail or send Trojan horses to other computers. They should investigate and stop the activity. If nothing else, you'll feel better for trying to do something about the intrusion attempt.

Here is a copy of the message I sent to Korea Telecom regarding their IP address, with the heading "Hack Attack From Your IP Address"

```
To whom it may concern,

          An IP address registered to your company,
          61.77.116.98, attempted to send the NetBus Trojan
          horse to my computer at 3:17 p.m. today, May 27,
          2004. To date, my firewall program has blocked 12
          intrusion attempts from this IP address. I would
          appreciate it if you could investigate and stop
          this activity as soon as possible.

          Sincerely,

          Greg Holden
```

When you do send an e-mail message reporting your break-in, don't use your primary e-mail address. Use the one you have designated for spam and other disposable e-mail messages, just to be on the safe side.

Ping sweeps and port scans

Attempts to send you Trojan horse programs are only the most obvious kinds of attacks you can face. You're more likely to encounter the common ping sweeps and port scans that many computers launch on the Internet. A ping sweep occurs when a series of ICMP ping messages is sent out to a range of IP addresses, one after another. Any computer that responds to the request with an acknowledgement gives the potential hacker a valid computer that can be targeted for a more specific attack.

A port scan, mentioned in Chapter 1, occurs when a single computer attempts to connect to a series of ports on a given machine. It may be a follow-up to a ping sweep — after a hacker has a valid IP address, a port scan can reveal an open port. The open port can then be targeted with a Trojan horse or other program. These two types of events aren't attacks in and of themselves: They fall under the heading of reconnaissance. Norton Internet Security blocks them automatically because they can lead to more damaging attacks later on.

A Web browser that wants to communicate with a Web server uses port 80 on a computer; outgoing e-mail uses port 25, incoming mail uses port 110, and instant messages are sent over a variety of different ports, depending on the application (MSN Messenger uses TCP ports 6891–6900). Each port on a computer is assigned a number between 0 and 65,535.

Deciding when to disable your firewall

By now, you probably realize the need to keep your firewall operating as long as you are connected to the Internet. If you want to test connectivity among computers on your network, you can disconnect from the Internet and turn off Norton Personal Firewall. To disable the firewall, open the main NIS window, single-click Personal Firewall, and click the Turn Off button in the right-hand column. When you click Turn Off, the button changes to Turn On. Be sure to turn the firewall back on before you connect your computer to the Internet.

Using Symantec Security Check

All of the configuration options discussed in this chapter and Chapter 3 may leave your firewall with a very different configuration than when you began. If you're ever in doubt about the security of your firewall's configuration, you can perform a security check: Open the main NIS window, single-click Security, and click the Check Security button on the right-hand side of the window. Your browser connects to the Symantec Security Check page (`http://security.symantec.com/sscv6/default.asp`). Click Go to have Symantec check Personal Firewall to make sure it is providing adequate protection.

Part II
Handling Viruses and Malicious Code

The 5th Wave   By Rich Tennant

"A centralized security management system sounds fine, but then what would we do with the dogs?"

In this part . . .

When most people think about computer security, they immediately think about viruses — programs that people you've never met try to sneak into your computer without your knowledge. When they find a home on your file system, they can do any number of things you don't want them to do, ranging from recording the keystrokes you make on your keyboard to e-mailing themselves to all of the names in your e-mail software's address book.

This part of the book examines the many types of threats you need to guard against and shows you how to put Norton Internet Security to work to handle them. You'll discover not only how to handle viruses, worms and other obviously harmful code, but programs that invade your privacy in a more subtle way, such as spyware and adware, which track the Web sites you visit and automatically present you with advertisements you never asked to see. You find out how to keep Norton AntiVirus, Ad Blocking, and Privacy Control up to date to combat the latest types of harmful code, and you also find out how to quarantine suspicious programs.

Chapter 5

Working with Norton AntiVirus

. . . .

In This Chapter

▶ Familiarizing yourself with viruses

▶ Exploring Norton AntiVirus's configuration options

▶ Conducting automatic and manual virus scans

▶ Responding to viruses

. . . .

A nti-virus software is a must-have for every computer that has access to the Internet. Malicious code can find its way into your computer by any number of means. You may already know not to click on an e-mail attachment that you don't recognize, but some viruses can enter your computer through open ports, on floppy disks or CDs, in compressed files such as Zip archives, and by other means.

Norton AntiVirus can detect and delete viruses and other harmful code, but not if you let the program run automatically all the time without any management or updating. This chapter tells you how to get the most out of this powerful protection component.

Recognizing Viruses and Their Notorious Relatives

The term virus is a sort of catchall that describes various types of programs that perform actions on a computer without the computer's approval or, often, knowledge.

A *virus* is a program or code that replicates; that is, infects another program, boot sector, partition sector, or document that supports macros, by inserting itself or attaching itself to that medium. Most viruses only replicate, although many do a large amount of damage as well.

If you scan the various threats listed in the Symantec Virus Encyclopedia, you find a number of different malicious programs that fall under the virus category:

- **Worm.** A program that makes copies of itself; for example, from one disk drive to another, or by copying itself using e-mail or another transport mechanism. The worm may do damage and compromise the security of the computer. It may arrive in the form of a joke program or software of some sort.

- **Trojan horse.** A program that neither replicates nor copies itself but causes damage or compromises the security of the computer. Typically, an individual e-mails a Trojan horse to you — it does not e-mail itself — and it may arrive in the form of a joke program or software of some sort.

Viewing the Newest Viruses

You can always find new things on the Internet — new Web sites, discussion groups, music files to download, and new viruses. At any time, you can connect to the Symantec Security Response Web site and view the viruses that have been most recently reported. Just make sure you're connected to the Internet and that you have your Web browser open. Then open the main Norton Internet Security window and do the following:

1. **Click Norton AntiVirus in the left-hand column of the main window.**

   The Norton AntiVirus options (Auto-Protect, E-mail Scanning, Script Blocking, and Full System Scan) appear on the right side of the window.

2. **Click Reports.**

   The Reports options appear.

3. **Click View Report next to Online Virus Encyclopedia.**

   Your browser displays the Symantec Security Response – Search, and the Latest Virus Threats Page appears.

4. **Scroll down to the heading Latest Virus Threats.**

   You see a list of the most recent malicious codes that have been detected and reported to Symantec (see Figure 5-1).

You can click on the names of each of these threats to find out more about how they are spread and what they do. In case you don't want to pursue this step (which can be anxiety-producing), Table 5-1 presents a random sampling from a visit I made early this year.

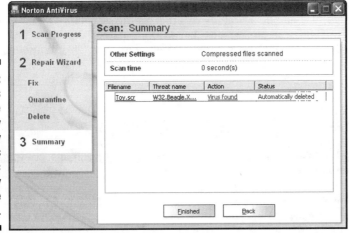

Figure 5-1:
New virus
threats are
listed nearly
every day
on this
Symantec
Security
Response
Web page.

Table 5-1	Viruses and How They Propagate		
Name	**Type of Threat**	**How It Spreads**	**What It Does**
W32.NetsupA@mm	Worm	E-mail attachment	Mails itself to all names in Outlook address book
W32.Korgo.D	Worm	Enters through port 445	Opens back doors on TCP ports 113 and 3067
W32.Antinny.Q	Worm	Spreads via a Japanese peer-to-peer file sharing application called Winny	Attempts to delete files on the C: drive and steal information
BAT.Sebak	Trojan Horse	N/A	Displays a message claiming credit for creation and disables functions such as mouse, keyboard, and possibly the operating system, on the infected computer
W32.Gaobot.FO	Worm	Spreads through network shares	Allows access to another computer through an Internet Relay Chat channel

The second worm on the list, W32.Korgo.D, doesn't seem all that dangerous by itself. But it can be a prelude to a more serious attack. Opening ports such as 113 and 3067 can enable a hacker who has gained control of another computer to send a Trojan horse to the target computer. This happened with the infamous Sendmail and NetBus Trojans.

Identifying Expanded Threats

Expanded threats fall outside the category of commonly-known definitions of viruses, worms, and Trojan horses that may provide unauthorized access, threats to system or data security, and other types of threats or nuisances. You may unknowingly download expanded threats from Web sites, e-mail messages, or instant messengers. You can also install them by accepting the End User License Agreement from another software program related to or linked in some way to the expanded threat. The following list describes some expanded threats:

- ✔ **Remote Access Programs.** Programs that may allow another computer to gain information or to attack or alter your computer, usually over the Internet. Remote access programs detected in virus scans may be recognizable commercial software, which are brought to the user's attention during the scan.

- ✔ **Joke Programs.** Programs that change or interrupt the normal behavior of your computer, creating a general distraction or nuisance. Harmless programs that cause various benign activities to display on your computer (for example, an unexpected screen saver).

- ✔ **Hack Tools.** Tools used by a hacker to gain unauthorized access to your computer. One example of a hack tool is a keystroke logger — a program that tracks and records individual keystrokes and can send this information back to the hacker.

- ✔ **Dialers.** Programs that use a system, without your permission or knowledge, to dial out through the Internet to a 900 number or FTP site, typically to accrue charges.

The Symantec Security Response newsletter (`http://securityresponse.symantec.com/avcenter/newsletter.html`) reported in its March/April 2004 edition that 2,636 new vulnerabilities were reported in 2003, or an average of seven new threats per day. The number of mass-mailing worms reported in the first half of 2004 was an increase of 61 percent over those reported in the first half of 2003.

Configuring AntiVirus

Like Norton Personal Firewall, Norton AntiVirus has many configuration options. In most cases, the default options will be adequate for your needs. Occasionally, though, you need to change how often the program runs its automatic virus scans and how it responds when a virus is detected. Changing your options as a preventative measure is far better than reacting to a successful virus infection. The following sections explain what your options are and why you might choose one over another.

Deciding how to respond

AntiVirus gives you several configuration options to fit your protection needs. You can change automatic protection options, the way the program blocks scripts, and how manual scans are conducted. In the following sections, I give you more details about these options.

Enabling Auto-Protect

You can't always tell when a virus is about to infect your computer. When you receive an e-mail attachment that has a virus in it, the virus is usually concealed inside a compressed file. The file you see as the attachment doesn't have an "obvious" name along the lines of `virusinfection.exe`. Rather, it might be called `hi.vbs` or `greetings.scr`. Some viruses can enter through open ports on your computer, or in other compressed files you download.

That's why taking advantage of AntiVirus's Auto-Protect feature is important. Auto-Protect is enabled by default and starts up when Windows starts up. Its icon appears in the Windows system tray alongside the Norton Internet Security icon and indicates that your computer is protected all the time. You can, however, turn Auto-Protect off or change other settings by following these steps:

1. **Open the main NIS window, click Options, and select Norton AntiVirus from the drop-down list that appears.**

   The Norton AntiVirus Options window appears (see Figure 5-2). By default, the Auto-Protect options are on top.

2. **Deselect Enable Auto-Protect (recommended).**

   Auto-Protect turns off. The other two boxes in the first section (How to Stay Protected) cause Auto-Protect to start when your system starts, and display the icon in the system tray, respectively.

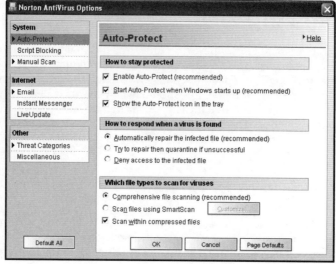

Figure 5-2:
You can
change the
way Norton
AntiVirus
auto-
matically
protects
your file
system
using these
options.

3. **Click Try to Repair Then Quarantine If Unsuccessful to tell AntiVirus not to automatically repair all files.**

   The second button in the How to Respond When a Virus Is Found section is selected. The third option, Deny Access to the Infected File, doesn't allow it to be quarantined and is risky because it doesn't really give you protection; the file can still execute automatically and infect you.

4. **Click the Scan Files Using SmartScan button if you want to scan only those types of files contained in AntiVirus's Program File Extensions List.**

   This turns off comprehensive file scanning, which causes all programs and types of files to be scanned.

5. **Click Customize next to the SmartScan option.**

   The Program File Extensions dialog box appears (see Figure 5-3).

Windows uses file extensions to determine what a file is and what application should be used to process it. By default, the file extensions in the Program File Extensions dialog box are ones that NIS searches for when it conducts a scan. You can delete extensions you don't think you need to look for, but unless you really know what each of the extensions means, it's probably best to leave the list alone.

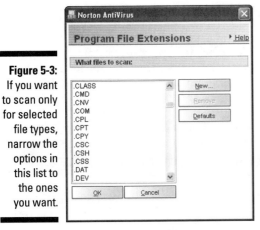

Figure 5-3:
If you want
to scan only
for selected
file types,
narrow the
options in
this list to
the ones
you want.

If you click on the arrow next to Auto-Protect in the Norton AntiVirus Options window, a set of three subcategories appears: Bloodhound, Advanced, and Exclusions. These are all advanced configuration options that casual users won't want to adjust. In general, they give you ways to fine-tune automatic virus scanning in order to exclude file types that definitely are not viruses, and catch files that are viruses — even if those files don't fit into any currently known virus definitions. (Click on the arrow next to Auto-Protect to close the subcategories.)

Note: Bloodhound is a technology developed by Symantec to detect previously unknown viruses. Norton AntiVirus uses the Bloodhound method and Bloodhound is enabled with a default level of protection. You can find out more about Bloodhound technology at `http://securityresponse.symantec.com/avcenter/venc/data/bloodhound.html`.

Blocking scripts

A script is a set of commands written in a programming language that are designed to be executed, sometimes with a user's interaction, and sometimes not. In a sense, any computer program you use on your computer is a script. Most scripts are configured to execute when something happens. Usually, a user has to perform some sort of action in order for the script to execute.

Scripts that cause trouble are those that are executed (in other words, carry out the task that their programmers have built into them) without the user doing anything. They start themselves automatically, run in the background without your knowledge, and perform functions you never asked them to do.

Script Blocking is the component of Norton AntiVirus that detects scripts written in two languages that are sometimes used to create malicious code: Visual Basic and JavaScript. (These languages are used more often to create applications both on the Web and in computer operating systems.) To change the options for Script Blocking, open the main Norton Internet Security window, click Options, and select Norton AntiVirus from the drop-down list that appears. Click Script Blocking to view the three options:

- **Enable Script Blocking (recommended).** This option is checked by default; deselect it to disable script blocking.

- **Ask Me What to Do (recommended).** This causes alert messages to appear when a potentially malicious script is detected.

- **Stop All Suspicious Activities and Do Not Prompt Me.** This blocks all scripts without informing you. Since some programs you download from the Internet are potentially helpful and not harmful, this option isn't recommended.

If you're writing scripts either for a Web site or for another application, be sure to turn off Script Blocking or your scripts might be prevented from functioning.

Configuring manual protection

When you conduct a manual scan, you are performing the same activity as AntiVirus when it scans automatically. Therefore, it's not surprising that when you click Manual Scan in the Norton AntiVirus options, you see options that are virtually the same as those for automatic scans. One difference is that you can deselect Boot Records and Master Boot Records under the heading What Items to Scan In Addition to Files. These are records that the system keeps when determining how to start up your computer. You should choose to scan these files for viruses unless you have a compelling reason not to.

Inoculation is an additional feature available on versions of Norton Internet Security 2004 that is designed to run with Windows 95, 98, or Me. Inoculation displays an alert message if one of your system files changes. Many viruses make changes to important system files such as Win.ini, so a change to such files can indicate that a virus is present. Such protection is incorporated into versions of Norton Internet Security for Windows 2000 and XP.

Protecting yourself from Internet threats

Viruses, worms, and Trojan horses usually infect computers by familiar means such as e-mail attachments. Two of the applications that are frequently compromised by attackers, e-mail and instant messaging, have configuration options that are covered in the sections that follow. You may want to change the options if you don't want to see alert messages notifying you that AntiVirus is scanning e-mail messages for example, or if you use an instant messaging program that isn't covered by default.

Responding to e-mail attacks

E-mail is one of the easiest ways to reach people around the world — a fact well known to marketers as well as hackers. When it comes to e-mail, Anti-Virus's default configuration provides the maximum amount of protection. Every time an outgoing e-mail message leaves your computer, an alert message appears, notifying you that it's being scanned for viruses (see Figure 5-4). You should change that option only if you want to adjust the way AntiVirus responds to threats that it detects, or if you want to turn off scanning e-mail because you are conducting a test of your network.

Figure 5-4:
By default, alert messages appear for all of your outgoing e-mail messages.

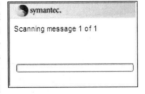

When you click E-mail on the left-hand side of the Norton AntiVirus Options window, options appear that let you deselect (and thus turn off) scanning incoming or outgoing e-mail. You can also change the way the software responds when it detects a virus. By default, AntiVirus automatically attempts a repair, but you can change this to "Repair then quarantine if unsuccessful." If you never want to see messages reporting that viruses were found but could not repaired, and then asking you to quarantine them, another option is available: "Repair then silently quarantine if unsuccessful."

Scanning your outgoing and incoming e-mail for viruses is important. Many malicious programs try to spread themselves by e-mailing themselves to other users listed in your address book. If such an attack occurs, the viruses would be sent out in your outgoing e-mail. You could conceivably be subject to litigation if you're found to be the source of the infection and you didn't take due diligence to protect your system.

Blocking instant message infections

The Instant Messenger options in AntiVirus are especially critical if you use AOL Instant Messenger or Yahoo!Messenger. These two applications aren't covered by default by AntiVirus; only Windows Messenger is protected. Because the people you communicate with via IM can send you attachments, it's important to provide protection for these popular applications, if you use them.

MSN Messenger is also supported by AntiVirus, but only versions 4.6, 4.7, 4.8, and 6.0; version 5.0 is not supported. Other popular instant messaging applications such as ICQ aren't going to have virus scanning provided by AntiVirus, either.

To configure AntiVirus for AOL Instant Messenger or Yahoo Messenger, open Norton AntiVirus Options, click Instant Messenger under the heading Internet, and select the box next to the program you use. Click Configure New Users if you need to set user options for one of these programs.

Note: The options in the AntiVirus Options window only let you control whether or not AntiVirus scans messages for viruses as they enter or leave your computer. If you have identified information that you want to keep private when you send information via IM or other software, that information will be blocked whether or not you scan the messages for viruses.

Enabling LiveUpdate

Frankly, LiveUpdate can be annoying from time to time, but it's a necessary irritation. This module regularly checks to make sure you have the latest virus definitions and other data like intrusion detection signatures installed. You also may see warnings from the program if you don't have the latest version of the LiveUpdate module *itself* installed. All these requirements and reminders may tempt you to click LiveUpdate in the Norton AntiVirus Options window and deselect one of the options that keep your copy of NAV equipped with the latest supporting information:

- ✔ **Enable Automatic LiveUpdate (recommended).** This keeps LiveUpdate checking for new information on the Symantec Web site.

- ✔ **Apply Virus Protection Updates.** This incorporates new virus definitions into NAV's database.

- ✔ **Notify Me of Norton AntiVirus Program Updates (recommended).** This tells you if any new versions of NAV have been released.

Deselecting any of these options reduces the number of "update needed" messages you see but it also makes your version of NAV less secure, which can potentially undo the protection you wanted when you originally installed the software.

Running Your Own Virus Scan

On occasion, manually scanning your computer to make sure that you don't have any infections is a good idea. You might do this if you have downloaded a number of files from the Internet, or if you have installed new communications software such as an Instant Messaging program — or if you received an alert of a possible virus infection and the file was quarantined or repaired.

Before you run a virus scan, you need to disable the System Restore feature. To find out how to disable System Restore, you can go to a Web page on Symantec's Web site (`http://service1.symantec.com/SUPPORT/tsgen info.nsf/docid/2001012513122239?OpenDocument&src=sec_doc_nam`), or choose Start⇨Help and Support, search for System Restore, and click Change System Restore Settings. Then follow the instructions for Turning Off System Restore.

System Restore is included only with Windows Me or XP. These operating systems use the feature to restore files on your computer if they are corrupted or damaged in some way. If any of the files backed up by System Restore were infected by a virus, System Restore will back up the virus as well and it can potentially infect your computer after repairs are made.

Running a full system scan

In order to catch all possible infections, it's better to scan your entire file system for viruses rather than only part of it. Open the NIS window, click Norton AntiVirus, and click Scan for Viruses. When the Scan for Viruses options appear (see Figure 5-5), leave Scan My Computer highlighted, and then click Scan. The Scan for Viruses window appears, letting you know how many files have been scanned so far.

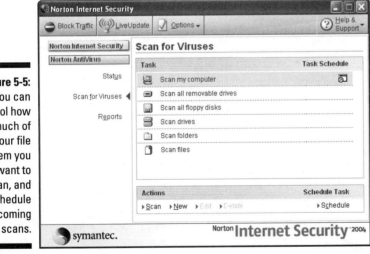

Figure 5-5: You can control how much of your file system you want to scan, and schedule upcoming scans.

Unfortunately, the Scan for Viruses window doesn't indicate what percentage of your computer resources has been scanned at any given moment, and what percentage remains. For large file systems with several gigabytes of data, NAV may well have to go through tens of thousands of files.

Scanning selected files

Suppose you don't want to scan your whole file system, but you only need to scan for viruses on a new hard drive or CD-ROM you have obtained. Or suppose you want to exclude a part of your hard drive that has already been scanned recently. You can do both by creating a custom scan.

You can choose to perform a custom scan by using the Norton AntiVirus Scan Wizard. The wizard lets you configure a scan that includes only the files or folders that you're most concerned about. Follow these steps:

1. **When the Scan for Viruses window is open, click New.**

   The Norton AntiVirus Scan Wizard opens.

2. **Click Next.**

   The second screen appears, in which you select the items you want to scan.

3. **Click Add Files or Add Folders.**

   If you click Add Folders, the Scan Folders dialog box opens (see Figure 5-6); if you click Add Files; the Scan Files dialog box opens.

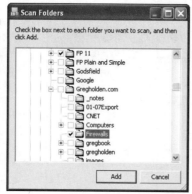

Figure 5-6:
You can make a virus scan go more quickly by specifying individual files to inspect.

4. **Select a file or folder, then click Add.**

   You return to the wizard, where the selected files have been added.

5. **Click Next.**

   A new wizard screen appears, asking you to specify a name for the scan you have created.

6. **Enter the scan name in the box provided, and then click Finish.**

   The wizard closes and you return to the Scan for Viruses options, which now include the name of the custom scan you created.

The advantage of using the wizard is that it lets you limit the scan to individual folders rather than an entire disk drive, for example. The wizard prompts you to give the scan a name, and the scan is added to your list of other scans.

The other option for doing a partial system scan is to select a resource in the Scan for Viruses options and then click Scan.

Scheduling automatic virus scans

The Scan for Viruses options also enable you to schedule when you want a custom or scheduled scan to occur. Open the Scan for Viruses window as described in the preceding section, select the resources you want to scan (such as your entire computer, or a disk drive, or a custom scan you have created), and click Schedule. The Norton AntiVirus - Scan My Computer dialog box appears (see Figure 5-7).

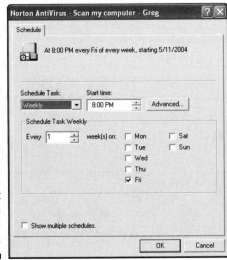

Figure 5-7:
After you create a custom scan, you can schedule it to occur on a periodic basis.

As you can see, you can schedule a scan to occur at a convenient time. Because virus scans do consume some of your computer's processing resources and can slow down the speed of your computer, you might schedule them to occur in the middle of the night, when they won't interfere with your other work.

Responding to Virus Alerts

After you install Norton Internet Security, the AntiVirus component runs once a week to do an automatic full system scan. You can also perform manual scans yourself. Occasionally, you'll be surprised to see a Norton AntiVirus Repair Wizard alert message appear after the scan like the one shown in Figure 5-8.

Figure 5-8:
A message alerting you to a virus infection can leave you wondering how to respond.

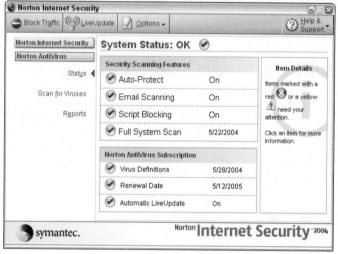

Such a message can be bewildering at first. Naturally, you wonder what this threat is and what you need to do about it. The dialog box tells you that one file was deleted; you assume it was the same threat mentioned earlier, but you don't know that for sure. If you click the name of the file itself, you get more information.

The more detailed alert message informs you that the infected file is called Toy.scr. It was probably an attachment to an e-mail message. (Whether or not you actually clicked on the suspicious attachment to open it, the attachments can be stored in your e-mail folders such as your Deleted Items folder until you empty the folder's contents.) The attachment contained the virus W32.Beagle.X..., and it was automatically deleted by Norton AntiVirus.

If you click the name of the virus, your browser connects to the Symantec Security Response - Search and Latest Virus Threats page where it displays information about the virus. You discover that its full name is W32.Beagle. X@mm, and that it is a mass-mailing worm. It opens a backdoor port on an infected computer through which a hacker can gain access to your file system.

If you automatically configured AntiVirus to place viruses that it can't repair in Quarantine, you'll see the Repair Wizard window with information to that effect. However, if you don't have Auto-Protect automatically configured, you'll see a Repair Wizard dialog box giving you the option to quarantine the file or skip it. If a virus has been found, you should definitely quarantine it. If AntiVirus finds a piece of harmless Ad-ware, click Skip. But when in doubt, click Quarantine.

If the virus is repaired

By default, if a virus is found during an automatic scan, it will be deleted or repaired automatically if possible. You can configure AntiVirus to do automatic virus removal and repair during a manual scan as well. Suppose AntiVirus reports that a virus was found and then repaired. You might think, "That's nice. I'll just click OK to close this window and go on with my work." You'll be better off taking a few minutes to configure the program so AntiVirus knows how to handle such attacks in the future. Here are the steps to follow to configure AntiVirus:

1. **Set AntiVirus's Auto-Protect options so that files that cannot be repaired are automatically placed in a secure area called Quarantine.**

   (See "Enabling Auto-Protect," earlier in this chapter.)

2. **Run a full system scan manually to make sure you don't have any other infections.**

3. **Follow any recommendations made by the Repair Wizard so your computer is protected from any other infected files.**

If you haven't configured the program to handle malicious code automatically, the Repair Wizard opens and prompts you to make decisions. Your options are described in the sections that follow.

If NAV can't repair or delete the file

Norton AntiVirus can't repair or delete every file it encounters. If a virus or other malicious program is found during a scan and can't be repaired or deleted, you'll see a message like the one shown in Figure 5-9.

If a virus is found, AntiVirus gives you the option of quarantining the file. But if the file is Ad-ware or another type of program, you see the option shown in Figure 5-9 — and you can tell AntiVirus to not handle the file and continue scanning. Alternatively, you can find out more about the file and how to handle it, as recommended by the Repair Wizard (notice the message at the bottom of the Repair Wizard screen shown in Figure 5-9). Click on the name of the file and your browser connects to the Symantec Security Response site, where you can find out more about the file and what to do. You may, for example, be able to download a special tool to remove the file, or you may read instructions on how to remove information about the file in the Windows registry or other locations.

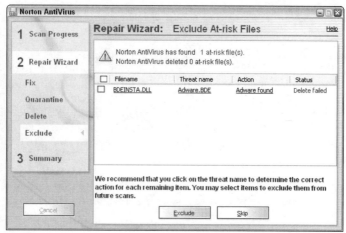

Figure 5-9: Sometimes viruses or other files cannot be repaired and you must determine how to handle them.

If NAV places a file in Quarantine

Quarantine is a part of your hard drive that Norton AntiVirus sets aside for storage of viruses, Trojan horses, and other files that it cannot repair or delete. Files in the Quarantine storage area cannot harm other files and cannot be executed.

You can view and work with the harmful files isolated in the Quarantine area. Quarantine options are discussed in detail in Chapter 8. For now, you should know that you can view a list of all the files that are in Quarantine and delete the files if you want. Just follow these steps:

1. **Open the main NIS window, and click Norton AntiVirus.**

   The Norton AntiVirus System Status set of options appears.

2. **Click Reports.**

   The Reports options appear.

3. Click View Report next to Quarantined Items.

The Norton AntiVirus Quarantine window appears.

When the Quarantine window is open, you can click Quarantined Items to see a list of any files that have been placed there. You can either delete the files, repair them, or leave them as is.

If you see a malicious worm alert

It sounds like something out of a bad 1950s science fiction movie. If Norton AntiVirus displays an alert message informing you that a malicious worm has been detected and you aren't using your e-mail software, you should be concerned. The message appears when a worm tries to send itself to others' computers by e-mail. Many worms that are spread around the Internet attempt to propagate themselves by using all of the addresses found in Outlook or Outlook Express's address book as destinations. (The problem seems to affect Microsoft's e-mail clients more often than Netscape or other e-mail programs.)

The Malicious Worm alert gives you a number of options from a drop-down list:

- ✔ **Quarantine This Program (Recommended).** This is the recommended option because it places the worm in the Quarantine area and blocks the e-mail transmissions that are going on.

- ✔ **Stop This Program from E-mailing Itself.** Choose this option if you suspect that a legitimate program is doing a mailing (for example, if you have created an e-mail newsletter or mailing list and your mailing list software is automatically sending out information to members). If a worm is at fault, this option will stop it.

- ✔ **Allow This Program to E-mail Itself.** Choose this option only if you're absolutely sure the program that is doing the e-mailing is legitimate, or if you are conducting a controlled test to see how a worm operates.

- ✔ **Always Allow This Program to E-mail Itself.** Obviously, this option only makes sense if the program that is doing the mailing is legitimate.

After you quarantine the worm, you should run LiveUpdate to download any new virus definitions. The fact that the worm began to mail itself is a clear warning sign that AntiVirus did not detect it to begin with, probably because it's a type not included in your software's virus definitions. You should send the file to Symantec so they are aware of the infection; if the file is in Quarantine, select it and choose Action⇨Submit to Symantec to send the file.

Viewing Reports

As you read earlier in this chapter, clicking the Reports link under Norton AntiVirus in the main Norton Internet Security window lets you take a peek at the spyware and viruses that NAV placed in your computer's designated Quarantine area. If you click View Reports next to Online Virus Encyclopedia, you go to a page on the Symantec Security Response Web site that provides you with information about the latest virus attacks.

The third Reports option also deserves a brief mention. If you click View Reports next to Activity Log, you open the Log Viewer. This utility is an essential part of any computer protection system: A log file is a record of all of the activity that has taken place on a computer system or network. When you click View Reports, you access the Norton AntiVirus section of the Log Viewer (see Figure 5-10).

You can use the Log Viewer to review any threat alerts you have received. If you have scheduled a virus scan to occur when you are not at your computer, you can use the Activity Log to verify that the scan actually took place and that it was done completely. Scans are listed under Application Activities.

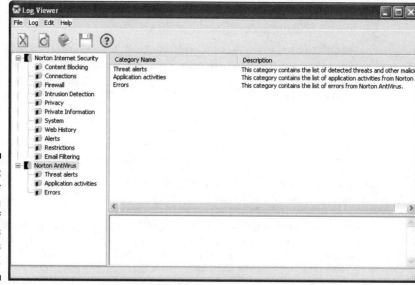

Figure 5-10: Log Viewer keeps a record of any viruses it has deleted.

Infamous malicious code attacks

Virus attacks crop up nearly every day. But most viruses come and go without gaining much attention. Once in a while, though, an attack gets national attention and computer users around the country are made aware, however briefly, of the need for virus protection. Some of the virus attacks that have become famous over the last two decades include

- On November 2, 1988, the first documented virus (technically, a worm) was sent out over the Internet by a graduate student at Cornell University named Robert Tappan Morris. The program became known as the Morris Worm. The computer security organization called CERT (Computer Emergency Response Team) was formed in order to deal with subsequent attacks. Morris became the first person to be tried and convicted under the Computer Fraud and Abuse Act of 1986.

- Melissa, which hit the Internet in March 1999, was the first virus to infect corporate and government networks and get the attention of mainstream media. Its author, David L. Smith, was caught within days and pleaded guilty to disrupting and damaging computer networks. The infection started when Smith posted an infected Word document on the newsgroup alt.sex.

- In May 2000, millions of computer users around the world clicked on the attachment of an e-mail message bearing the harmless-looking message ILOVEYOU.

Their computers became immediately infected with a virus that was eventually called the Love Bug or the I Love You virus. The virus's creator was never conclusively identified, but was believed to be a hacker based in the Philippines who was later nicknamed The Terminator.

- In February 2001, the AnnaKournikova e-mail worm infected thousands of computers whose users clicked on an attachment that they thought was a photo of the attractive tennis star.

- Just after the September 11, 2001 terrorist attacks in the United States, the Internet was hit by a series of virus attacks, the first of which was called Nimda. Nimda took advantage of a flaw in the Microsoft Windows operating system. Nimda infected an estimated 160,000 computers and crippled the federal courts system in Florida, among other computer networks.

Nimda was particularly harmful for a number of reasons: It could infect computers through an e-mail attachment, through scanning networks for vulnerable versions of Microsoft's Internet Information Server, through network shares, and through visits to a Web page that was hosted by an infected computer. The distribution method was so effective that Nimda spawned a variety of other viruses, with names like BadTrans.B and SirCam.

Chapter 6

Blocking Other Weapons of Mass Insecurity

• •

• •

*E*veryone knows that Norton AntiVirus blocks viruses from entering your computer: You can tell that from the program's name, after all. But new to the 2004 version of Norton Internet Security is the capability of blocking other threats such as downloaded files, spyware programs that attempt to track what you type on your keyboard, and other files that reduce your privacy — not only the ones that are already known and documented, but those that may turn up in the future. This chapter describes a variety of different threats that are, in some ways, more dangerous than viruses because they aren't as well known, and they aren't always taken seriously. Some enter your file system through the very software you use to connect to the Internet. Others enter through files you download or applications you use every day. By observing a few simple procedures, you can block these weapons of insecurity and keep your homeland secure from spies and hackers.

Surfing the Web Safely

It seems ironic. Your Web browser is the primary way you connect to the Internet. You use your browser to bring the world into your home. This very openness, however, has its dark side as well.

Blocking Web browser information

Whenever you surf the Web, your browser leaves a trail behind it that others can follow. Most times, the trail is a harmless one. Web site administrators analyze their log files to see how many people visited their Web pages, and they compile reports showing what kind of browser those visitors use and where the visitors surfed just before they arrived. Someone who really wants to find out about you can mine the data your browser reveals and use it as a starting point for further reconnaissance or even an attack.

Testing your browser privacy

Norton Internet Security includes a component called Browser Privacy. This component is intended to prevent your Web browser from sending out information to the Web sites you visit. You can test this component's operation by visiting a Web page like Symantec's own Security Check. To go there, follow these steps:

1. **Double-click the Norton Internet Security icon in your system tray.**

   The main NIS window opens.

2. **Double-click Security.**

   Your browser connects to the Symantec Security Check Web page shown in Figure 6-1.

3. **Click Go.**

   A browser window appears briefly (see Figure 6-2). The page notifies you that the Symantec Web site is checking your browser's scripting capabilities (your browser's ability to execute scripts written in programming languages like JavaScript). This inconspicuous note gives you an insight into the kinds of things that Web servers can detect when a browser connects to them: In this case, Symantec's server can detect whether your browser is running JavaScript.

   Note: Some sites use Java, ActiveX, or JavaScript to retrieve information from your browser. If they can't retrieve any information that way, they use the last piece of browser information that they received instead. You may see the information from the last person who viewed the site.

4. **Click Start under Security Scan.**

   A Web page appears with a progress bar informing you of the progress of the scan. This page also reveals a couple of bits of information gleaned from your browser: your IP address and the domain name of your Internet Service Provider. As shown in Figure 6-3, the ISP in this case is EarthLink.

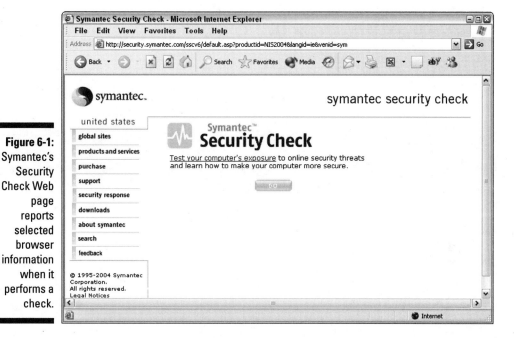

Figure 6-1:
Symantec's
Security
Check Web
page
reports
selected
browser
information
when it
performs a
check.

Figure 6-2:
Web
servers try
to determine
whether or
not your
browser
supports
scripting so
it can get
information.

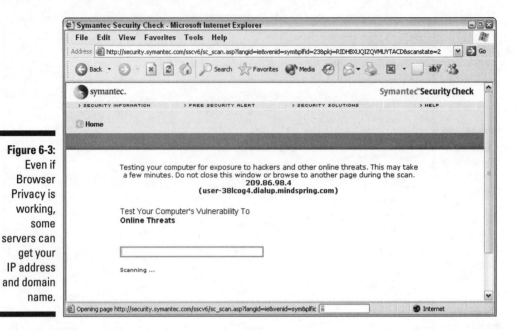

Figure 6-3:
Even if
Browser
Privacy is
working,
some
servers can
get your
IP address
and domain
name.

During a security scan, an Intrusion Detection alert box should appear. If you get details on this event by clicking Show Details in the Security Alert dialog box, you discover the following:

```
Intrusion: Portscan.
Attacker: 206.204.10.200
Risk Level: Medium
At least 11 ports were probed.
```

After the scan is complete, you'll hopefully see a Web page like the one shown in Figure 6-4 which reports that your browser security is adequate.

Boosting browser privacy settings

You may ask why Symantec's Web server was able to get *any* information from your browser in this situation. NIS's Browser Privacy settings, after all, are supposed to prevent your browser from sending browser information. However, some diagnostic sites on the Internet might report browser information even though the Browser Privacy settings are blocking it. Checking your Browser Privacy settings to make sure they are as strong as they can be is a good idea. Follow these steps:

1. **Open the main NIS window and double-click Privacy Control.**

   The Privacy Control window opens (see Figure 6-5).

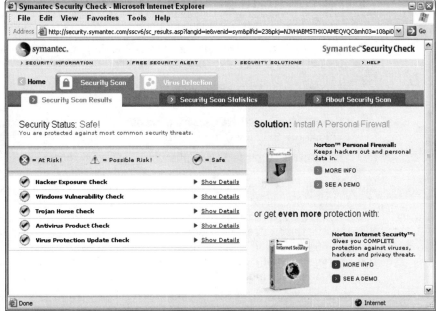

Figure 6-4:
The Security Check site should tell you Norton Internet Security is protecting your computer.

Figure 6-5:
You can adjust browser privacy settings to block scripts and other active content.

2. **Click Custom Level.**

   The Customize Privacy Settings dialog box appears (see Figure 6-6).

3. **Make sure Enable Browser Privacy is checked, then select one of the options from the Private Information drop-down list.**

   By default, the list is set to Medium. I recommend that you change the level to High.

4. **Click OK to close the Customize Privacy Settings dialog box, and OK to close the Privacy Control window.**

   You return to the main NIS window.

After you adjust your privacy settings, you can try an additional test: Go to a site that is especially designed to analyze your browser, such as the one provided by Privacy.Net (`http://privacy.net/analyze`). When you connect to this page, the site's server does a detailed analysis of all the information it can glean from your browser. It does *not* reveal the Web page you visited before you came to Privacy.Net. However, it does reveal your IP address, your domain name, your monitor type, your computer type, and more.

Figure 6-6:
Use this
dialog box's
settings to
boost your
level of
browser
privacy.

Blocking active content

The Privacy.Net page I describe in the preceding section also reveals that JavaScript and VBScript are enabled: These two languages may have allowed the site to find out so much information. You can return to the Privacy Control window and turn NIS's settings up another notch to block these types of content. Open the Privacy Control window as described in the preceding section and follow these steps:

1. **Click Advanced.**

   The Advanced dialog box opens.

2. **Click Global Settings if it is not already in front.**

   The Global Settings tab jumps to the front (see Figure 6-7).

3. **Click Block under Information About Your Browser, click Block under Information About Visited Sites, and then click Block under Scripts.**

4. **Click OK to close the Advanced dialog box, and OK again to close the Privacy Control window.**

   You return to the main NIS window.

Now, when you revisit the Privacy.Net screen, you discover that, while your IP address and domain are still sent to the site's browser, virtually no other information about your computer or your monitor is.

The problem with disabling scripts is that, while this makes your Web browser more secure, it also makes the many Web sites that use Java, JavaScript, and other scripting languages less functional. If you are unable to view content on Web pages, you may want to change the advanced setting under Scripts back to Permit.

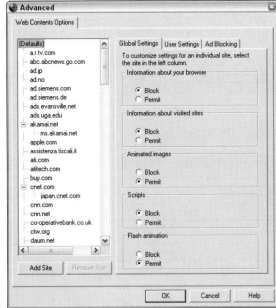

Figure 6-7: You can prevent your browser from processing scripts and giving out other information in Advanced options.

Working with compressed files

Even though some of the well-known peer-to-peer file sharing sites, such as Napster, don't give away music and software files for free, you can still download lots of files from sites around the world. Whether you're looking for a music file, a bootleg copy of a commercial application, or trial versions of software, you can find them somewhere on the Internet. Web sites like Software.com (`www.software.com`) or Tucows (`www.tucows.com`) make it particularly easy to find trial versions that you can use for a specified period of time (typically, 15 or 30 days) and then purchase if you want to keep them.

Making sure you know exactly what you're getting when you download compressed files is essential: Archives that contain a variety of separate files and that are created with applications like WinZip (for Windows) or StuffIt (for the Macintosh). You might download a compressed file that has a number of different files in it, including some that have harmless-looking files with names like `setup.exe`.

The file shown in Figure 6-8, for example, was downloaded from a file sharing Web site, and it claimed to be a trial version of a very expensive firewall program. Along with the official-looking files in the Zip archive, files like `setup.exe` and `click.exe` installed links in the computer's Start menu that led to an X-rated Web site. They could just as easily have contained viruses.

Norton Internet Security, by default, scans compressed files you download before you even extract the files within them. It makes sure none of the files in the compressed file contain viruses, and deletes them if necessary.

Note: The capability of scanning compressed files is available only on versions of NIS that run on Windows 2000 and XP.

Figure 6-8:
Norton
Internet
Security
inspects the
contents of
compressed
files to block
viruses.

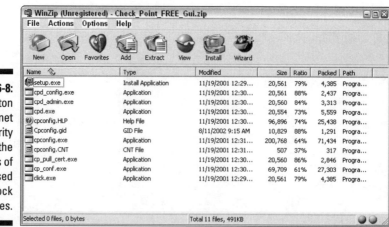

Protecting Microsoft Office Files

If you use popular Microsoft Office products such as Word and Excel, you notice something new as you open documents created in those applications. Before the file opens, the message "Running virus scan" appears in the status bar of any files you currently have open.

The virus scanning function is provided by an NIS component that works within Microsoft Office: the Office Plug-in. It protects Microsoft Office documents from viruses, worms, and virus-like activities. It scans documents whenever you open them in a Microsoft Office program. By default, the Office Plug-in is enabled. However, it does add some time to the process of opening Office files. If you want to disable the plug-in, you can follow these steps:

1. **Open the main NIS window and click Options, then select Norton AntiVirus from the drop-down list.**

   The Norton AntiVirus Options window opens.

2. **In the left pane of the Options window, under Other, click Miscellaneous.**

   The Miscellaneous options appear (see Figure 6-9).

3. **Deselect the box next to Office Plug-in.**

   The Plug-in is disabled.

4. **Click OK.**

   The Options window closes and you return to the main window.

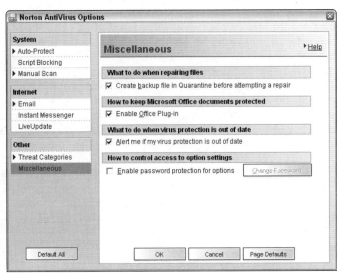

Figure 6-9:
You can disable the plug in, but you'll leave your Office applications vulnerable to viruses.

Viruses can infect Microsoft Office files, so you should avoid disabling the plug-in for any length of time as it provides you with valuable protection.

Keeping Spies and Hackers at Bay

One of Norton Internet Security's new features is its capability of blocking software programs that aren't obviously as harmful as viruses or worms, but that many Internet users consider invasions of privacy. Simply by clicking on an advertisement, downloading a piece of trial software, or visiting a Web site, you can download programs that connect to external computers without your knowledge and provide information about your computer and how you use it. The sections that follow describe the different types of programs you might encounter and the options NIS gives you for dealing with them.

Spyware

Spyware is software that provides tracking information about you and your computers to advertisers and others on the Internet. Spyware and can be unknowingly downloaded from Web sites (typically in shareware or free-ware), e-mail messages, and instant messages. Often a user unknowingly downloads Ad-ware by accepting an End User License Agreement from a software program.

Spyware that functions as advertising-supported software actually has a good aspect: It enables software developers to make money from their work and make their applications available to end users for free.

Suppose a programmer creates an application that lets you read your e-mail for free. In order to gain wide use for the application, the programmer needs to make the application freely downloadable on a shareware or trialware basis. If the customer decides to keep the software, he or she is asked to pay a fee to the program's creator. But many users never pay the fee. How can the developer make money for his or her work? By selling advertising. Often, the shareware applications force the viewer to view banner advertisements while they use the program. This enables customers to use the program without paying for it, and it provides compensation for the developers.

The "spyware" aspect of such programs comes not from the ads themselves but from additional tracking software installed on your system. This spyware is continually connecting to remote Web sites using your Internet connection. It reports information to the remote Web site (usually that of an advertiser, but possibly that of a hacker) about how you use the software.

Spyware is technically not illegal. Most spyware reports harmless data, such as different Web pages you view using the software, how often you start up the program, and so forth. But think about it: Do you want a piece of software sitting on your computer, acting as a server and transmitting information to people you know nothing about, and consuming your Internet connection's bandwidth? Many people would say no.

Spyware is also sometimes called *Ad-ware*. Advertisements can be blocked with Norton Internet Security's Ad Blocking component, which I discuss in Chapter 10.

Keystroke loggers

Spyware comes in different flavors. Much of it has to do with advertising, as I describe in the previous section. But a dangerous type of spyware is more intrusive: This is software that performs surveillance on a computer user, monitoring activities such as keystrokes on a keyboard, Web pages that have been visited, e-mail messages that have been sent, snapshots of a computer desktop taken periodically, and other activities.

Sometimes, this spy software has a legitimate purpose. Spectorsoft, for example (http://spectorsoft.com), produces a software program called Spector that takes periodic snapshots of a computer desktop so teachers and parents can keep track of what young people are doing with the machine. Businesses, too, often want to keep track of how their employees are making use of company resources.

The problem occurs with types of spyware known as keystroke loggers (also known as keyloggers): programs that run in the background, usually without your knowledge, recording all of the keystrokes you type on your keyboard. The keystrokes are then either saved on the computer so they can be retrieved later, or transmitted immediately to the hacker who planted the keylogger program in the first place. The hacker then has to peruse all of your keystrokes carefully, hoping to uncover passwords, usernames, credit card numbers, or other information.

Multimedia communications is increasingly popular on the Internet, and that includes keystroke loggers and other forms of spyware. Some programs, such as RemoteSpy (www.remotespy.com), can log chat conversations, or capture information from every window that has been open on your computer. A few products can even function as audio and video recorders, transmitting everything that occurs over your Internet connection.

Joke programs

Joke programs are like the whoopie cushions of the computer world. They do things that distract you and hopefully make you smile. They also distract you from your work, consume computer resources, and occasionally irritate you if you're not in the mood for opening unsolicited software. They can even cause you moments of great panic: The "joke" performed by the program called Joke.Amigo is that it pretends to delete all of the files and folders on your computer and reformat your hard drive as well. Ha ha!

Joke programs are generally not harmless; they are considered more of a nuisance than a destructive problem. But you should still handle them like a virus: Don't click on them or open them. Here are a few examples of such programs and what they do:

- ✔ **Joke.Apeldorn.** This program displays a series of dialog boxes in Dutch and causes your screen images to appear distorted. It pretends to restart the computer in MS-DOS mode and reformat your C: drive.

- ✔ **Joke.Flash.** This little program causes black and white flashing rectangles to appear on your Windows desktop.

- ✔ **Joke.Hikaru.** If you execute this program, nothing happens at first. After a period of time has elapsed, you see a picture of a woman and hear screaming sounds.

- ✔ **Joke.Irritant.** This well-named application causes small windows to open constantly that bear the title Irritant!

- ✔ **Joke.Trembler.** When you click on this file to manually execute it, the cursor appears to shake, making it difficult to point and click on objects.

As you can see, most joke programs are easy to identify because their file names begin with "Joke." Also, most of these applications must be manually executed in order to operate them: You have to click an attachment to open it, or double-click the executable file itself to start it. NIS regards these relatively harmless programs as an extended threat and removes the files automatically.

The Symantec Security Response Web site maintains a lengthy list of joke programs at http://securityresponse.symantec.com/avcenter/ expanded_threats/joke_programs/. Click on the name of the program to find out what it does.

Dialers

Most computers that are connected to the Internet are equipped with a modem of some sort, even if those computers go online by means of a T-1, DSL, or cable modem connection. Programs called *dialers* or remote access programs are designed to dial out to a remote site using your modem. Typically, they will dial to a 900 number in order to use X-rated phone services for free, or to an FTP site where software can be downloaded.

Dialer applications allow another computer to access yours over the Internet. Hackers can use such programs to gain information about you or your network, or to alter your computer configuration in some way. Like joke programs, dialers have predictable names beginning with "Dialer" (Dialer.LoveX, Dialer.Megateens, and so on), but you don't always have to manually execute the files in order to get them to work. Sometimes they're installed when you visit selected Web pages (though you must agree to the installation).

Symantec Security Response maintains a list of dialer applications at `http://securityresponse.symantec.com/avcenter/expanded_threats/dialers/`.

Hack tools

Some of the preceding programs are more of a nuisance than a threat. But hack tools (which are often called *rootkits*) definitely fall into the latter category. These are programs that are specifically designed to give someone unauthorized access to a computer or network. They attempt to scan a network for valid IP addresses. When an address is located, they attempt to find an opening through a port or a running server application. Hack tools are automatically blocked by NIS when they are detected.

Hack tools are described by Symantec Security Response at `http://securityresponse.symantec.com/avcenter/expanded_threats/hack_tools/`. But Symantec's list of hack tools is limited to programs that actually start with the term "Hacktool." There are many more programs, such as Nmap, that analyze entire networks and attempt to find points of entry. You can find out more about such tools and how easy it is to download them at `www.infosyssec.net/infosyssec/tools2.htm`.

Handling Security Threats

Norton Internet Security gives you a number of options to deal with threats you uncover. If NIS blocks a piece of spyware, a joke program, or a hack tool, you can respond in a number of ways. You can do nothing, of course, and feel good that your security software prevented serious damage. But if you report the software to Symantec, you might help improve security on the Internet in general. You can also block all traffic to and from your computer with a single click of your mouse button, giving you time while you determine the source of an infiltration.

Sending a file to Symantec over the Internet

Most of the time, the viruses, spyware, and other threats that NIS blocks are well known to Symantec. You don't need to send such files to the manufacturer. However, you might want to send a file under the following circumstances:

- ✔ A Symantec employee tells you to send in the file.
- ✔ Norton AntiVirus detects the same viruses every time it performs a scan.
- ✔ You believe that a file is infected even though Norton AntiVirus reports that no viruses were found after a scan.

You can always send a virus or a file you think is infected on a floppy disk through the mail. But you won't get any response for several weeks. The faster and more efficient way is to send the file to Symantec over the Internet. You can do this easily for items that have been placed in Quarantine:

1. **Open the main NIS window, click Norton AntiVirus, and click Reports.**

   The Reports set of options appears.

2. **Click View Report next to Quarantined Items.**

   The Norton AntiVirus Quarantine window opens.

3. **Right-click the name of the item you want to submit.**

   A shortcut menu appears.

4. **Select Send to Symantec from the shortcut menu.**

   The file is sent to Symantec.

If the file you want to send is not in Quarantine, you can use a utility called Sarcret.exe to send the file to Symantec. Go to the Symantec Security Response site, click Support, and search for the document entitled "Submitting a file to Symantec Security Response over the Internet," which has a document ID of 1999052109284606, or go directly to `http://service1.symantec.com/SUPPORT/nav.nsf/docid/1999052109284606`.

Note: Games that your kids play over the Internet give remote users another way to connect to your computer. You may want to block such applications using Norton Parental Control, as described in Chapter 13.

Protecting against timeouts

By default, Norton AntiVirus scans both incoming and outgoing e-mail messages for viruses. But sometimes, timeouts can occur. A *timeout* is a halt in a process caused because a specified amount of time has passed without any activity. Either the e-mail attachment that AntiVirus is attempting to scan is multiple megabytes in size, or an e-mail folder contains a large number of messages. A timeout is more of an inconvenience than a harmful event: You might lose your connection to the Internet, if you are on a dialup line, and you'll have to reconnect.

To prevent connection timeouts while receiving large attachments, enable timeout protection. Timeout protection causes Norton AntiVirus to confirm on a periodic basis that your e-mail software has an active Internet connection. To enable timeout protection, Choose Options⇨Norton AntiVirus, click E-mail on the left-hand side of the window, then choose Advanced. When the Advanced E-mail Options dialog box opens, make sure Protect Against Timeouts (recommended) is checked.

Hitting the panic button

Sometimes, if you know an attacker has gained access to your computer and is either copying software or files or an application is in the process of sending data out over the Internet, you need to pull the plug on the Internet connection as quickly as possible. By breaking the connection, you prevent the attacker from doing any further damage. You can then do a scan for infected files or close any vulnerable ports or services.

To block your Internet connection, you can unplug the computer from the network or turn off your computer altogether. But a simpler and less disruptive way is to click NIS's Block Traffic button at the top of the main NIS window (see Figure 6-10).

Figure 6-10:
Block Traffic
instantly
breaks your
Internet
connection
so you can
repair a
problem
safely.

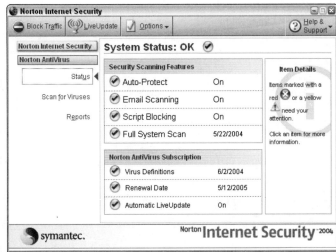

When you click the button, its name changes to Allow Traffic. After you have repaired the problem, you can click the Allow Traffic button to re-establish your connection.

Block Traffic is only intended to be used as a temporary measure while you address a security problem. If you restart your computer, Norton Internet Security automatically allows all incoming and outgoing communication.

Chapter 7

Performing Updates and Other Housekeeping

*E*very large-scale facility, from schools to hospitals, checks its security and safety systems periodically. You may or may not conduct in-home fire drills; you check your smoke detectors every six months, and you should check your computer firewall and anti-virus software even more frequently.

Do you change the batteries in your smoke detectors every six months? If so, my hat is off to you. Because Symantec knows that periodic maintenance is often hard to remember, it builds automatic updating procedures into Norton Internet Security. That doesn't mean you can ignore upkeep and updates, however. By spending a few minutes each week, you can keep hackers, spammers, marketers, and other intruders at bay so you can keep computing happily and efficiently.

Working with LiveUpdate

LiveUpdate is the component of Norton Internet Security that checks for updates to the software and downloads it to your computer on a periodic basis so NIS can keep up with the latest threats. It locates and obtains files from an Internet site, installs them, and then deletes the leftover files from your computer. LiveUpdate obtains two kinds of files:

- ✔ **Product updates:** Updates to the software itself, commonly called patches.

- ✔ **Protection updates:** New intrusion signatures and virus definitions that keep NIS able to recognize the newest versions.

With other firewall products, you have to check the manufacturer's Web site yourself for periodic updates. LiveUpdate does the checking for you; however, running the program manually or scheduling updates is still up to you.

Running LiveUpdate

You can run LiveUpdate in either of two modes: Interactive mode or Express mode. If you are a "hands-off" computer administrator and don't feel you need to know many details about NIS's operation, use Express mode. LiveUpdate automatically installs all updates that are available. Otherwise, you can use Interactive mode, where you see a dialog box that lists available updates and gives you the chance to choose the ones you want to download. You get a list of available updates when you click LiveUpdate in the NIS main window, and then, when the LiveUpdate application opens, click Next to check for new software (see Figure 7-1).

Figure 7-1:
In Interactive mode, you control which updates to download, in case you are short on time or disk space.

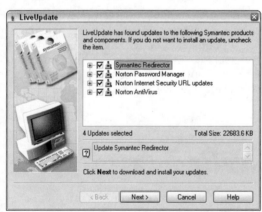

To switch between Interactive mode and Express mode, you open the main NIS window, click LiveUpdate, click Configure, and then click the mode of your choice on the General tab (see Figure 7-2). Then click Apply.

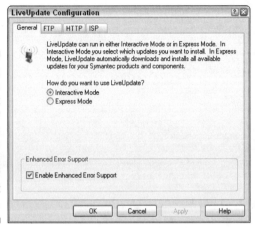

Figure 7-2:
LiveUpdate
isn't
completely
automatic;
use these
controls to
specify how
you want it
to operate.

You should leave Enable Enhanced Error Support checked; it gives you access to a self-help Web site if you run into an error while using LiveUpdate.

To run LiveUpdate in either mode, you first need to be connected to the Internet. If you have a DSL or cable modem connection that is "always on," you don't have to do any special configuration. If you connect to the Internet manually through a dialup connection and you want LiveUpdate to connect to Symantec's Web site automatically, you may need to configure the application to use a particular connection method, as provided for on the other tabs in the LiveUpdate Configuration dialog box. Click FTP if you want LiveUpdate to connect using File Transfer Protocol; click HTTP if you need to change your HyperText Transfer Protocol settings, which enable you to connect to the Web; or click ISP if you need to connect to America Online or another Internet Service Provider and you need to enter a phone number, username, or password so LiveUpdate can make a connection (see Figure 7-3).

Updating manually

After you configure LiveUpdate, click OK to close the LiveUpdate Configuration dialog box and then follow these steps:

1. **Open the main NIS window and click LiveUpdate.**

   The Welcome to Live Update window appears.

2. **Click Next.**

   LiveUpdate connects to Symantec's Web site and locates any available updates.

3. **Deselect any files you do not want to download, and then click Next.**

   The updated files are downloaded.

4. **When the downloading is complete, click Finish.**

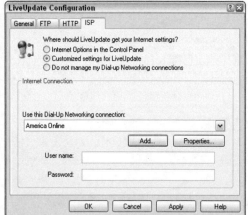

Figure 7-3:
Use the
ISP tab to
enter your
Internet
connection
information
so Live-
Update can
connect
auto-
matically.

You may be prompted to restart your computer after you install the available updates. Keep in mind that you don't need to do this immediately; be sure you save any work you have in progress and close open files before you restart.

Keep an eye on the Total Size figure just beneath the list of updates in the LiveUpdate window. You may want to make decisions based on available disk space. In Figure 7-1, a full 22MB of updates have been specified. Click the plus sign (+) next to each item to get more detailed information on its size. You can deselect an item if you want to save hard drive space — but you should probably download Norton AntiVirus and Norton Personal Firewall updates, as these are what protect your computer.

Updating automatically

Norton recommends that you run LiveUpdate once a week. If you have a direct connection to the Internet, no worries about available hard drive space, and want to keep on top of the latest security threats, you may decide to have LiveUpdate run automatically. Automatic LiveUpdate checks every five minutes until you're connected to the Internet; after you're connected, it checks for new definitions and other data every four hours.

To run LiveUpdate automatically, open the main NIS window, click Options, and select Norton AntiVirus from the drop-down list. Click LiveUpdate under the Internet heading to view the Automatic LiveUpdate options (see Figure 7-4).

If you click the button next to Notify Me When Updates Are Available, a miniature LiveUpdate icon appears in your Windows system tray (see Figure 7-5). Click on the icon to launch LiveUpdate.

Note: In order to perform LiveUpdate on a computer running Windows XP or Windows 2000, you need to be logged on to the computer with Administrator access privileges rather than PowerUser or user privileges.

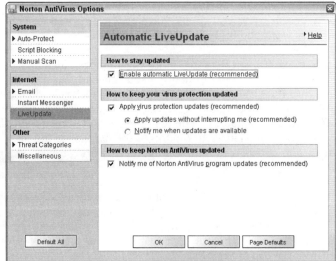

Figure 7-4:
Use these
options to
disable or
enable
automatic
updates.

Figure 7-5:
If you don't
want to run
automatic
updates
immediately,
you can
have Live-
Update
notify you
from the
system tray
that new
files are
available.

Reviewing Your Firewall Rules

In Chapter 4, you found out how to establish rules for Norton Personal
Firewall. Over time, you might create a number of specific rules in response
to intrusion alerts. When you start accumulating dozens of separate rules,
the firewall can slow down. After all, every time a connection attempt is
made, the firewall has to run through each of the rules in turn and evaluate

whether it can be applied. Ideally, all of the rules in your firewall's rule base should be necessary, and you should have as few as possible. This makes the firewall do less work and improves performance.

You can also make Norton Personal Firewall run more efficiently by making sure the most important and frequently used rules appear near the top of the rule base rather than the bottom. Most firewalls check rules in top-to-bottom order until a match is found. If the firewall has to go through rules 1 through, say, 12 before finding a match, it spends unnecessary time moving from rule 1 to 12. Moving the rule closer to the top of the list makes the match occur more quickly and allows traffic through your network gateway in a more efficient fashion.

In order to determine which rules are most frequently used, you need to review your Event Log as described in Chapter 16. Also consider that one of the most frequent sources of traffic into and out of your computer is e-mail, so any rules that allow your computer to check your mail server for e-mail should go near the top of your list.

To review your current set of firewall rules, open the main NIS window, double-click Personal Firewall and, when the Personal Firewall options open, click Advanced. When the Advanced Firewall options appear, click General. After a few seconds, the General Rules dialog box appears (see Figure 7-6). Click the ones you want to adjust; for each one, click Remove to take it off the list altogether, or click Move Up or Move Down to reorder the rule within the list.

Figure 7-6:
Reorder and trim your firewall rules to improve performance.

Managing Passwords

One of the most difficult things to remember when it comes to periodic maintenance is the need to change your passwords once in a while. I can tell you from personal experience that remembering this is difficult, especially when I have different passwords for e-mail, online banking, cellphone, *The New York Times,* eBay, and many, many other sites and services.

Nevertheless, changing your passwords every few months is a good idea. One of the passwords you can change — or perhaps set for the first time — and that's directly relevant to your security — is your Norton Internet Security options password. This password protects Norton Internet Security so only you, and no one else who has access to your computer, can change rules or options. You're required to enter a password every time you want to change options. But this option provides good protection in an environment where multiple individuals have access to your machine. To change or set the password for the first time, follow these steps:

1. **Open the main NIS window and click Options.**

   A drop-down list appears.

2. **Select Norton Internet Security.**

   The Norton Internet Security Options window appears.

3. **On the General tab, check the box next to Turn On Password Protection if you have not yet set a password.**

   A dialog box appears prompting you to create a password (see Figure 7-7).

4. **Click Yes.**

   A dialog box appears prompting you to enter and then confirm a new password.

5. **Enter the password, and click OK.**

   You return to Norton Internet Security Options.

If you already have a password and want to change it, open Norton Internet Security Options and click Set Password. You'll be prompted to enter the current password and then create a new one.

Creating an Emergency Disk

Firewalls and anti-virus programs are primarily intended to prevent everyday risks rather than help you recover from severe disasters. But the potential for real disaster is on everyone's mind these days. NIS has the capability of creating emergency disks that can help you restart your computer in case the system is corrupted or critical files are erased, or in the unlikely event that a virus gets past NIS and brings work to a screeching halt.

Nobody likes to create emergency disks. You may think, "Oh, I'll never need them anyway." Having neglected to create my own set of Windows emergency disks and later been faced with the dreaded "blue screen of death" (the screen that appears when Windows is seriously disabled and can't function), I'll never neglect to create such disks again. The NIS emergency disks have different files than the ones Windows creates, but they perform similar functions. They give your computer just enough information to boot up, so you can use NIS or other software to solve the problem you are experiencing.

The emergency files are on the NIS CD, so you could try to boot from that disk drive in case of disaster. But a computer that's in major disrepair won't be able to use the CD-ROM drive, either. If you're using a computer that can't start from a CD, you need to have a set of Emergency Disks available — floppy disks — that you can use to start your computer and scan for viruses.

Note: You need a program called NED.exe to create these disks. The NIS help files claim that you can find it on your computer in the location where you downloaded the rest of the software. I couldn't find NED.exe there; however, I did find it online at `ftp://ftp.symantec.com/public/english_us_canada/tools/win95nt/ned_2001.exe`.

From the CD

If your computer can start from a CD, you can use the Norton Internet Security CD in place of Emergency Disks. You'll need three floppy disks (1.44MB in storage capacity) ready. To create the disks from the CD, insert the NIS CD in your CD-ROM drive and follow these steps:

1. **If the Welcome screen appears because you have just inserted the CD in your drive, click Browse CD.**

   Windows Explorer displays the contents of the drive.

2. **Double-click the Support folder, then double-click the Edisk folder.**

   A dialog box appears welcoming you to the Norton Emergency Disk Creation Utility.

3. **Insert the first floppy disk in your computer's floppy disk drive and click OK.**

   The files are copied to the floppy disk.

4. **Take out the first disk when prompted to do so and insert the second disk into the floppy disk drive.**

5. **Repeat Steps 3 and 4 for the other two disks.**

6. **When the disks have been prepared, click OK and remove the final disk from drive A.**

When you're done and you have some time, close your open files, shut down your computer, insert the first disk in the set, and restart your computer to make sure it will boot up your machine.

From the Symantec Web site

Alternatively, you can go to `www.symantec.com/techsupp/ebd.html` and download the Emergency Disk program. Follow the instructions included in the page, which is entitled How to Create Emergency Disks by Downloading a Program from the Symantec FTP Site, to create the floppy disks.

Even though the "How to Create Emergency Disks" document instructs you to download a file called NED_2001.exe, which might seem a few years out of date, it still contains the files you can use to restart your computer in case of serious trouble.

Housecleaning: Do You Really Need All This Stuff?

When you install new software, you want to know exactly what it's doing and how much memory it needs. If you look on your Norton Internet Security packaging, you see very clearly that the program requires 200MB of hard drive storage space. What the packaging doesn't tell you is that 200MB is the amount of space the software files *initially* consume. As it blocks files, places files in Quarantine, accumulates new virus definitions and intrusion signatures, and records events in the Event Log, it stores an ever-increasing amount of information. A little bit of housecleaning can make the program run more efficiently and conserve disk space, too.

Cleaning out the Quarantine folder

My Quarantine folder probably isn't like yours. The items there accumulated over several years. Having just installed Norton Internet Security, you may only have a handful of files in Quarantine. But you can still follow these steps to see how much space the program is *really* using:

1. **Choose Start➪All Programs➪Accessories➪Windows Explorer.**

   The Windows Explorer window opens.

2. **Find the Norton AntiVirus folder where you installed the program.**

   If you installed the program in the default location, you'll find it in C:\Program Files\Norton AntiVirus.

3. **Click the plus sign (+) next to Norton AntiVirus.**

   The Quarantine folder within it is displayed.

4. **Single-click the Quarantine folder.**

   The folder's name is highlighted. Wait a few seconds, and the complete list of all the files in the folder appears. The total number of files appears in the bottom left-hand corner of the window (see Figure 7-8).

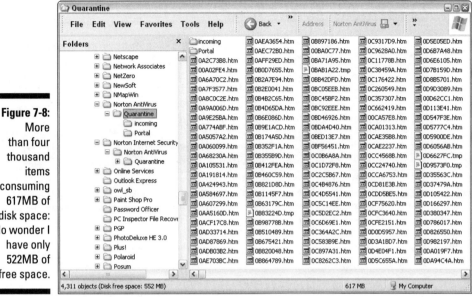

Figure 7-8:
More
than four
thousand
items
consuming
617MB of
disk space:
No wonder I
have only
522MB of
free space.

Hopefully, you won't have more than 4,000 items in your own Quarantine folder. But even if you have a few hundred, cleaning them out as long as you no longer need them is worth it. You could choose File⇨Select All to select all the items in the folder, then choose File⇨Delete to delete them, but it's not the approved way. To clean items out of Quarantine, follow these steps:

1. **Open the main NIS window and click Norton AntiVirus.**

   The Norton AntiVirus options appear on the left-hand side of the window.

2. **Click Reports.**

   The Reports options appear.

3. **Click View Reports next to Quarantine.**

   The Quarantine window opens.

4. **Select the items you want to delete, then click the red X (Delete Item) on the Quarantine window's toolbar or choose Action⇨Delete from the menu bar.**

   The item is deleted.

Be careful when removing files from Quarantine. When you remove files, they aren't placed in the Recycle Bin; they are immediately deleted from your computer.

Emptying Event logs

With enterprise-level firewalls, managing log files can be a time-consuming and important activity because of the sheer size of the files. Log files for a large-scale network contain so many records of events that they can quickly grow many gigabytes in size. Log files often have to be rotated — moved to a storage area and replaced by newer log files. Outdated log file records are either archived on tape or CD or overwritten by newer records.

With Norton Internet Security, log files are kept relatively small in size by default: between 64K and 512K. When a log file reaches its maximum size, the newer events simply overwrite the oldest ones automatically. Over time, you may find that you actually want to *increase* rather than decrease the size of certain logs in order to view a wider range of events. When files accumulate, you can do two things to manage them:

- ✔ Export them to another location so they don't take up so much space on your computer.
- ✔ Clear the log files altogether.

If your log file is at the default size of 64K or so, there isn't much benefit to completely clearing out log files. The primary benefit is that you can see the most recent events more easily. However, if you have increased the log files' sizes to the maximum size of 2,048K, you can save many megabytes of space.

To clear a single log, follow these steps:

1. **Open the main NIS window, click Norton Internet Security, and click Statistics.**

   The recent attack and traffic statistics for your computer appear.

2. **Click View Logs.**

   The Log Viewer window opens.

3. **Clear the logs in one of two ways:**

   - To clear an individual log, right click the type of log you want to clear and then choose Clear Category from the shortcut menu (see Figure 7-9).

   - To clear all of the log files at once, right-click either Norton Internet Security or Norton AntiVirus and choose Clear All Categories from the shortcut menu.

4. **When you are done, choose File⇨Exit.**

   The Log Viewer closes and you return to the main NIS window.

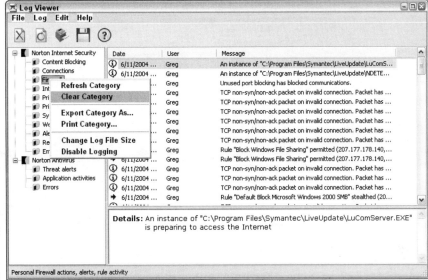

Figure 7-9:
You can
save hard
drive space
by clearing
out log files,
but not if
they're at
the small
default size.

When you specify that the size of one of your log files should change, you automatically erase all information from the log files and start fresh. If you have some information you want to preserve, you should export it to a text file, as described in Chapter 16.

Chapter 8

Welcome to the Land of Quarantine

*I*n the real world where viruses like SARS are a problem, quarantining is one way of stopping the spread of infections. In the world of your computer file system, Quarantine is the area where Norton Internet Security places infected files and encrypts those files so other files cannot be infected. Some of the quarantined objects are viruses; some are your own files that have been infected with viruses and that cannot be repaired.

Most computers probably have the impression that Quarantine is simply a sort of "isolation area" and that files placed there should simply be left alone. But Norton AntiVirus gives you a great deal of control over Quarantine — which, in turn, gives you a greater degree of control over how your computer is protected. You can add files to Quarantine, restore files placed there, submit them for analysis, and more. This chapter gives you a rundown of the basics as well as some of the complications that can arise when working with quarantined files. Finally, you find out how to restore your computer system to its previous, stable condition if a disaster such as a crash or virus befalls it.

Quarantine Basics

You may wonder why viruses and other files are placed in Quarantine in the first place. It may seem safer to simply delete the file altogether, rather than leave it in an area of your file system where you can see it and work with it. Placing the file in Quarantine ensures that you won't delete a file you actually need; there's a chance (however small) that Norton AntiVirus or Norton Personal Firewall will attempt to quarantine a file you actually need and that isn't a virus at all.

Quarantined files can be held for retrieval or restoration to their original state. Quarantined files that AntiVirus can't repair immediately can be sent to Symantec for analysis, and this can result in new virus definitions. I describe some of the strategies for beginning to work with quarantined files in the sections that follow.

Knowing when to quarantine a file

Most of the time, you don't have to make a conscious decision to quarantine a file. Norton AntiVirus automatically makes the decision for you. Occasionally, you encounter a suspect file on your own and you can manually add it to the Quarantine area. When the file has been isolated in this protected area where malicious code cannot replicate or execute, you may think you can forget about it. When you view the contents of the Quarantine folder using Windows Explorer or My Computer, the objects in the folder appear as encrypted codes rather than filenames (see Figure 8-1).

Figure 8-1:
The Quarantine folder's location isn't a mystery, but the files within it are encrypted.

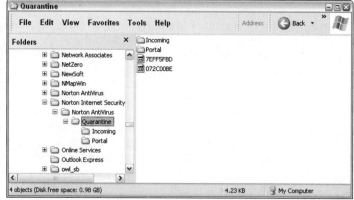

Because the files in Quarantine are encrypted, they can't infect other objects in your file system. And the Quarantine area is supposed to function as sort of a digital "isolation chamber" that keeps potentially harmful files away from your computer.

The problem is that you don't really know what the quarantined file is or what it does. Is it a virus? A worm? Or is it just a file that Norton AntiVirus doesn't know how to handle? After a file is quarantined, you need to do three things:

✔ **Watch out for applications that don't run correctly.** The infected file was possibly a critical part of an application's operation. If an application doesn't function correctly after the file is placed in Quarantine, then you'll need to repair the file or restore an uninfected copy.

✔ **Do some research on the quarantined file.** You should find out what the program is and how it functions. After you find out more about the file, you can see if the program is needed by one of your applications or whether you should delete the file from Quarantine.

✔ **Delete infected backup copies.** If the file placed in quarantine was a backup made before AntiVirus attempted to repair a file — and if the file was actually repaired — the infected backup copy should be deleted from Quarantine.

Keep in mind that Quarantine is just a holding area; files should either be restored or deleted altogether and not allowed to pile up so they can consume disk space. I talk about two options for handling quarantined files in the sections that follow.

There isn't any hard and fast rule about handling quarantined files, because they only accumulate when you encounter viruses or other files that NIS cannot handle. Check the Quarantine area every few weeks to see what's there.

Researching quarantined data

Norton AntiVirus makes decisions to quarantine files based on settings in AntiVirus options. By default, AntiVirus attempts to repair all the viruses it finds automatically. But you can also specify that AntiVirus should automatically quarantine files if they cannot be repaired. Figure 8-2 shows your options for getting a notification message when a file goes into Quarantine or its placement there without notice.

Figure 8-2:
You can
specify
whether or
not you are
notified
when
files are
quarantined.

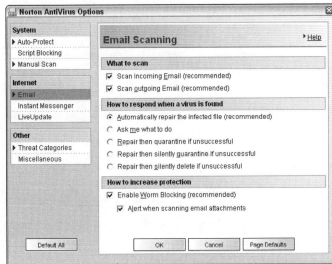

You may want to opt for a notification message rather than have AntiVirus silently place files in Quarantine. Why? Because knowing about a file's existence there helps you decide how to handle it. If you do decide to place files there "silently," you should make a point to check the Quarantine area for any new files after AntiVirus performs its regular scan.

AntiVirus puts the following kinds of files in Quarantine:

- ✔ A virus or other threat that AntiVirus can't repair immediately.
- ✔ A backup of a file that was made before AntiVirus attempted to repair the file.
- ✔ A file, virus, or Trojan horse that you submitted to Symantec Security Response for analysis. You send the original, but a copy remains in Quarantine. After Symantec provides you with an analysis, you can determine how to handle the file.

To research a file placed in Quarantine, you first have to view it and get its name. Follow these steps:

1. **Open the main NIS window and click Norton AntiVirus.**

   The AntiVirus options appear.

2. **Click Reports.**

   The Reports options appear.

3. **Click View Report next to Quarantine.**

   After a few seconds, the Quarantine window opens (see Figure 8-3).

Figure 8-3:
The Quarantine window lists the files that have been placed there and provides you with options for researching them.

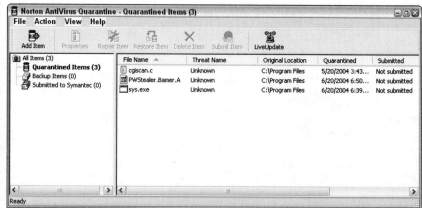

4. **Write down or make note of the names listed in the File Name and Threat Name columns.**

   File Name is the name of the file that contained the virus, Trojan horse, worm, or infected file; Threat Name lists the name of the virus or malicious program involved, if it is known. (If it isn't, you'll see "Unknown.")

5. **Start up your Web browser, if necessary, and connect to the Symantec Security Response Search and Latest Virus Threats Page (**www. symantec.com/avcenter/vinfodb.html**) shown in Figure 8-4.**

6. **Enter all or part of the filename in the search box near the top of the page.**

   If you're sure the file is a virus, Trojan horse, worm, or macro, uncheck the Vulnerabilities and Exploits check box to refine the search. If you're sure the file is a vulnerability or exploit, uncheck Viruses, Trojan horses, Worms and Macros. If you're not sure, leave both options checked.

7. **Click Search.**

   In a few seconds, a set of search results appears. Click on the list item that seems most relevant to find out more about the threat.

Figure 8-4:
Search the
Symantec
Security
Response
database for
instructions
on how to
handle a
quarantined
file.

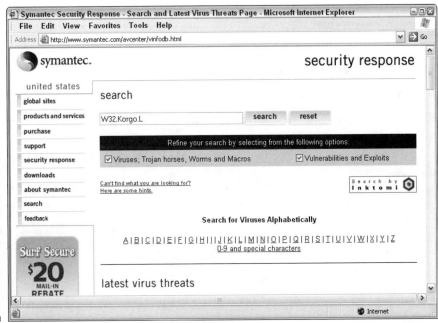

The Symantec Security Response page contains information about how widespread the threat is, what it does, and what files it adds to your computer. Scroll down to the "removal instructions" heading to read how to remove the file. In some cases, a special removal tool will be available. In other cases, you'll be instructed to delete the file from Quarantine or manually repair the file. I cover both options later in this chapter.

The Symantec Security Response page contains information about how widespread the threat is, what it does, and what files it adds to your computer. Scroll down to the "removal instructions" heading to read how to remove the file. In some cases, a special removal tool will be available. In other cases, you'll be instructed to delete the file from Quarantine or manually repair the file. I cover both options later in this chapter.

Manually repairing viruses or Trojans

If some files in your computer are infected by viruses or Trojan horses and AntiVirus places the infected files in Quarantine, you may discover that some — or all — of your applications won't start up. In that case, you need to manually repair the infected file.

Follow these steps to have AntiVirus repair the file:

1. **Right-click the file's named in the Quarantined Items list.**

   A shortcut menu appears (see Figure 8-5).

2. **Choose Repair.**

   A dialog box appears asking if you want to repair and restore the file.

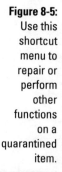

Figure 8-5:
Use this shortcut menu to repair or perform other functions on a quarantined item.

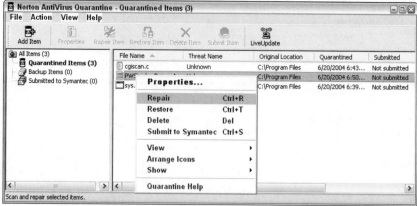

3. Click Yes.

The dialog box closes. The file is either repaired or a dialog box appears telling you that the file could not be repaired.

If you're lucky, AntiVirus will repair the file automatically. If the file can't be repaired automatically, you need to repair it manually.

Repairing the file manually is a complex and advanced procedure. Don't undertake the procedure lightly, because it requires you to edit the Windows Registry. Quarantining an infected file is like putting a bandage on a wound. It doesn't repair or treat any underlying infections or problems that can't be seen immediately. In the same way, an infection may also change parts of the Windows Registry. The registry itself may need to be cleaned out in order to completely remove the effects of the infection.

Working with Quarantine

You can't work with the files in Norton AntiVirus's Quarantine area the way you would in My Computer or Windows Explorer. For one thing, you can only view the files through the Quarantine window. The window's menu bar and toolbar let you perform the main functions, which I describe in the following sections.

Adding files to Quarantine

Sometimes, you may encounter a file that Norton Internet Security has missed. Suppose you have a network of several computers. You perform a virus scan on one machine and detect a virus; you search one of your other machines for the same file and find that it's also present on the other machine.

You can add a file to the Quarantine area by opening the Quarantine window (see the section, "Researching quarantined data," earlier in this chapter) and then clicking the Add Item toolbar button (or choose File⇨Add Item or press Ctrl+A). The Add to Quarantine dialog box appears. Click the down arrow next to Look In and locate the file you want to add, either in your own computer or a network share. Click Add to add the item to the Quarantined Items list.

Submitting files with Scan and Deliver

Sometimes, Norton AntiVirus turns up the same infections repeatedly with each regular virus scan. Or you may encounter a file that AntiVirus didn't repair and you think the file may still be infected. In either case, you can submit the object to Symantec for analysis using the Scan and Deliver Wizard. You may have uncovered a virus (or a variation of a virus) that Symantec hasn't encountered yet. To submit a file, follow these steps:

1. **Select the file that you want to submit in the Quarantined Items list.**

   The item's name is highlighted.

2. **Click Submit Item in the Quarantine toolbar (or right-click the highlighted item and choose Submit to Symantec from the shortcut menu).**

   The first screen of the Scan and Deliver Wizard appears (see Figure 8-6).

3. **Click Next.**

   Norton AntiVirus quickly scans the file. If the file does not appear to be infected, a message appears stating that the file was rejected and asking, "Would you like to submit this file today?"

4. **Click Yes, and then click Next.**

   The User Information screen appears, asking for your contact information.

5. **Continue with the wizard, filling in the contact information in each of the next three dialog boxes, and finally reviewing the information.**

6. **Click Finish in the last dialog box.**

   Your virus sample is sent to Symantec Security Response.

Symantec Security Response will e-mail you a summary of the analysis. If their response indicates that the file was a Trojan horse or worm and recommends that you delete and replace it if necessary, you should delete the file.

If the quarantined file was part of a legitimate software program or a Windows system file and is infected by a virus that can't be repaired by Norton AntiVirus, you should restore a clean copy of the file from a backup or from the original software installation CD.

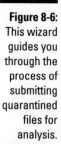

Figure 8-6:
This wizard guides you through the process of submitting quarantined files for analysis.

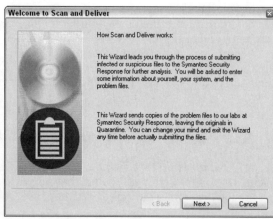

Restoring files from Quarantine

If you submit a file to Symantec and the analysis determines that the file was harmless, you can remove it from Quarantine and restore it to its previous location on your computer. Simply right-click the file's name in the Quarantined Items list to highlight it, and choose Restore from the shortcut menu (or press the Restore Item toolbar button). The Restore Results dialog box appears, notifying you that the selected file has been restored to the previous location on your computer.

Viewing Properties

If you want to view a quick summary of data about a file in Quarantine, right-click the file's name in the Quarantined Items list and choose Properties from the shortcut menu that appears. The Properties dialog box for the item opens. Click the General tab to see the file's name, its type, and the other information you see in the Quarantined Items list. The Properties sheet, however, contains the file size of the item and a recommendation for what to do with it (see Figure 8-7).

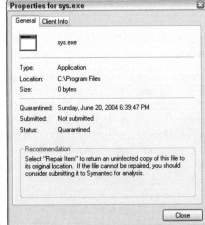

Figure 8-7: The Properties sheet for a quarantined item contains a recommendation for what to do with it.

If you want to save a list of the files that have been placed in Quarantine, open the Quarantine window and choose File➪Export (or press Ctrl+E). The Export dialog box opens. Choose the location where you want to save the exported list of quarantine files. Click Save, and the list is saved as a text file (the default name is Quarantine.text) that you can open later with Notepad or another text editor. The text file contains detailed information about the file that was quarantined, its size, the original location, and the date and time when it was isolated.

Dealing with quarantine errors

If your virus definitions become corrupted or Norton AntiVirus itself becomes damaged, you'll see a dialog box informing you of the problem. For example, you may attempt to open the Quarantine folder and instead see the dreaded dialog box shown in Figure 8-8.

This dialog box is truly bad news: It requires you to uninstall and then reinstall AntiVirus. That may not sound difficult, except that AntiVirus is integrated with the entire Norton Internet Security package, and you'll need to uninstall and reinstall the entire NIS program. This happened to me, and the process took several hours (I cover this in painful detail in Chapter 14). If you must perform an uninstall and reinstall, the process goes something like this:

1. I tried to remove NIS using Windows' Add/Remove Programs program in the Control Panel. At first this seemed to work, but after restarting Windows, the original NIS CD behaved as though the program was still present: It gave me the option of removing NIS or modifying it, even though I had supposedly removed it. In fact, although the program had been removed, many traces of it remained in the Windows registry and in other locations.

2. I had to read several documents on the Symantec Web site and follow a series of steps to remove all traces of NIS, such as folders, temporary files, and shortcuts.

3. I had to restart the computer and reinstall the program, reconfiguring passwords, and running LiveUpdate once again.

4. I added a test file to Quarantine, closed Quarantine, and then reopened it to see whether the problem was resolved.

Note: If you have items in Quarantine that you don't want to delete, move the *contents* of the folder to another location and then continue as instructed. When you finish with the process, you can move them back to the new Quarantine folder and then attempt to restore them.

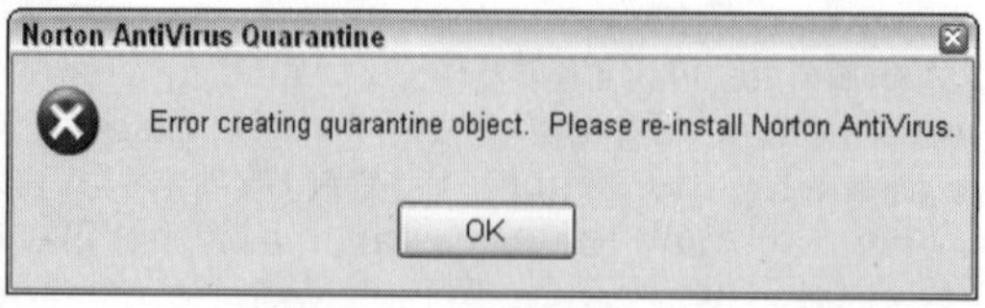

Figure 8-8:
Bad news:
If the
Quarantine
folder
cannot be
created, you
need to
reinstall
AntiVirus.

Norton AntiVirus Quarantine

Error creating quarantine object. Please re-install Norton AntiVirus.

OK

Deleting original e-mail files

If you choose the option Repair Then Quarantine If Unsuccessful or Repair Then Silently Quarantine If Unsuccessful, Norton AntiVirus places infected e-mail attachments that it can't repair in Quarantine. As you've already discovered, you can research the attachments and then restore them, delete them, or submit them to Symantec for further analysis.

What do you do with the original e-mail messages that contained the attachments? They remain in your e-mail inbox until you delete them. The original attachment is replaced by a textual note from Norton AntiVirus, indicating that the attachment was deleted or quarantined. The original message can no longer harm you; if you respond to it, you may or may not get a response. It's possible the sender was completely innocent and that his or her e-mail program sent you the attachment automatically as a result of a Trojan horse or virus infection. If the sender is someone you know, you may want to tell the individual that the message contained an infected file, because the person may be unaware that his or her address book was hijacked and used to distribute infections. Otherwise, you can safely delete the original e-mail.

System Restore and Quarantine

When your computer is infected with a Trojan horse or virus and you get removal instructions from Symantec's Security Response Web site, you see a note about System Restore. This is a Windows system utility that can restore your system to a previously known stable condition if you run into a crash or other disaster (such as a virus infection). The first step in the removal instructions typically begins with this one-line instruction:

```
1.   Disable System Restore
```

You may ask what System Restore has to do with Norton Internet Security. According to Symantec, Windows Me and XP use System Restore to restore files if they're damaged. If a virus, worm, or Trojan horse was the original source of the infection, the danger is that System Restore may back up the virus, worm, or Trojan horse on the computer. Because Windows prevents anti-virus applications and other programs from modifying System Restore, those programs cannot remove any threats that may have been inadvertently placed in the System Restore folder. As a result, System Restore has the potential of restoring an infected file on your computer, even after you have cleaned the infected files from all the other locations. Also, a virus scan may detect a threat in the System Restore folder even though you have removed the threat.

Microsoft's Web site presents a different picture. In fact, document 831829 in the Microsoft Knowledge Base is entitled "How antivirus software and System Restore work together." It states that system restore creates a backup of a file before it is infected with a virus. Symantec states that infected files can be mistakenly backed up by System Restore, thus keeping a virus present on the computer that AntiVirus might pick up during a scan.

A problem occurs when a file cannot be repaired and it is put in Quarantine. In this case, restoration to a previous uninfected state doesn't work. Then, you need to remove infected files from the System Restore data archive. In Windows Me, System Restore files are contained in a volume called _RESTORE. In Windows XP, they're contained in the System folder. For Windows XP users, System Restore is disabled as follows:

1. **Close all open programs and then, on the Windows desktop, right-click My Computer.**

   A shortcut menu appears.

2. **Choose Properties.**

   The System Properties dialog box appears.

3. **Click the System Restore tab.**

   The tab jumps to the front.

4. **Check the box next to Turn Off System Restore.**

   The box is checked.

5. **Click OK.**

   A dialog box appears asking you to confirm that you want to turn off System Restore.

6. **Click Yes.**

   System Properties closes and you return to the Windows desktop.

7. **Restart your computer.**

   This disables the System Restore feature and purges the contents of the System Restore folder.

After restart, open Norton Internet Security and click the LiveUpdate button to run LiveUpdate and download the latest virus definitions. After LiveUpdate is complete, make sure that NAV is set to scan all files and all drives. (Click Norton AntiVirus, click Scan for Viruses, and then click My Computer.) Then click Scan.

If you want to be absolutely sure you remove all viruses in the System Restore folder and elsewhere, open Norton AntiVirus Options. Click Manual Scan in the options on the left side of the window. Click Bloodhound, then click Highest Level of Protection. Click OK to close Options, and then start the scan. The scan will take longer but it will include the maximum number of files.

After you clean the infected files, be sure to turn System Restore back on again. Repeat the preceding set of steps but, in Step 4, uncheck Disable System Restore.

If you use Windows Me and you want to clean out the contents of the System Restore folders, refer to document 2000092513515106 of the Support area of the Symantec Web site (http://service1.symantec.com/SUPPORT/nav.nsf/docid/2000092513515106). The document is entitled "Cannot repair, quarantine, or delete a virus found in the _RESTORE or System volume information."

Part III

Safeguarding Your Privacy and Your Network

The 5th Wave   By Rich Tennant

"We take network security very seriously here."

In this part . . .

*H*ackers and viruses are only two types of threats to your home or office computer systems. Norton Internet Security also helps improve the way you experience the Internet to make it more enjoyable, not to mention less intrusive.

This part examines Norton Internet Security components that help streamline your entire online experience. You find out how to cut down on unsolicited e-mail messages that are clogging your inbox. You also discover how to prevent ads from popping up and cookies from being placed on your hard disk without your knowledge.

You also examine a type of privacy invasion that's becoming more common as people access the Internet from public spaces, such as coffeeshops or "hot spots," using their laptops. When your home or office network extends to such remote locations, you need to protect yourself there, after all.

Chapter 9

Canning Spam

. . . .

. . . .

*T*he World Wide Web may get all the attention, but e-mail is what gets the job done and really delivers, both literally and figuratively. E-mail is probably the most popular part of the Internet, a communication method used for both work and pleasure, for exchanging files and holding discussions on mailing lists.

Because its use is ever more central to business, e-mail ought to be secure. But it isn't. The very qualities that make it ubiquitous — its openness and convenience — make e-mail a tempting target for anyone with a product to sell or a message to get out.

E-mail is widely used to disseminate unsolicited commercial e-mail, otherwise known as spam. Recent legislation that was supposed to regulate spam has only increased it, at least in the United States. More than ever, programs like NIS and its component Norton AntiSpam are needed to preserve privacy. This chapter examines how to help Norton AntiSpam do its job. It also gives you strategies for handling e-mail that will cut down on unwanted messages.

The Web and Privacy: An Oxymoron

You can argue that the Web was created to make the world less private. Rather than a bunch of isolated computers and disconnected networks, the Web helps participants share their information freely. By its very nature then, e-mail is insecure.

Where does spam come from?

As many of its devoted followers know, the processed meat product called SPAM comes from the Hormel Food Corporation's processing plants in Austin, Minnesota. Unwanted e-mail was dubbed "spam" in reference to a skit by the well-known British comedy troupe Monty Python. In the skit, a couple wandered in to a small café where everything on the menu had multiple helpings of SPAM. Whether they wanted it or not, they had to accept the SPAM. The spam you know about from your e-mail inbox comes from a variety of sources:

- Computer programs that scour the Web, scanning the contents of Web pages for e-mail addresses

- Businesses that gather e-mail addresses from individuals who register for services online and sell those addresses to marketers

- Marketers who buy huge lists of e-mail address so they can send out mass mailings

Big-time purveyors of spam regularly send out thousands or even millions of messages at a time. It might seem like a wildly un-businesslike and time-consuming way to reach people — after all, do *you* know anyone who has ever responded to one of those messages, or have you ever done so yourself? But mass e-mailings are a very cost-efficient way to get a message before potential customers. Sending mass e-mail is far cheaper than sending bulk snail mail. Only a few people out of a million have to respond in order to make the mailing worthwhile: The marketer gets paid by companies advertising their services based on the number of eyeballs that will see it.

Some spam merchants have gotten rich from their efforts, but they don't always keep their gains. In recent years, the popular ISP EarthLink has won judgments against e-mail spammers who have used EarthLink's mail servers to send spams. In 2002, EarthLink won a $25 million judgment against spam merchant K. C. Smith, who allegedly sent out as many as one billion unsolicited e-mail messages using EarthLink accounts. In May 2003, EarthLink won a $16 million judgment against the so-called "Buffalo Spammer," Howard Carmack, who allegedly sent more than 825 million e-mails from EarthLink accounts.

Whenever you sign up for a newsletter or product or register for something online, your contact information can potentially be shared with others. Some companies boost their income by selling the e-mail addresses, street addresses, and other information to direct marketers. Some spammers use e-mail programs called *spiders* that scour the Web and scan the contents of millions of Web pages at a time, looking for e-mail addresses published openly on those pages.

Some spammers act like hackers, bombarding an e-mail provider with pass-words in an attempt to crack into the server and retrieve all of the cus-tomers' contact information. Some even send viruses that rifle through the e-mail addresses in your address book, sending them back to the spammer.

Don't respond to spam e-mail messages. Doing so only communicates that your e-mail address is valid, and this sets you up to receive more unsolicited e-mail. If you want people to reach you by e-mail, don't publish your address on your Web page; make a link on the page that says "Contact me" or some-thing similar; in the HTML for the page, use the mailto command to make a reference to your e-mail address.

Recognizing spam

You probably know from your own experience that spam e-mail messages typically encourage you to try out new pharmaceutical products that will make you lose weight fast or cause you to feel younger and more vigorous in some way.

Some spam is more subtle. You may also see e-mail messages that promise to speed up your e-mail, or that offer you a new software solution for cutting back on spam itself. The most devious tell you that you have experienced a security breach with your account at a popular online service like the auction site eBay (`www.ebay.com`) or the payment service PayPal (`www.paypal.com`). They instruct you to click on a link in order to verify your username, pass-word, and other information. As you can guess, they are not representatives of the company in question, but spammers or criminals who want to misuse your personal information.

Spam often appears to come from someone with a real name, but the person's e-mail address does not contain recognizable English words: `t49xvgh9eioc@yahoo.com`, for example. Often the domain name used in the sender is foreign, originating from China, South America, or another overseas location where spammers face less stringent regulations than in the United Kingdom or (to a lesser extent) the United States.

Working with Norton AntiSpam

You don't necessarily have to do anything to start using AntiSpam. The com-ponent starts working when you set up Norton Internet Security. Look at your Outlook Express folder: You notice a new toolbar button labeled Norton AntiSpam as well as a Norton AntiSpam folder (see Figure 9-1).

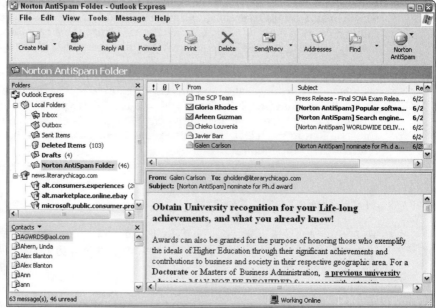

Figure 9-1:
Norton
AntiSpam
starts
working
when you
first set
up NIS.

Changing default options

Norton AntiSpam has a default set of criteria that it begins to use right away.
Monitoring what the program begins to do to make sure it doesn't delete any
e-mail messages you actually want is a good idea. I spotted a "real" e-mail
amid the junk, but not until a few days after it had been sent. You can view
the options by opening the main NIS window, and double-clicking Norton
AntiSpam. The Norton AntiSpam window opens (see Figure 9-2).

You can also open Norton AntiSpam Options by clicking the Norton AntiSpam
button in your e-mail program's toolbar, then Open Norton AntiSpam from
the drop-down list that appears.

The slider the General tab is described in the section "Adjusting spam protection" that follows. If you click Allowed List, you can review the list of e-mail
addresses that you marked as approved when you first installed Norton
Internet Security. You can review the list to make sure there aren't any spammers buried within it. If you find one, select the name to highlight it, then
click Delete.

Figure 9-2:
Turn spam
protection
on and off
and change
the default
settings in
this window.

Adjusting spam protection

The Norton AntiSpam window contains a slider that enables you to specify
the level of spam filtering you want. The higher the level of protection, the
greater the range of e-mail messages that will be filtered (and, correspond-
ingly, the greater the chances that the program will delete a message you
actually want to keep). The slider has three settings:

✔ **High:** Norton AntiSpam uses the strictest set of criteria that it has available to filter e-mail and throw spam in the trash. The Help files state only
that "Most spam is correctly identified," not all spam, because spam characteristics change constantly in order to bypass filters like this. Check
your Norton AntiSpam folder periodically if you use this setting; you may
discover that some legitimate personal e-mail has been filtered out.

✔ **Medium:** This is the default setting. AntiSpam will filter out most, though
not all, spam e-mail. On the other hand, the program is also less likely to
delete legitimate e-mail messages you really want.

✔ **Low:** If you aren't having a problem with spam (lucky you!) or you want
to try alternate methods of blocking spam, such as a "mail washing" service that processes your e-mail and deletes spam before it reaches your
computer, either choose this setting or turn off AntiSpam altogether. The
chances are low that you'll have legitimate e-mail thrown out if you
choose this setting.

AntiSpam uses pattern-matching software to identify spam. It scans the subject line, sender, body, and other characteristics of e-mail messages and compares them to a set of known spam characteristics. The more matches that are found, the more likely the message is to be spam. Setting the AntiSpam slider to high means that a message does not have to contain a high number of matches to be identified as spam. Setting it to low means that only messages with many matches will be identified as spam and placed in the Norton AntiSpam folder.

Training AntiSpam

AntiSpam uses a default set of spam definitions that are similar in some ways to virus definitions: They are sets of characteristics that help the program recognize spam when it arrives at your inbox. You update such definitions automatically when you run LiveUpdate and obtain new software from the Symantec Web site. You can help AntiSpam even further by training the component to recognize spam.

You're probably used to deleting spam e-mail messages when you see them. After AntiSpam is present in your e-mail toolbar, you can use it to dispose of your unwanted communications more efficiently.

Using the This Is Spam option

Suppose a spam message shows up in your inbox because it was not filtered out by AntiSpam. You can change the AntiSpam settings to a higher level if you want, but this is likely to delete legitimate e-mail messages that you really want. You get a finer-grained level of control by identifying the message's characteristics as spam:

1. **Select the message's subject line in your inbox.**

   The message is highlighted.

2. **Click Norton AntiSpam in your browser's toolbar, or right-click the message's subject line and choose Norton AntiSpam⇨This Is Spam from the shortcut menu.**

   A drop-down list appears (see Figure 9-3).

3. **Choose This Is Spam.**

   After a few seconds, a progress bar appears briefly, followed by a Norton AntiSpam dialog box asking you how you want to handle such messages in the future.

4. **Click OK to block messages from this sender in the future.**

   The dialog box closes and you return to the e-mail window. The message is added to your Norton AntiSpam folder.

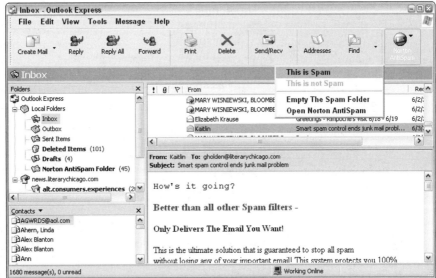

After you add a message to the Blocked Senders list, you can view it by open-ing AntiSpam and clicking Blocked List. The name of the sender should appear at the bottom of the list.

You can continue to scroll through your inbox, choosing each unsolicited commercial e-mail message and repeating the previous steps. As a further training measure, you can also go through the messages that the component has placed in your Norton AntiSpam folder. If you see any that should not have been placed there, select them, click Norton AntiSpam, and select This Is Not Spam from the drop-down list. (The This Is Not Spam option is only active when you are scrolling through the Norton AntiSpam folder.)

Selecting the box next to Always Use This Action means AntiSpam will auto-matically block every message you identify as spam. Chances are you want AntiSpam to do this. But when you check this option you do give up a mea-sure of control. There's a small chance that subsequent messages from a sender you block will not be spam. To be on the safe side, don't select Always Use This Action, and instead manually block messages you identify as spam.

By selecting a message's title in your inbox list and clicking AntiSpam, you essentially tell the program: "This e-mail is spam: Delete any other messages that have the same characteristics." I talk about the characteristics that AntiSpam uses to identify unsolicited e-mail in the sections that follow.

Creating AntiSpam rules

Suppose you have configured AntiSpam to block e-mail messages that have a broad set of characteristics — for example, every message that has the word "Viagra," "Cialis," "Lipitor," or another pharmaceutical product in the subject line. At the same time, there are certain e-mail messages that mention such products that you do want to receive, such as joke messages regularly sent from one of your friends, or special offers from an online drugstore you frequent. If that's the case, you can customize AntiSpam by creating a custom rule. Open Norton AntiSpam Options as described in "Changing default options," earlier in this chapter. Then follow these steps:

1. **Click Spam Rules.**

   The Spam Rules tab jumps to the front.

2. **Click New.**

   The Custom Spam Rule dialog box appears (see Figure 9-4).

> **Norton AntiSpam - Spam Rules**
>
> **Custom Spam Rule**
>
> What word or phrase should Norton AntiSpam search for when it scans your incoming email?
>
> Search for...
>
> Keywords: | Viagra
>
> Examples: XXX
> make money fast
> mortgage
>
> Tip: Norton AntiSpam ignores punctuation and capitalization. The word "mortgage" will also match: Mortgage, MORTGAGE, M.O.R.T.G.A.G.E, m-o-r-t-g-a-g-e.
>
> Step 1 of 4
>
> < Back | Next > | Cancel

3. **Type a word or phrase in the Keywords box.**

   The word or words should be part of the e-mail messages you want AntiSpam to recognize. You can use a single word such as "pharmacy" or a phrase such as "hot deals for you."

4. **Click Next.**

   The next Custom Spam Rule appears with the heading "Which part of the e-mail should Norton AntiSpam search?" Select one of the options based on where the keywords normally appear (Entire E-mail, From, Recipient, Subject Line, or Body Text).

5. Click Next.

In the next window, specify whether the keyword or phrase identifies the e-mail as spam.

6. Click Next.

Read the summary of the rule characteristics you have created, and then click Finish. The Custom Spam Rule Wizard closes and you return to the Spam Rules screen, where the rules you have created are listed.

After you create rules, you can order them in the list by clicking Move Up or Move Down, respectively (see Figure 9-5). You can change the characteristics of each rule by selecting it and clicking Edit. When you're done, click OK to exit the Custom Spam Rule dialog box.

What's the difference between selecting a message and choosing This Is Spam, or creating a custom rule to cover such messages? The custom rules are generally used to overrule AntiSpam's own set of built-in spam matching characteristics. Usually, you create a rule to identify an exception, and you choose This Is Spam to block types of spam messages.

Make sure the user next to Norton AntiSpam Settings For is the one whose settings you want to change. (You probably want to select your own Norton Internet Security account name from the Norton AntiSpam Settings For drop-down list.) The rules you create will only apply to this user.

Figure 9-5:
You can reorder your custom spam rules so the ones you use most frequently appear first.

Allowing e-mail addresses

When you first configure Norton Internet Security, you identify a group of e-mail addresses that you want to allow. You may choose to import your entire address book or select addresses from it and add them selectively. The addresses you add will be put on your allowed list and not treated as spam. Addresses you don't add won't necessarily be blocked and thrown in the Norton AntiSpam folder; they will be subject to the same matching rules that AntiSpam uses for all of your e-mail correspondence.

Note: One exception exists, however. If you open Norton Internet Security Options, click the E-mail tab, and select Block E-mail from Anyone Not In the Allowed List, NIS will delete any e-mail that you haven't specifically marked as "Allowed."

To add someone to your Allowed List, open Norton AntiSpam options, click Allowed List, click Add, and enter the individual's name and e-mail address. Then click OK to close Add Address to Allowed List and OK to close Norton AntiSpam Options.

Cutting Down on Spam

Norton AntiSpam can cut down much of the unwanted e-mail you receive. But no solution is guaranteed to eliminate all of it. Some common-sense practices on your part can keep spam from reaching your e-mail inbox in the first place, so AntiSpam has less mail to filter. The most obvious step you can take is to avoid responding to spam, even if you only want to send an angry message telling the sender to stop bothering you. This only tells the mailer that you exist, and guarantees that you'll get even more spam. I offer some other suggestions in the sections that follow.

Reducing registrations

The most effective single thing you can do to reduce spam is to refrain from registering online. If you don't sign up for anything, don't submit your e-mail address to any Web site, don't include your e-mail address on a paper form you fill out, and avoid publishing your e-mail address in the body of a Web page, you probably will get significantly less spam.

Of course, you won't get any information or be able to buy anything online. More and more Web sites require their users to identify themselves just to read articles, download software, or perform any number of functions. Registration means they know something about who visits their site. It also means they have a way to tell you about new products and special sales, and send you a newsletter if they have one available.

If you want to sign up freely as you surf the Web but don't want spam, you can do one of two things: surf anonymously or create a special e-mail address simply for junk e-mail.

When a business that seems to have nothing to do with the Internet asks for your e-mail address, you can be reasonably certain that they want to send you spam. When I had my car repaired recently, I filled out a customer contact form that asked for my e-mail address. Why? I asked. "So we can send you some promotional offers," I was told. I left the space blank. You should, too.

Anonymizing your browser

"Surfing anonymously" means you use a software program or an online service that processes all of the information going out of your Web browser before it gets to a Web site. The software erases any information that can possibly identify you. As you surf the Web, you leave a trail of data behind you, including your computer's IP address and records of pages you view. Examples of such programs include Anonymizer, which functions as a toolbar added on to your browser's usual toolbars (see Figure 9-6).

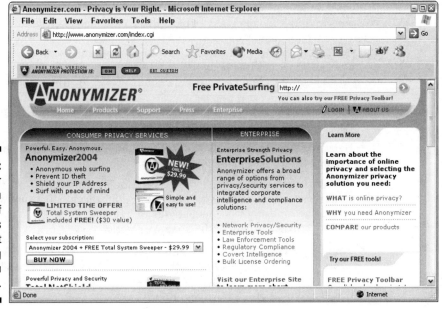

Figure 9-6: Anonymizer enables you to surf Web sites without revealing who you are.

The downside of using a program like Anonymizer is that it slows down your surfing experience. That's because the software acts like a proxy browser, processing your request before it sends it on to the remote Web service. If you get tired of slowly but anonymously browsing the Web, you can set up a special e-mail address to handle junk e-mail you receive for registering for things like the Anonymizer free toolbar itself.

Note: Anonymizer's browser toolbar comes in two versions. The free version has fewer features than the commercial, full-featured version. To download the free version, go to the Anonymizer home page (www.anonymizer.com) and click "try our free privacy toolbar." Ironically, you have to submit your e-mail address to Anonymizer to download the software.

Creating a junk e-mail address

You may not be able to prevent Web sites from getting your e-mail address, but at least it doesn't have to be your private e-mail address that you use most of your time. If you create an e-mail address using a free e-mail service provider, you can use that address whenever you sign up for anything online. You can keep your primary e-mail address in reserve for your normal correspondence.

Using a spam e-mail address doesn't cut down on the amount of junk e-mail you receive, but it makes you feel better to gain a measure of control over where the e-mail goes. You don't have to open your junk mail often, or at all, and you don't have to read what goes there if you don't want to. The number of organizations providing truly free e-mail addresses is small, but you only need one account to handle your junk e-mail. Consider these options:

- **America Online.** For a single account, you get as many as seven screen names, each with its own e-mail address.
- **Netscape.net.** If you use Netscape Messenger, you can create a free e-mail address ending in netscape.net.
- **G-Mail** (http://gmail.google.com). Google, the world's most popular search service, has started a new free e-mail service that offers customers an amazing 1,000 megabytes of free storage space, so you never have to throw out any of the spam you get.
- **Yahoo! Mail** (http://mail.yahoo.com). Shortly after G-Mail took off, Yahoo increased the storage capacity of its free e-mail service to 100 megabytes. If you already have a Yahoo account that you use often, this is a convenient and free e-mail option.

Microsoft, of course, offers its free Hotmail service, but I find the requirement to sign up for a Passport password cumbersome. Hotmail isn't my first choice; the preceding options are much easier to use.

I personally use a special e-mail address with Netscape.net when I sign up for mailing lists, make purchases, and create accounts with utilities, banks, and other institutions so I can check accounts and pay bills online. To create your own account, open Netscape Messenger, click Netscape WebMail in the list of accounts on the left side of the window, and then click Create a New Account (see Figure 9-7).

The nice thing about this e-mail account is that I don't have to check it all the time. Rather than have an alert message appear every time a new message arrives, I close the e-mail inbox altogether. I only check e-mail in that account when I need to confirm a registration. That way, when I receive a "you've got mail" type of alert, I can be reasonably sure it is legitimate and not spam.

Opting to opt out

When you register and submit your e-mail address to a Web site, that doesn't necessarily mean the site's managers have to send you e-mail. The Direct Marketing Association (DMA) has devised a Mail Preference Service that lets you opt out of receiving direct mail from many participating companies for five years. (Companies that don't register with this service will still send you unsolicited mail and e-mail, however.) The service blocks not only mail you get in your home mailbox, but also e-mail.

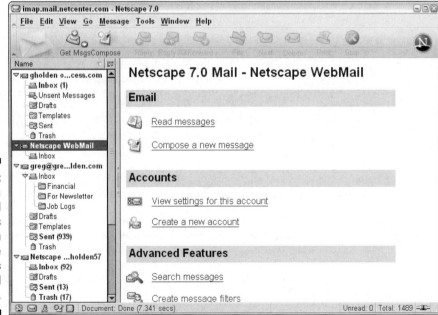

Figure 9-7:
Creating a free e-mail account is easy if you already use Netscape's e-mail client.

To register for the Mail Preference Service's opt-out provision, fill out the form at www.dmaconsumers.org/cgi/offmailinglistdave. You can read about ways to opt out of credit card applications and other marketing efforts on the Federal Trade Commission Web site at www.ftc.gov/bcp/conline/pubs/alerts/optoutalrt.htm.

In December 2003, the U.S. Congress passed the CAN-SPAM Act, which requires businesses to provide an opt-out provision for unsolicited e-mail they send. Opinions differ widely as to whether this bill actually reduced unsolicited commercial e-mail; many observers believe it opened the floodgates for marketers to send as much spam as they want as long as it includes a provision for recipients to say they don't want any more. Whatever the result, the important thing is that you do opt-out — and use Norton AntiSpam to block any mail that still gets through.

Note: If you don't see the opt-out options, look for them in a Web site's privacy policy. Some companies may hide them in the privacy document in the hopes that you will overlook them.

Canning Spam: More Approaches

You can block e-mail addresses that you know are sending you unsolicited e-mail you don't want, either using your e-mail program's own settings or Norton AntiSpam's advanced options.

All the spam blockers, filters, and safe e-mail practices in the world can't protect you from an employee at an Internet Service Provider who decides to make a quick buck using your personal information. As I was working on this chapter, news reports surfaced about an employee of America Online (AOL) who allegedly sold an estimated 92 million screen names and corresponding information to — guess who? — a spammer. There isn't much you can do to protect yourself from this invasion of privacy, but having two or more e-mail addresses to switch among is a good idea.

Blocking addresses

You can use the Advanced Norton AntiSpam window to modify the list of e-mail addresses the program uses, or text strings that you see repeatedly in the subject lines of spam e-mail messages. When you add an address or text string to the advanced options, the program will recognize a message as spam based on your settings.

You can also use Advanced Options to identify e-mail as legitimate rather than spam. If Norton AntiSpam has been deleting messages that you don't consider spam, add the sender's address or a text string in the message (such as the title of a newsletter that is being sent to you. In that case, AntiSpam will bypass its normal spam settings and treat e-mail messages as legitimate rather than spam.

To add an e-mail address to AntiSpam's Blocked List, select it, click Norton AntiSpam, and choose This Is Spam. When a dialog box appears asking if you want to block e-mails from this address, click OK. This adds the address to the list of blocked addresses.

If you are really disgusted with a direct marketer, you can give them a double-whammy of sorts: Block them by adding their e-mail address to AntiSpam's Blocked List, and also use your e-mail software to block them. It may be overkill, but in case you ever turn off AntiSpam — or if the program's Subscription runs out and you are slow about renewing it — your e-mail software can block spammers as a backup.

Microsoft Outlook Express has a quick and convenient way to block e-mail from a single address:

1. **Select the message in your inbox.**

   The subject line is highlighted.

2. **Choose Tools⇨Block Sender.**

   A dialog box appears asking if you want to remove all messages from this sender from your current mail folder (see Figure 9-8).

3. **Click Yes.**

   A dialog box containing a progress bar appears indicating that any messages from this individual are being deleted. Then a dialog box appears informing you that the messages have been deleted.

4. **Click OK to close the dialog box and return to the Outlook Express window.**

Figure 9-8:
Outlook
Express
makes it
easy to
block a
sender.

Outlook Express	
ⓘ	'rygm85@cs.com' has been added to your blocked senders list. Subsequent messages from this sender will be blocked. Would you like to remove all messages from this sender from the current folder now? [Yes] [No]

The problem with blocking an individual sender is that almost all spam comes from fictitious e-mail senders. The name is usually one that looks like a real person's, but the address has nothing to do with that person; it's the address of an e-mail server that is most likely relaying bulk e-mail from the original mail server, thus shielding the original mail server and preventing it from being traced. Blocking the spam sender in the event the same name is used again, however, is a good idea.

Note: Netscape Messenger doesn't have a command equivalent to Outlook Express's Block Sender menu option. You have to set up a filter rule to block a sender.

Setting up filters

A filter is a set of e-mail message characteristics used to create a rule for processing incoming messages. If a message matches a rule, an action is performed. For example, you might set up a special folder for e-mail messages pertaining to a project you are working on, or messages from your supervisor. Both Netscape Messenger and Microsoft Internet Explorer have the capability of creating such rules.

Filters can also be created to delete messages based on the sender's name, a keyword or phrase in the subject, a word in the body of the message, or other attributes. You can try to create a filter for blocking spam, but it's very difficult. That's because spammers create their marketing messages in such a way that they specifically circumvent e-mail filters. Sender's names often appear to be the names of real people, and those names change constantly. E-mail addresses usually contain gibberish of the sort that won't be caught by a rule set up to block a particular sender. Subject lines vary also.

If you want to create a filter in Netscape Messenger, you can select the spam message and choose Message⇨Create Filter From Message from Messenger's toolbar. The Filter Rules dialog box appears, which lets you specify the way you want Messenger to handle such rules in the future. In the case of spam, you should select Delete the Message from the Perform This Action drop-down list (see Figure 9-9).

In Outlook Express, you follow a similar process. Select the message that has the attributes (sender, subject, or body text) that you want to block in the future. Choose Message⇨Create Rule From Message. When the New Mail Rule dialog box appears (see Figure 9-10), select Delete It in the Select the Actions for Your Rule box.

If you want to create a filter rule without having to select an individual message beforehand using Netscape Messenger, choose Tools⇨Message Rules and create the rule from scratch. In Internet Explorer, choose Tools⇨Message Rules⇨News to open the New Mail Rule dialog box, where you san specify attributes and an action for your rule.

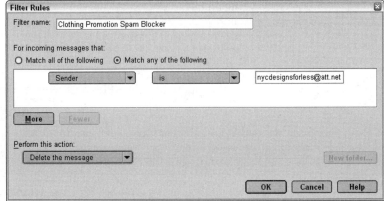

Figure 9-9:
Netscape
Messenger
lets you
create a
filter rule
from a
specific
message.

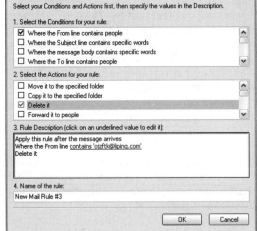

Figure 9-10:
Outlook
Express lets
you create
filter rules
from
scratch or
based on a
message
you receive.

Practicing Safe E-Mail

Norton AntiSpam deletes much of the unwanted commercial e-mail you
receive. Setting up filters and blocking senders will help to an extent. To
maintain your privacy and decrease the chances that someone will obtain
your valid e-mail address in the first place, you should follow the e-mail best
practices I describe in the following sections.

Clearing your mail folders

Your e-mail inbox should be cleaned out on a regular basis for reasons that have to do with good file management as well as security. If you start running short on disk space, some of the first places you should look are your Inbox, Sent Items, and Deleted Items folders to delete files and reduce your usage of disk space.

Cutting down on unneeded e-mail messages also helps maintain your privacy: It keeps hackers and other intruders from looking over your e-mail. Suppose you are late for a meeting and run out the door without logging off or closing your e-mail application. While you're gone, your co-workers, family members, or supervisors can look through your e-mail inbox and see who you've been talking to. Permanently deleting messages from your Sent Items and Deleted Items folders can protect you even further, especially in a work environment.

After you select a message and delete it, it's not necessarily deleted from your computer. Even the messages placed in the Norton AntiSpam folder are placed in a holding area rather than deleted permanently. This is a safety feature that prevents you from deleting legitimate e-mail messages. After a while, though, the contents of those folders (especially Sent Items) grows as you send and receive e-mail. Emptying your trash folder and compressing e-mail folders so they consume less disk space is a good idea.

In Netscape Messenger, the e-mail application that comes with Netscape Communicator, you choose File⇨Compact Folders and File⇨Empty Trash to perform these respective functions. In Microsoft Outlook Express, you can right-click the Deleted Items folder and choose Empty 'Deleted Items' Folder from the shortcut menu. As you can see from Figure 9-11, even items deleted from the Norton AntiSpam folder are not removed from your computer completely unless you empty Deleted Items.

For other folders, such as Sent Items, you need to open the folder, choose the messages you want to delete, and press the Delete key to manually send them to Deleted Items.

If you want to have Outlook Express empty the Deleted Items folder automatically whenever you quit Outlook Express, follow these steps:

1. **Choose Tools⇨Options.**

   The Options dialog box opens.

2. **Click Maintenance.**

   The Maintenance tab jumps to the front.

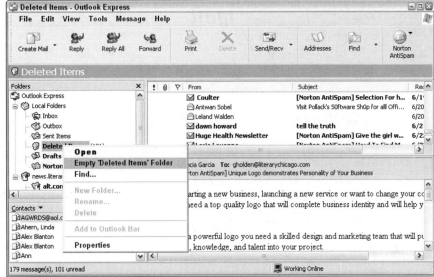

3. **Check Empty Messages from the 'Deleted Items' Folder On Exit (see Figure 9-12).**

4. **Click OK.**

   The Options dialog box closes and you return to the Outlook Express window.

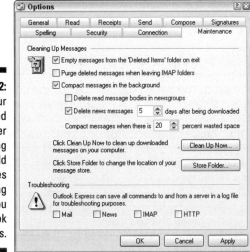

Your employers probably maintain backup copies of your e-mail correspondence, and they probably have the legal right to view all of your office e-mail. Even deleting your local e-mail might not protect you from prying eyes in the workplace. Never send sensitive or potentially damaging e-mail using your office e-mail account.

Washing your e-mail

If you want to conceal your e-mail address and maintain privacy for all of your online correspondence, sign up with a service that processes your e-mail before it even reaches you. My brother is a customer of the service called SpamCop.net (www.spamcop.net), and he is satisfied with their ability to cut down on the junk e-mail he receives. If you sign up with a service that processes (you might say launders) your e-mail before it gets to your computer, Norton AntiSpam will have less work to do, and Norton Internet Security can devote more processing power to protecting your computer in other ways.

Another e-mail laundering option is encryption. Rather than having to purchase and install software that encrypts your e-mail on your desktop, you send it to a service such as Hushmail (www.hushmail.com). Hushmail works through its Web site: You send your e-mail to Hushmail where it is encrypted and sent to the recipient. When it reaches its destination, the e-mail is automatically decrypted; the recipient doesn't have to install special software or follow special steps to read what you have sent. Hushmail comes with a free version that requires you to view advertisements when you retrieve your e-mail. This prevents anyone from intercepting your e-mail and reading it without your knowledge. A Premium account that is ad-free costs $29.99 per year.

Concealing your e-mail address

Some spam-conscious Internet users try to conceal their e-mail address as much as possible so spammers cannot find it. When they post messages to discussion groups, they add a line to the subject: x-no-archive-yes. This tells the newsgroup that your message should not be stored in an archive where spammers can find it. When they send e-mail and need to use a "real" e-mail address, they add some text that computer programs won't be able to interpret but that humans can understand.

For example, if your legitimate e-mail address is meg@website.com, you can change it to meg#website.com (change @ to #) or meg@website.com_no spam.com (delete "_nospam" before replying). Include the parenthetical addition to the e-mail address when you post, so readers know for sure which part you should delete.

Trying to trace your spammer

In Chapter 4, you find out that it's possible to trace someone who attempts to make an unauthorized attempt to connect to your computer through the originating computer's IP address. This doesn't lead you to an individual sitting at a particular computer, but it does indicate the part of the world where the person is situated, and can lead you to the attacker's domain name and Internet Service Provider (ISP). But if the hacker has gained control over someone else's computer and uses that machine to launch an attack, he or she is shielded from detection.

It's just as difficult to find the legitimate domain name or IP address of a spam e-mail marketer. Such individuals hide behind other spammers, and the computers from which millions of spam e-mails originate are shielded behind other servers. The chances of locating the source of a piece of spam are slim. Complaining to a spammer or his or her Internet Service Provider can be time-consuming and possibly fruitless.

Nevertheless, you can trace a spam e-mail by viewing the e-mail header of a message you receive. In Outlook Express, you select the message, then choose File⇨Properties. When the properties sheet for the e-mail message appears, click Details to view the message header. The Return-Path and Received lines near the top of the header details indicate where the mail came from. You can use the header or IP address to create a custom filter rule as described earlier in this chapter, or a custom rule for Norton Personal Firewall as described in Chapter 4. The header shown in Figure 9-13 indicates that the spam message came from a sender with the e-mail address of wtfprx51dwdt@syix.com, and that the sender's computer was at IP address 207.155.248.19. You can use the IP address to create a firewall rule blocking all inbound traffic from this computer.

Figure 9-13:
You can trace a spammer's supposed e-mail address and IP address, though they're not likely to be the ultimate source of the mail.

China, which has an estimated 68 million Internet users and is second only to the United States in its "online population," recently launched a crackdown on spam. In autumn 2003, it reportedly blocked 127 servers that were sending spam to Chinese citizens. But Spamhaus, a London-based organization, has ranked China as the number two source of spam around the world. An article in PCWorld.com (www.pcworld.com/news/article/0,aid,116300,00.asp) reported that many American spammers hire local Chinese spammers to install and run servers and send out spam. A survey by the Internet Society of China estimated that an estimated 47 billion pieces of spam were received by Chinese Internet users in 2003, and the hours spent reading or deleting spam resulted in an economic loss of $581 million.

Chapter 10

Blocking Weapons of Mass Distraction

● ●

In This Chapter

▶ Stopping pop-up ads that slow down your Web surfing

▶ Blocking cookies that Web sites try to place without your knowledge

▶ Finding ways to surf the Web anonymously

▶ Keeping your Web site communications confidential

● ●

Many of the previous chapters in this book discuss actual weapons that can cause destruction to your financial and personal information as well as your computer. These are hardly the only kinds of threats you face from the Internet, of course. Because your computer and your network have a connection to a worldwide network increasingly populated by marketing experts, aggressive businesspeople, and advertisers, you also have threats to your privacy, your attention, and your experience of the Internet.

Without some sort of software protection, you're going to see Web pages you don't want to view, advertisements that delay the content you really want to read, cookies that track your activities, and marketers who take advantage of the contact information you submit in order to send you information you don't necessarily want. Luckily, Norton Internet Security has several components that are specially designed to block these distractors and marketing tools to make your journey through cyberspace more enjoyable. This chapter tells you how to use them.

Halting Advertisements

If you've ever tried a device called TiVo or even videotaped a few television shows, you know how much more enjoyable that medium is without commercial advertisements. It only stands to reason, then, that the World Wide Web would be more enjoyable and less time-consuming to navigate without ads cluttering up Web pages or forcing your browser to launch new windows. The following sections describe how to do just that by using Ad Blocking, the Norton Internet Security component that prevents ads from appearing on the Web.

Using Ad Blocking

Advertising on the Web is still in its early stages. Traditional advertisers are still trying to figure out what works best online. They still use the "billboard" approach to advertising, which holds that, as long as you can get your product before the eyes of a captive audience, some users will buy that product. They try to throw up cyber-billboards — new Web pages that appear either on top of or behind the content you really want to view. They fall under the general description of *pop-up* ads. A few variations exist, such as:

- ✔ Under ads. These are pop-up ads that appear underneath the Web page you want to view.

- ✔ Interstitial ads. These are ads that appear before you connect to the desired Web page.

- ✔ Ads that cover up part of the Web page you are trying to view. Amazon.com is known for these.

Freeing disk space by blocking ads

There's also a security aspect to blocking ads. Some ads aren't just simple, static images. A few use animation that can only be produced by having your browser process commands that are written in the Web page language JavaScript or the much more complex and processor-intensive language called Java. Not long before I installed the latest version of Norton Internet Security, I noticed that my computer was crawling at the proverbial snail's pace. I closed as many open browser and other windows as I could, trying to determine what the problem was. At the bottom was an animated advertisement, along with an alert message indicating that some scripts embedded in the ad were consuming nearly all of my computer's resources. When I closed the ad, the machine started operating normally again.

Some Java scripts (which are called Java applets) are even more harmful: They function as Trojan horses, attacking browsers or servers or planting viruses on your hard drive.

In addition, some businesses will send you ads to try to get you to install new software on your system. In reality, you may be installing spyware. You should be especially wary of ads that invite you to install novelty cursors or other entertaining software. These frequently include user agreements that require you to allow companies to track your browsing or to provide them with information about where you go online, among other things. Such clauses are typically hidden deep in the agreement where many users will overlook them.

In addition to pop-up ads, some ads appear in the body of Web pages. These are much like the ads you see in newspapers and magazines. The Norton Internet Security component that is designed to block both pop-up and Web page ads is called Ad Blocking. It takes advantage of two characteristics of the aforementioned ads:

✔ They tend to appear in standard sizes. The standard sizes help Web content providers charge standard rates to the advertisers.

✔ They use standardized HyperText Markup Language (HTML) commands. Ad Blocking recognizes the HTML and uses it to block specific ads. Specifically, Ad Blocking compares the Web addresses of ads that are being downloaded by your browser with its own list of ads to block. If it finds a match, it removes the ad so that it does not appear in your browser, leaving the rest of the Web page intact.

Ad Blocking gives you several options for keeping ads out of your eyeball space. You can throw individual ads in an Ad Trashcan after they appear on a page; you can prevent ads from appearing in the first place; or you can set up configuration rules to block ads. All three options are described in the sections that follow.

Using HTML to block ads

HyperText Markup Language (HTML) is the primary language used to mark up Web pages. These days, Web pages also contain commands in languages such as JavaScript and a more complicated version of HTML called eXtensible Markup Language (XML). But HTML is all you really need to create your own Web page or to block ads on other site's pages using Norton Internet Security's Ad Blocking component.

HTML is a standardized set of instructions for marking up documents so that many different types of computers (Macs, PCs, laptops, or handhelds) can process the code, whether those computers are located on one network within a building or a giant set of networks such as the Internet. Web browsers can interpret and then display Web pages the way their authors intended.

One type of HTML command that browsers can display is a hyperlink. A hyperlink is a reference to a file that is separate from the Web page you are viewing. The file might be in another directory on the same computer the file is in; it might also be located on a completely different computer located elsewhere on the Internet. Hyperlinks to such resources are made by means of another standard type of identifier called a Uniform Resource Locator (URL). A URL describes the location of an object, such as an image, like this: `www.wiley.com/nis/book/cover.jpg`.

Ad Blocking has the ability to scan the HTML code that underlies the Web page you are trying to load in your Web browser. It looks for URLs that are linked to the current page and that are commonly used for advertisements. If it finds all or part of a URL and that URL is contained on its list of ad URLs to block, it blocks the link from being made to the ad, and the ad does not appear in your browser window.

Throwing ads in the Ad Trashcan

Sometimes you are looking at a Web page, and an ad just offends you for some reason. Perhaps the colors are too garish, the illustration is sexist, or the slogan is just plain dumb. If you want to delete just the ad and leave the rest of the page alone (and if the ad isn't already included on Ad Blocking default block list) you can throw the ad in the Ad Trashcan.

The Ad Trashcan is a feature of Ad Blocking that lets you selectively delete ads or create rules based on the ads you see on a particular Web site. By creating rules, you can keep similar ads from appearing on the site in the future. If you are viewing a Web page that contains an ad you don't want to see, follow these steps to throw that single ad in the trash:

1. **Open the Norton Internet Security window and double-click Ad Blocking.**

   The Ad Blocking window opens. You may have to manipulate the Ad Blocking window so that the ad you want to block is still visible, at least partially, on-screen.

2. **Make sure Turn On Ad Blocking is checked, and then click Ad Trashcan.**

   The Ad Trashcan dialog box appears (see Figure 10-1).

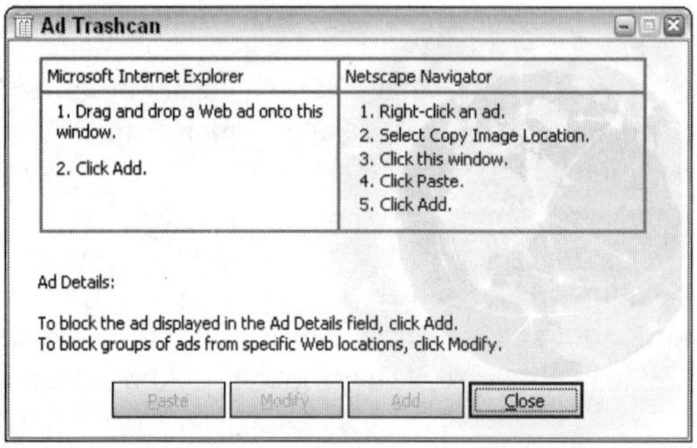

Figure 10-1:
You can block ads from appearing in the future by dragging them into this dialog box.

Ad Trashcan

Microsoft Internet Explorer	Netscape Navigator
1. Drag and drop a Web ad onto this window. 2. Click Add.	1. Right-click an ad. 2. Select Copy Image Location. 3. Click this window. 4. Click Paste. 5. Click Add.

Ad Details:

To block the ad displayed in the Ad Details field, click Add.
To block groups of ads from specific Web locations, click Modify.

[Paste] [Modify] [Add] [Close]

3. **If you're using Microsoft Internet Explorer, click the ad with your mouse and drag it atop the Ad Trashcan dialog box (see Figure 10-2).**

   As you drag the image, the mouse pointer turns into a circle with a line across it. When the ad is atop the Ad Trashcan, the circle turns into an arrow and a plus sign.

4. **When you see the arrow, release the mouse button.**

   The ad is "dropped" into the trash.

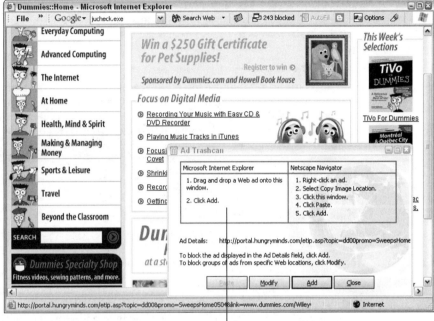

Click and drag an ad into the Ad Trashcan

Figure 10-2:
Use the
Trashcan to
interactively
block
ads from
appearing in
the future.

 5. **Click Add.**

 The ad is deleted.

 6. **Click Close.**

 The Ad Trashcan dialog box closes.

If you click Modify, the Modify HTML string dialog box appears (see Figure 10-3). The dialog box displays the URL for the ad you have placed in the Ad Trashcan. By clicking Add, you add the URL to Ad Blocking so it will be blocked automatically in the future and you won't have to throw the ad in the trash manually.

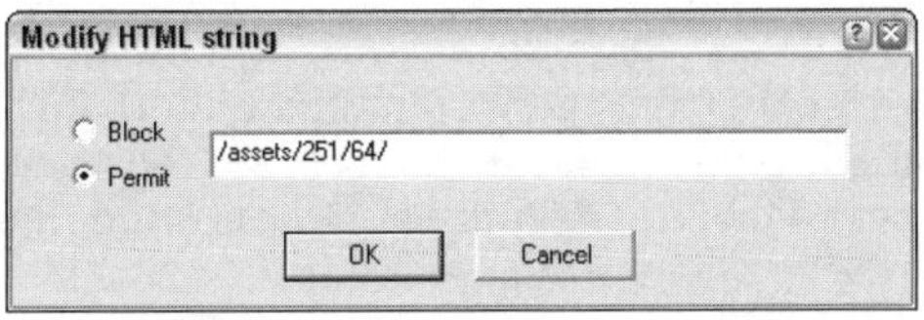

Figure 10-3:
Use Ad
Blocking to
manually or
automati-
cally
prevent
ads from
appearing.

Note: You can throw ads in the Ad Trashcan from Internet Explorer: Click the down arrow the Web Assistant toolbar, choose Open Ad Trashcan, and then follow the instructions in the Ad Trashcan window.

Ad blocking criteria

As indicated in the sidebar "Using HTML to block ads," URLs (also called Web addresses) are used to make links to text and image files. When you view a Web page, your computer connects to the address you request and displays the file that is stored there. If the page includes graphics, audio files, and other multimedia content, your browser displays the files as part of the page.

When you view a Web page that includes an ad, the instructions used to display the page might include the following:

```
<p>Be sure to visit our Web site<img
      src="http://www.intrusiveads.com/images/image.jpg"
      > </p>
```

Your browser displays the text "Be sure to visit our Web site" on the screen. Then it connects to www.intrusiveads.com and requests a file called /images/image4.jpg. (The suffix .jpg indicates that this is a Joint Photographic Experts Group file, a common image file format.) The computer at www.intrusiveads.com sends the file to the browser, which displays the image.

When Ad Blocking is enabled and you connect to a Web site, it scans Web pages and compares their contents to two lists. One is the default list of ads that Ad Blocking maintains on its own. This list is kept current using Norton Internet Security's LiveUpdate component. The other is the list you create yourself as you view Web pages and manually add files to the list of blocked ads.

Ads can also be blocked by their physical dimensions. Most of the ads you see on the Web are presented in one or more standard sizes. Ad Blocking is able to block images and other Web page contents based on these standard ad dimensions. The dimensions, like other Web page contents, are listed in the HTML or XML for a page so a browser can display them.

Viewing the default Ad Blocking list

By default, Ad Blocking comes with a set of default text strings that it looks for. If it finds a match on the Web page your browser is in the process of opening, it will remove the HTML from the Web page's underlying code before the page loads in the browser window; as a result, the ad won't be included in the page. You can view the default list by following these steps:

1. **Open the main Norton Internet Security window and double-click Ad Blocking.**

   The Ad Blocking window appears (see Figure 10-4).

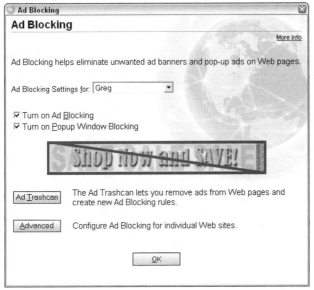

Figure 10-4: Use this window's controls to turn Ad Blocking on or off or customize options for specific sites.

2. **Click Advanced.**

   The Advanced dialog box appears with the Ad Blocking in front (see Figure 10-5).

The information shown in the Advanced dialog box may seem highly technical and confusing. But it isn't that hard to understand. The left side of the dialog box contains a long list of Web site URLs and domain names: These are sites that are known for producing pop-up ads and other ads. The list on the Ad Blocking tab contains bits of URLs that are used by the sites in the left-hand list to link to ads. Ad Blocking looks for matches to these partial URLs to block the ads.

Ad Blocking gives you the option of blocking all ads on a Web site. But keep in mind that stopping all images on a particular site from appearing may make that site unusable. A good compromise is to block only the directories that contain ads. For example, if `www.intrusiveads.com` stores its ads in `/images/` and its navigational images in `/nav_images/`, you could block `www.intrusiveads.com/images/` without impairing your ability to use the site.

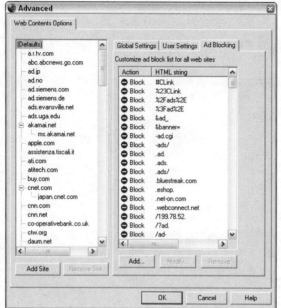

Figure 10-5:
The
Advanced
dialog box
gives you
fine-grained
control over
the ads you
block.

Modifying how much Ad Blocking really blocks

The way that you define Ad Blocking strings affects how restrictive or unrestrictive Ad Blocking is when filtering data. For example, if you add the string intrusiveads.com to the (Defaults) block list, you block everything in the intrusiveads.com domain. If you are more specific and add the string images/image4.jpg to the site-specific block list maintained for www.intrusiveads.com, you block only that single image.

To change how restrictive Ad Blocking is, open Ad Blocking, then click Advanced. The Advanced dialog box opens. Click the site whose ads you want to modify. Then click the Global Settings tab. As shown in Figure 10-6, Global Settings controls which information is blocked by Ad Blocking and which is not.

Overriding block rules

You can also create permit strings that allow Web sites to display images that match the string. This allows you to override the blocking effect of any string in the (Defaults) block list for individual sites. Permit rules take precedence over Block rules on any site. In order to set rules, you have to view the current blocking rules as well as the default block list. Open Ad Blocking and click Advanced. The Advanced dialog box displays the list of default domains and partial URLs that are blocked by default.

Such domains and URLs are a mixed bag: Some are from well-known companies like Apple Computer (apple.com) and eBay (ebay.com), while others are from domains that are notorious for junk advertising and intrusive marketing (such as iwon.com, thaigaming.com, and kazaa.com).

You may see some URLs on the default block list that you want to unblock (for example, google.com or media.wiley.com). Follow these steps to allow the previously blocked ads:

1. **Single-click the domain to highlight it.**

   The domain name is highlighted. The HTML string that is associated with ads generated by that domain appears in the Customize Ad Block List for Selected URL box on the right half of the Advanced dialog box (see Figure 10-7).

2. **Click the URL string.**

   The URL string is highlighted.

3. **Click Modify.**

   The Modify HTML String dialog box appears.

Figure 10-6: Control how much information (from advertising or not) Ad Blocking prohibits from a given Web site.

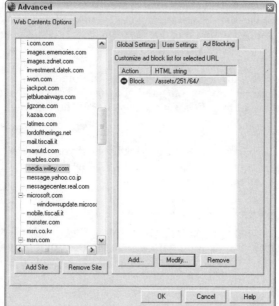

Figure 10-7:
You can modify ads generated by a domain on a case-by-case basis.

4. **Click Permit.**

   The Permit radio button is selected.

5. **Click OK twice.**

   The Modify HTML String dialog box closes, and the Advanced dialog box closes.

Ad Blocking can't block all ads, because some ads are text messages; they don't use images that are linked to remote Web sites by means of URLs. Ad Blocking only prevents linked images from appearing.

If you ever want to view an ad that has been blocked, you can temporarily disable Ad Blocking. To enable or disable Ad Blocking, in the main window, double-click Ad Blocking. In the Ad Blocking window, select or deselect Turn On Ad Blocking. Then click OK.

Adding content to be blocked

You can block either individual ads with specified text strings, or entire Web domains. Suppose, for example, that you like to look up books and make purchases from the popular online bookstore Amazon.com at www.amazon.com.

But you're tired of waiting for the site's home page to load while various pop-up ads appear. You can block all pop-up ads from this site by following these steps:

1. **Open Ad Blocking, and click Advanced.**

   The Advanced dialog box opens.

2. **Click Add Site.**

   The New Site/Domain dialog box opens. Type the domain name of the site in the text box provided. The prefix www is pre-entered for you. In this case, type **amazon.com** after www.

3. **Click OK.**

   The New Site/Domain dialog box closes and you return to the Advanced dialog box. The domain www.amazon.com is added to the Web Contents Options tab.

4. **Make sure the domain name you entered is highlighted, and then click User Settings.**

   The User Settings options appear.

5. **Deselect Cookies.**

   On Amazon.com, cookies are useful because they enable the site to "remember" who you are from previous visits. Cookies (as described in the following section) give you the ability to make "1-Click Purchases" from the site, among other things.

6. **Click Permit.**

   The Permit radio button is highlighted.

7. **Make any other changes you want, then click OK.**

   The Advanced dialog box closes and you return to Ad Blocking.

The User Settings tab gives you one level of control over the kinds of content a site is permitted to send you. Another set of controls is provided on the Global Settings tab. When you highlight a site or domain in Web Contents Options, then click Global Settings, you gain the ability to block or permit information about

✔ **Your Web browser.** Some sites have the ability to tailor content based on whether you're using Microsoft Internet Explorer, Netscape Navigator, or another browser.

✔ **Sites you visited before you came to the present site.** Some sites track "referring" sites so they can tell whether or not to advertise themselves on those sites.

✔ **Animated images.** Images that move are often entertaining and don't always take up much processing ability. But if they are created by Java applets, they can slow down your computer and you may want to block them.

✔ **Scripts.** This option covers not only scripts created in the Java or JavaScript language but other languages such as VBScript or JScript.

✔ **Flash animations.** These are animations that require you to load and use the Macromedia Flash player.

Selectively blocking some content while permitting other content can be a sensible approach to Web surfing. Blocking many different types of content can seriously degrade your experience of a site. Many sites generate pop-up windows in order to play music you want to hear or view demonstrations you want to follow, for example.

Spitting Out Unwanted Cookies

A cookie, as you well know, is something sweet and desirable that someone might well give you as a gift. On the Web, a cookie is also a gift. It's a small piece of binary information that a Web server transmits to your browser, and is stored on your hard drive.

One big difference between a chocolate chunk cookie that comes to you as a gift and a Web site cookie is the fact that you don't actually realize you are being given the Web site cookie. Another is that you don't know what the site that gave you the cookie is actually going to do with it.

Opinions differ as to whether cookies actually represent invasions of privacy, and whether or not they are potentially harmful in some way. The Web sites that issue cookies say that they do this so they can recognize you when you revisit the site. The cookie doesn't tell the site what your name is or where you live, exactly. It is just a bit of code that identifies you on subsequent visits to the site, or during the current visit to the site. Cookies are generally a convenience rather than a nuisance: Many Web sites that require you to enter a username and password offer you the option to "remember" your username and password so you don't have to enter them every time you revisit. The option is made possible by a cookie the site places on your computer when you check the "Remember me" or "Remember information" option.

If the site is able to associate the cookie with information you provide through a form you fill out, it can indeed identify you by name when you revisit. Some of the more sophisticated sites, like Amazon.com, use cookies to greet visitors by name and make book recommendations based on what those individuals (the cookie-holders) have purchased in the past.

Just how many cookies do you have on your hard drive? If your browser has been configured to block all cookies, you won't have any. But if you've never paid attention to your browser's cookie settings and are using the default settings, you probably have a healthy selection. To view your cookies, do one of the following:

✔ If you use Microsoft Internet Explorer, choose Tools⇨Internet Options. On the General tab of Internet Options, click Settings. In the Settings dialog box, click View Files. A Windows Explorer window opens with your cookies displayed. (The cookies are the files that begin with the term "Cookie:".)

✔ If you use Netscape Communicator, choose Edit⇨Preferences, click the arrow next to Privacy & Security, click Cookies, and click Manage Stored Cookies. The Cookie Manager window opens with a list of stored cookies (see Figure 10-8).

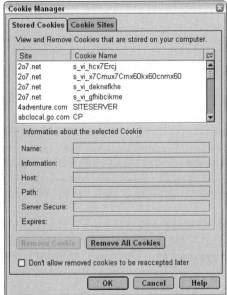

Figure 10-8:
If your browser stores cookies, you may find that you have quite a few on your computer.

Blocking cookies

You can control cookies using your browser's built-in controls. But when you choose Norton Internet Security to control cookies, you have the opportunity to make cookie control part of an overall browser privacy program. You gain the ability to accept or reject cookies from specific Web sites — a finer-grained level of control than you get with your browser. First, you need to make sure Norton Internet Security's Browser Privacy component is enabled:

1. **Open the main NIS window and double-click Privacy Control.**

    The Privacy Control dialog box appears.

2. **Click Custom Level.**

    The Customize Privacy Settings dialog box opens.

3. **Make sure the Enable Browser Privacy box is checked.**

After Browser Privacy is enabled, you can choose a global setting that is similar to your browser's controls, or you can block cookies on a site-by-site basis. The drop-down list under the Cookie Blocking heading in the Customize Privacy Settings dialog box contains three options:

- ✔ **None: Allow cookies.** Allows all the cookies that Web sites you visit want to send you.

- ✔ **Medium: Prompt me each time.** Prompts you whenever a cookie is being sent so you can decide whether or not to allow it.

- ✔ **High: Block Cookies.** Prevents all cookies from being sent to your computer.

These settings don't give you any advantage over your browser's controls. The Web Assistant toolbar provides a greater degree of control. The toolbar options include Block Cookies on This Site. Of course, if you've already chosen High: Block Cookies in the Customize Browser Settings dialog box, this option is irrelevant. It makes sense to choose None or Medium in the Customize Browser Settings dialog box and then block cookies on a site-by-site basis.

Viewing cookie alerts

In Chapter 3, I cover the different sorts of alert messages that Norton Internet Security presents you when external computers try to access your computer — or vice versa. When you change your privacy control settings, you prompt Norton Internet Security to alert you whenever an external Web site tries to connect to a cookie that has been placed on your computer. Open Privacy Control and move the slider to High. This setting produces an alert whenever a Web site attempts to connect with a cookie that has already been placed on your computer, or when a Web site attempts to place a cookie. Chances are that, as you surf the Web, you'll see an alert message like the one shown in Figure 10-9.

To find out more about what this connection attempt means, click Alert Assistant. A separate window opens with information about the alert message.

It's enlightening to see just how many cookies are communicating with Web sites, even when you aren't doing anything with your browser. An image (spacer.gif, an empty space created by a blank image file) on a Web page that is open in a browser window is connecting to a cookie placed on my computer. I decide to block the cookie, as recommended in the alert box. I click OK to close the alert box, and a succession of other alerts appears, one after another — so many that I decide to reduce the privacy level back to Medium just to stop them.

Figure 10-9:
Web sites connect to cookies that have been placed on your hard drive.

Keeping Your Web Activity Confidential

The individuals who organize and maintain Web sites have many tools at their disposal in order to find out who visits their sites. The most direct way is to require visitors to register for something. As part of registration, visitors are made to give out much personal data. A more subtle approach is to view the information in the packets that are exchanged by a Web server and a Web browser when a connection is made. A part of the packet called the header can tell the server what IP address your computer has been assigned, where you came from just before you visited the current site, what type of Web browser you are using, and possibly what part of the country you live in based on the domain name used by your ISP's servers. For example, if one of the servers has the name dsl1.server-ch-il.com, the Webmaster can surmise that you live in Chicago.

Some Web surfers don't want the sites they visit to know anything about them unless they willingly volunteer personal information. They prefer not to have their IP addresses tracked and records kept of the Web pages they view on a site. They don't want to be statistics used to set advertising rates or develop marketing programs. Such privacy-minded surfers can have NIS block transmissions of such info through Privacy Control.

You can see how much information your browser is giving out by going to the Qualys Browser Checkup site (`http://browsercheck.qualys.com`). Click a single button, and you'll see how much information the remote Web server can detect about your browser, including what scripts it is able to run. If a remote computer can see that your browser can execute Jscripts, for example, a hacker can learn the same information and attempt to send malicious Jscripts to your browser.

Adding or changing your private information

Chances are you fill out online forms all the time. You register for services, you pay your bills online, and you download trial versions of useful applications. Whenever you submit information to a remote Web site, the information should be encrypted. You can always tell whether the information is being encrypted or not by checking the security icon in your Web browser's status bar.

If you don't check the security icon all the time, your information can go out unprotected to sites that don't have encryption set up. NIS can prevent the information from going online. In Chapter 2, you found out how to create a file of sensitive data that NIS protects. You can add to or delete that information by following these steps:

1. **Open the main NIS window, and double-click Privacy Control.**

   The Privacy Control dialog box opens.

2. **Click Private Information.**

   The Private Information dialog box appears (see Figure 10-10).

3. **Do one or more of the following:**

   • **Click Add if you want to add a new bit of information.**

   • **If you want to delete a bit of information, highlight it and then click Remove.**

   • **If you want to change information you have already entered, highlight the current information and click Modify.** The Modify Private Information dialog box appears; enter the different information and click OK.

4. **Click OK to close the Private Information dialog box, and click OK to close the Privacy Control dialog box.**

   The two windows close and you return to the main NIS window.

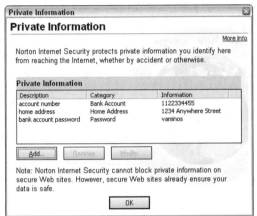

Figure 10-10:
You can add passwords or financial data you want Norton Internet Security to protect.

For even greater security, you can download an install a program called Anonymizer. It prevents your IP address and other information from being detected while you surf. A free version is available as a toolbar you add to your browser: Find out more on the Anonymizer Web site at `www.anonymizer.com`.

Deleting temporary Internet files

If you work in an office where supervisors and network administrators scrutinize your computer activity, or in another environment where others have access to your computer, you can give yourself an additional level of protection above and beyond what NIS's Privacy Control provides: You can delete the temporary files your browser creates, effectively "covering up your footsteps."

As you visit Web pages, your browser downloads image and text files and saves them on your hard drive. When you revisit the page, the files that have not changed are used again to save time. Internet Explorer describes them as Temporary Internet Files. Employers who are very inquisitive of how their employees use company resources can conceivably view the files to see what Web sites you have visited. You can prevent them from finding anything by deleting the files:

1. **Choose Tools⇨Internet Options from the Microsoft Internet Explorer menu bar.**

   The Internet Options window opens.

2. **Click the Delete Files button on the General tab.**

   A Delete Files dialog box appears.

3. **Click OK.**

   The files are deleted.

If you want to cover your footsteps and prevent others from seeing where you have been online, you also need to delete your browser's History file. (If you are at work, make sure this doesn't violate company policy first.) The History file keeps a record of all the Web pages you have visited in recent weeks. If you use Netscape Navigator, choose Go⇨History. When the History window opens, choose Edit⇨Select All, then choose Delete. In Internet Explorer, open Internet Options as described in the preceding set of steps. Then click the Clear History button on the General tab.

Chapter 11

Wireless and Laptop Security

. . . .

In This Chapter

▶ Detecting a new network so you can maintain security while traveling

▶ Keeping your laptop secure from thieves and snoopers

▶ Protecting your Internet-enabled handhelds

▶ Practicing basic security for your wireless network

. . . .

*N*orton Internet Security provides the same level of protection for laptop computers as it does for desktop computers. In this chapter, I cover how you use NIS's Network Detector component to connect to the Internet using a wireless modem. You can take advantage of Personal Firewall, Intrusion Detection, and the program's other components.

But consider this: These days, most people have more than one computer at their disposal. Suppose you have installed Norton Internet Security on your desktop computer. What level of protection does it provide for your laptop? With the activation feature that's new for the 2004 version, you can use the program only on a single computer that's connected to the Internet. That forces you to either buy a multilicense copy of NIS, or install other software. I discuss both options in this chapter.

Computers, of course, aren't the only devices that connect to the Internet. Cellphones and PDAs go online too, and they're beginning to encounter the first viruses made for those devices. Lastly, I describe some options for protecting your security with handhelds in this chapter as well.

Network Detector

When you leave your home and connect to the Internet from a new location, you may be connecting to the same Internet and accessing the same resources as usual, but Norton Internet Security regards you as being on a different network. And in a sense, you are: You're in a new location and you're using a new Internet connection. For example, you may be taking advantage of a wireless hotspot in a coffeeshop. In any case, whenever you make a new network connection, you need to use the Network Detection component. This compo-nent streamlines the process of creating security settings for the new network. The sections that follow describe how to use Network Detector to make a secure connection from your wireless device or laptop.

Understanding Network Detector

In the language of Norton Internet Security, a new location isn't just a seat on a park bench or a table at the public library where you get online. A location is a set of security settings that can contain one or more networks. Whenever your computer connects to a network in one of these locations, Norton Internet Security automatically switches to the security settings that are associated with that location. (If you just think "set of security settings" when you see the word "location" in the pages that follow, the distinction will be easier to under-stand.) Network Detector lets you customize Program Control and Trusted Zone settings so you can take advantage of NIS's protection in those different locations.

If you connect to the Internet from a bookstore, a coffeeshop, and a library, those are technically three different locations and three different networks. If you want the same level of security in each location, you could place those networks in a single location (in other words, a single set of security settings). If you want a higher level of security in, for example, the bookstore, you could create a location (set of security settings) for that network that has more secu-rity. The potentially confusing thing is that you can add new networks to a single location; you would do this if you want the new network to have the same set of security settings as the other networks in that location.

The four possible locations and their corresponding level of predetermined security are found when you double-click Personal Firewall from the main NIS window, then click the Locations tab. They break down as follows:

✓ **Default.** This security level is based on the settings you have chosen for your default user account.

✓ **Office.** This is a low security setting because it assumes you're on a cor-porate network that has its own hardware firewall. NIS gets out of the way and lets the hardware firewall do much of the work.

✓ **Home.** This medium security setting lets you access the Internet with minimal restrictions.

✓ **Away.** This high security setting provides extra protection for public locations.

Why the extra security for public places? A relatively new breed of hacker trolls for wireless networks, trying to gain high-speed access to the Internet using someone else's account. When the hacker is online, he or she can download X-rated material, attack other sites, or perform other unpleasant tasks, all on your dime. You could get in trouble with your ISP, who might think you're actually doing the dirty work.

Getting started with Network Detector

When you want to use NIS in a new physical location, you have to consider whether that new location needs the same security settings as an existing location or whether it needs different settings. Why? Because you can get started in one of two different ways:

- ✔ Create a new location/set of security settings.
- ✔ Add a new network to an existing location/set of security settings.

If your home setting is used for your home computer and you think this medium level of security would work for the public library, you could add the new network to the Home location. If the library needs higher security than any other network you currently use, you can designate it as a new location with higher security.

Consider the second option first: You want to add a new network (such as the library, or a coffeeshop) to one of the four preconfigured locations mentioned earlier: Default, Home, Office, or Away. You don't need to start Network Detector. The component starts up automatically for you. When you attempt to connect to the Internet from the new location, you see the Network Detector alert shown in Figure 11-1.

If you want to add the new network to a pre-existing location, just choose that location from the drop-down list.

Figure 11-1: Network Detector presents this alert so you can configure a set of security settings for it.

Norton Internet Security

Network Detector

⚠ New Network Detected

To join this network, choose the security settings you want to use.

Show Details

What location do you want to use?

[Make a Selection] ▼

OK

If, on the other hand, you want to assign the new network to a new location, click Use Custom Settings. Then click Wizard. The Network Detector Wizard opens. Follow the steps shown in the wizard to create a new location: In the first screen of the wizard, you decide whether or not Automatic Program Control applies for the new location; in the second screen, you create a name for the location (see Figure 11-2); and in the third screen, you finish setting up the network.

You can choose a third option: You can assign the new network to a custom set of security settings that applies to that place and no other. In this case, click Use Custom Settings, and click the custom location that you have already created.

If you ever want to review the current locations you have in place and their associated settings, follow these steps:

1. **From the main NIS window, double-click Personal Firewall.**

   The Personal Firewall options open.

2. **Click the Locations tab.**

   The Locations options appear.

3. **Review the list of locations and highlight one; click Delete to remove a location, Clear to remove networks from a location, or Wizard to create a new location.**

   Figure 11-3 shows that four networks are associated with the Home location.

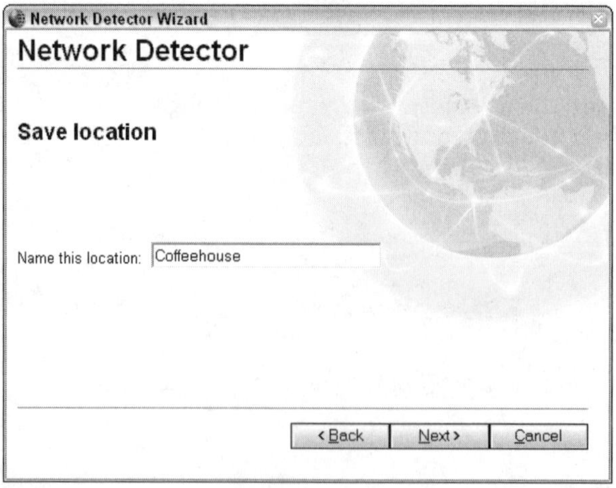

Figure 11-2: You can assign a new network to a new location using the Network Detector Wizard.

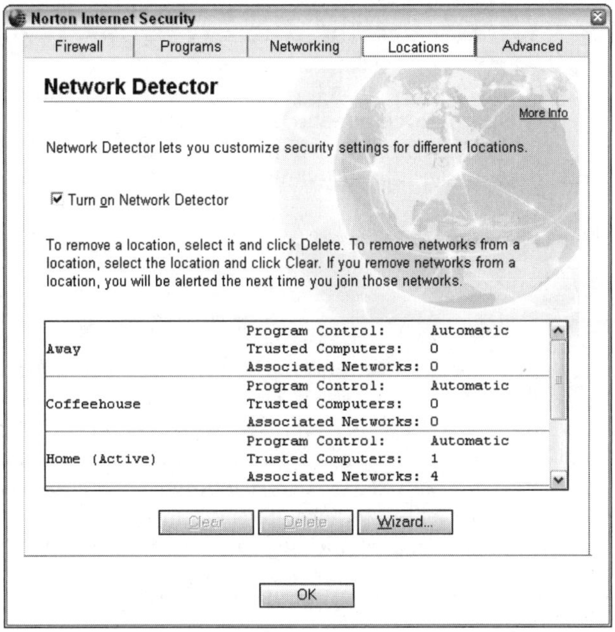

Figure 11-3:
Use the
Locations
window to
create or
change
locations.

4. **When you create a location, select it in the Locations window, and then use the Networking window to identify trusted computers for that location.**

   Use the Programs window to set up program control for that location.

   If you're using Windows XP, the Network Detector alert will specify whether the connection is physical or wireless (that is, as long as you have selected the Turn On Network Detector box). If you're using Windows 98, Windows Me, or Windows 2000, this nature of the connection may not be specified.

Laptop Security

Laptops are an everyday part of business, and because of the sensitive corporate and personal data they contain, they need to be protected. If those laptops have wireless modems and can connect to the Internet through places that use the wireless Wi-Fi protocol *(hotspots),* you need to install software of the sort described in the sections that follow.

Note: The software described in the sections that follow will provide added protection to desktop computers as well as laptops.

Installing third-party security software

Although this is a book about Norton Internet Security, you still need to install other firewall, spam blocking, and anti-virus programs on your laptop computer. At the very least, though, you need to install software such as the following on your portable computing device:

✔ Personal Firewall software

✔ Anti-virus software

✔ Spam blocking applications

✔ Keeping your operating system up to date with security patches

The software you install doesn't necessarily have to come from Symantec. Freeware and shareware programs also provide protection, though these programs are rarely as full-featured or user-friendly as NIS. Besides these programs and patches, you need to activate the built-in security features of your laptop. I describe the various add-ons in more detail in the sections that follow.

Personal firewall software

A variety of shareware and commercial firewalls are available that monitor traffic seeking to pass through your network gateway. If you want to purchase a second copy of Norton Internet Security, you'll either pay $69 or $99, depending on the version you buy. (Rebates are frequently available to reduce this cost.) You may want to consider the following alternate firewalls, which are less expensive and, in some cases, available in stripped-down versions:

✔ Sygate Personal Firewall (www.sygate.com). If I didn't have NIS, I'd be using the freeware version of this program (shown in Figure 11-4), which is easy to install and effective.

✔ Zone Alarm (www.zonealarm.com). This popular firewall package is available in a free version as well as much-more-capable Plus and Pro versions. I've used this program myself and don't find it as user-friendly as Sygate Personal Firewall.

✔ Agnitum Outpost Firewall (www.agnitum.com).

✔ Kerio Personal Firewall 4 (www.kerio.com).

Each of these firewall products comes in a freeware version that you can download, install, and use indefinitely at no charge — but they don't have as much functionality as the commercial versions. Sometimes you have to do a bit of searching on the manufacturers' Web sites to find these applications (at least, the free versions). The free software is not as easy to use as a commercial application, but such programs do provide a measure of protection at a price you just can't beat.

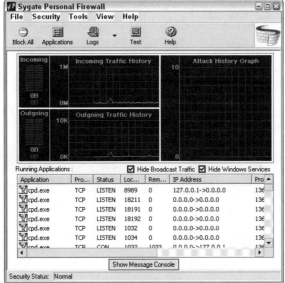

Figure 11-4:
Sygate
Personal
Firewall can
protect
laptops on
which NIS
is not
installed.

Testing your firewall that's in place either on your desktop computer or on your laptop is always a good idea. Visit Gibson Research Corporation's Web site and use their free Shields UP! analysis tool: (`http://grc.com`). The tool enables you to analyze the commonly-used ports on your system to see which ones are currently open and therefore accessible to outsiders. Also try out other utilities available from the same company to test for well-known vulnerabilities in Microsoft Windows operating systems. Shoot The Messenger tests for Windows Messenger vulnerabilities, while The DCOMbobulator (`www.grc.com/dcom`) tests for problems with the Microsoft Distributed Component Object Model (DCOM) system. All three programs are at `www.grc.com/stm/shootthemessenger.htm`; the latter two require you to download and install them.

Anti-virus software

Even with a firewall, you will want some form of active protection to make sure that any data that does make it through the firewall cannot harm your computer. Many anti-virus programs are available on the market today. Free anti-virus programs include:

✔ AntiVir Personal Edition (`www.free-av.com`)

✔ GriSoft AVG Free Edition (`www.grisoft.com/us/us_dwnl_free.php`)

Both of these freeware packages are also available in commercial versions with a wider range of features.

Spam blocking software

Spam blocking software is especially important because the majority of viruses are being transmitted as seemingly-innocent attachments to e-mail messages that appear to be coming from known-good sources. With the combination of anti-virus and spam blocking software, you will be able to prevent almost all of these from ever reaching your inbox.

MailWasher, a service I mention in Chapter 9 is available in a freeware version at www.mailwasher.net/download.php).

Free Web-based e-mail providers, such as Hotmail and Yahoo Mail, have options that you can activate to turn on spam blocking (referred to by Hotmail as "Junk Mail settings").

Securing your system

Other ways to secure your laptop don't require you to install software. Instead, you have to apply some common sense and care when creating security features like passwords, for example.

Setting passwords

The best approach to take for this is to activate the BIOS password protection features that every laptop has. You need to read your laptop's user guides to find out how to enter the BIOS to do this.

The most important password that you will want to set is your hard drive's password. By activating the hard drive's password feature, you prevent anyone without that password from being able to power up and access your hard drive. Even if the hard drive is removed from your laptop computer and installed into another computer, it cannot be accessed without the proper password.

If you do activate any of the BIOS passwords, you will need to use them every time you power up your laptop. But this is probably a minor inconvenience when you consider the protection it gives.

Investing in a laptop/notebook computer cable lock to secure the laptop when you need to leave it somewhere for even a few minutes (such as a hotel room) is also a good idea. Do a search for "cable lock" on Google's shopping service Froogle (http://froogle.google.com) to compare prices.

Updating your system

Hackers and virus creators take advantage of security vulnerabilities in your computer's operating system and in the programs that you run on your computer. To reduce the risk, you should always update your operating system whenever a new security patch is released. For Windows operating systems, this process is made easier by the Update Wizard.

Configure your Windows Update Wizard to automatically check for updates, and to download them for you automatically, while also prompting you first before they are installed.

Creating a new location for your laptop

Besides adding new networks to the four default locations, you can also create new locations with customized settings and names. For example, you could create a low-security Hotels location you use while traveling and a high-security Coffeeshop location for the wireless network access points provided by many such businesses. If you regularly switch between several networks, you may find that this gives you a greater degree of control over your protection.

You can create a new location from a Network Detector alert and from the main Norton Internet Security window. To create a new location from a Network Detector alert, follow these steps:

1. **When you connect to the Internet from a new location and the Network Detector alert appears, select Use Custom Settings from the Which Location Do You Want to Use drop-down list.**

   The Use Custom Settings window opens.

2. **Click Create New Location, and then click Next.**

   The Setup Program Control window appears.

3. **Do one of the following:**
   - Click Yes (recommended) to turn on Automatic Program Control so you get fewer security alerts.
   - Click No to turn off Automatic Program Control. You will be alerted the first time an application attempts to connect to the Internet.

4. **Click Next.**

   The Save Location window opens.

5. **In the Save Location window, type a name for this new location.**

6. **Click Next.**

   Your settings appear so you can review them.

7. **Click Finish.**

   You return to the desktop.

You can also create a new location from the main NIS window by double-clicking Personal Firewall, clicking Locations, clicking Wizard, and following the instructions in the screens that follow.

Using your laptop in a hotspot

If you use your laptop to connect to the Internet from home, from work, and from a neighborhood coffeeshop, you are actually connecting to at least three different networks. If you want the same level of security in both your home and office, you can place both networks in a single location. If you want more security in the coffeeshop, you can create a high-security location for that network.

A high-security location is one that has no computers identified as trusted, no networks associated with it, and Automatic Program Control enabled. For public locations, choosing a high-security location such as the default Away location is a must. You also need to protect the machine, as much as possible, from thieves and over-the-shoulder peepers.

Protecting your laptop from theft

The big problem with laptops and other portable devices is simple: Because they're small and portable, it's easy for a thief to walk away with them. You can't always chain them down to a table or other piece of heavy furniture — but you *should* try to lock them whenever possible. Don't keep sensitive information such as your PIN numbers or financial data on your laptop or PDA; don't leave your laptop out in the open where someone can see it easily.

Encrypting data on a device is important so that the data on it is secure if the device is stolen. You can use the powerful and popular personal encryption method called Pretty Good Privacy (PGP) to protect your information. You can also use the built-in encryption included with Windows XP and 2000, as long as it's on a disk that's formatted with the New Technology File System (NTFS).

Note: You can only encrypt files on hard drives that have been formatted with NTFS, not File Allocation Table (FAT). On an NTFS disk, you can enable encryption by right-clicking a file or folder, choosing Properties from the pop-up menu, and clicking Advanced. When the Advanced Attributes dialog box opens, click Select Encrypt Contents to Secure Data, and click OK.

Backing up the data on your laptop so it isn't lost forever if the computer itself is lost is also important.

Handheld Security

All of the security procedures that apply to laptops also apply to handheld devices that can get on the Internet. Physical security, passwords, and PINs are essential for obvious reasons. But in June 2004, a new threat emerged in the form of the world's first virus targeted specifically at cellphones: Cabir.

The first cellphone virus made it past software that is typically used to encrypt the identity of the user or the phone's unique ID number. Cabir used the Bluetooth wireless technology that some "smart" cellphones use to communicate with other wireless devices in order to spread itself. Cabir is regarded as relatively harmless because it required a user to download a file coming from an unknown source, which most users aren't likely to do. But future viruses are expected to be more insidious.

Protecting your cellphone

In Europe, where cellphone technology tends to run ahead of the U.S., cellphone hacking is also more prevalent. Thieves typically steal phones and change the unique phone ID number; they fill the phone up with prepaid minutes, and then resell them to make money.

Some cellphone providers let you create a PIN number that locks a phone when not in use. You can also avoid the transmission of sensitive information over cellphone networks. Besides these obvious strategies, there are a few other things that end users can do to protect their cellphones:

✔ Cellphones can be turned into microphones and used to eavesdrop on private conversations if someone can transmit a maintenance command to the cellphone on the proper channel. Don't turn on cellphones in court or any location where sensitive information is being exchanged.

✔ If someone intercepts your phone's unique ID number, he or she can assign the number to another phone to make it seem like yours. The thief can then place calls on the other phone and charge them to your account. Turn on your cellphone only when you need to make a call and turn it off when you're done to avoid having the ID number intercepted.

✔ Don't use the cellphone in the close vicinity of the shopping mall, sports stadium, or airport where lots of people congregate; radio hobbyists go to such locations to monitor cellphone conversations.

However, it's primarily up to cellphone manufacturers to provide protection against hackers. That may change if security companies like Symantec manage to create downloadable security software for cellphone, however. Encryption for cellphone conversations is available to businesses from companies like Global Teck (www.global-teck.com), but not to home users.

Protecting your PDA

PDA users can take advantage of a handful of products that let you encrypt or decrypt files that are transmitted online. Encrypt-it! (www.pocketiq.com/home/software/shareware.asp) is designed to work with a variety of handheld devices. It lets you overwrite the unencrypted portion of a file before you encrypt it, and launch a file immediately after it is decrypted.

Password-protecting a PDA also is essential. That way, if the device is lost, your data won't necessarily be free game. Password protection is integrated into the Palm OS. But you can also password-protect the contents of a PDA. A program called PDA Defense completely wipes the memory of a device if someone does not enter the password correctly for a specified number of times. Find out more about the program at www.pdabomb.com.

Wireless Security

Too many people buy wireless routers and adapters, bring them home or to their office, connect them, and never change the configuration from the default settings, which can be inherently insecure. In the following sections, I describe some options for strengthening those settings.

Obtaining an encryption key

Setting up a basic Wired Equivalent Privacy (WEP) encryption key keeps the casual visitor out. Most wireless routers come with a WEP key setting; the exact configuration method depends on the device. Such encryption will help keep out accidental intrusions and amateur hackers, although it may not be enough to deter anyone who has sufficient desire and the skill to get past its basic protection.

Securing your wireless router with an administrative password is also important. Choose a good password and change it regularly. You'll find this and other practical wireless security tips on the Practically Networked site (www.practicallynetworked.com/support/wireless_secure.htm).

Connecting to a Virtual Private Network

If you're concerned about hackers intercepting your wireless data transmissions, you may want to consider subscribing to a VPN (virtual private network) service that will allow you to encrypt your data no matter whether you're using WEP or not for the wireless transmissions. Normally, a VPN is set up by a company or organization that can afford the necessary hardware and bandwidth to handle the load. At each end of a secure connection, VPN hardware or software is placed that encrypts and decrypts as it passes into and out of a network.

Some businesses are offering VPN services as a subscription service for private individuals. HotSpotVPN (www.hotspotvpn.com) offers services for laptop computers as well as the Pocket PC. You use Windows' built-in Network Connection Wizard to set up a VPN connection to the service. Currently, HotSpotVPN charges an introductory price of $8.88 per month.

To find out more about wireless networking security issues, refer to *Wireless Home Networking For Dummies* by Danny Briere, Pat Hurley, and Walter Bruce, or *Wireless Networks For Dummies* by Peter Davis and Barry Lewis. Both are published by Wiley Publishing, Inc.

Part IV
Access Control

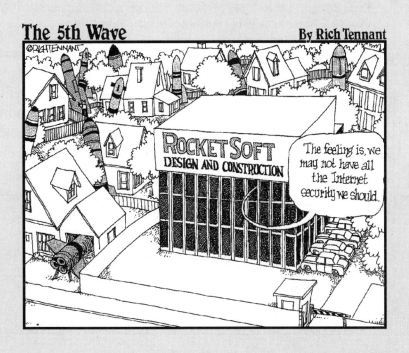

The 5th Wave — By Rich Tennant

ROCKET SOFT
DESIGN AND CONSTRUCTION

"The feeling is, we may not have all the Internet security we should."

In this part . . .

Chances are you aren't the only one who uses your computer or your network. If you have children, they'll need to go online to do homework assignments. Significant others and co-workers also need access to the Web as well as their own passwords and e-mail addresses. Even if you live alone, you probably have friends who come over to take advantage of your broadband connection or show you the cool new Web site they have discovered.

This part covers access control for computers or networks that are protected by Norton Internet Security. You find out how to set up accounts for multiple users and how to protect files that are shared by those users. For the business environment, I cover a special tool called Norton Productivity Control which gives employees access while blocking their ability to visit certain sites while on the job.

Parents of young children will be happy to find out about Norton Parental Control, a component that enables them to restrict what their children see or do online, and that gives them the ability to track where their kids have been — at least, while they're in your house and on the Internet.

Chapter 12

Issues for Networks with Multiple Users

· ·

In This Chapter

▶ Creating user accounts

▶ Establishing separate accounts for family members or employees

▶ Customizing privacy, spam, and ad blocking settings for individual accounts

▶ Configuring Norton Productivity Control for employees

· ·

*L*ife online is simple if you're the only person who ever uses your computer. If you're the only user, you don't have to use NIS's Accounts feature at all. You have a single account, which is both the startup account (the
account that NIS uses when it first starts up) and a Supervisor account (an
account with the highest level of privileges).

But suppose you have multiple individuals — your children or your co-workers
who go online using the same computer. If you're able to supervise them whenever they're at the computer, you can be sure they don't visit Web sites you
consider unsuitable or give out private information you want to keep private.
Constant supervision is impractical, to say the least, however. In that case,
you need to establish a user account for each person.

NIS user accounts are different from the user accounts that apply to your
Windows operating system. But the idea is the same. Each account is tied to
different preferences and applications. The primary difference between the
two types of accounts is that the Windows accounts are tied to the operating
system, while NIS's accounts determine the level of security restrictions each
person faces when going online. This chapter examines how to create and
customize user accounts in order to control how different people access the
Internet and take advantage of different levels of protection.

Understanding User Accounts

Your computer can't see or hear who is sitting at the machine and tapping away on the keyboard. It can't call out and say, "Is that you, boss?" or "Don't visit that Web site, young man!" Someday, computers may be able to scan and interpret thumbprints or other physical characteristics so they can identify people. Until then, you need to create user accounts. A user account is a set of data that applies to a single individual:

- A username
- A password
- A set of options or specifications that is tied to the username and password

Norton Internet Security uses accounts to set different access privileges for different users. Even if you don't bother to create accounts, Norton Internet Security uses default accounts to tell whether or not the Supervisor (that's you) is logged on or not.

Default accounts

Default accounts are ones that Norton Internet Security creates automatically when the program is first installed. You don't have to create them, and you can't delete at least one of them (the Not Logged On account), either. But you should know about the default accounts because, whether you realize it or not, you're using them when you work with NIS.

Protecting the Supervisor account

When you first install Norton Internet Security, the program creates a default account with Supervisor privileges. If no one else ever uses the computer's protected with NIS, the program assumes that the Supervisor is always present. This account gives you the maximum amount of access to the program: It lets you create firewall rules, set privacy options for individual Web sites, and all other options that NIS makes available to you.

Note: If you create an account for yourself when your first install NIS and you give yourself Supervisor privileges, you will, in fact, have two accounts that are labeled Supervisor. One has your own username, and the other has Supervisor as the username. You can delete the one with Supervisor as the username for greater security.

But the Supervisor account isn't necessarily secure because, by default, it is not password-protected. If an unauthorized individual gains access to your computer, he or she can disable NIS or change options without even having to crack a password. For better security, you should create a password for this account. Follow these steps:

1. **Open the main NIS window and click User Accounts under the heading Norton Internet Security on the left-hand side of the window.**

   The User Accounts window appears (see Figure 12-1).

Figure 12-1:
You can view, create, and change User Accounts settings using this window.

2. **Click the account labeled Supervisor in the Type column.**

   The account name is highlighted.

3. **Click Change Password.**

   The Change [*your username*]'s Password dialog box appears (see Figure 12-2).

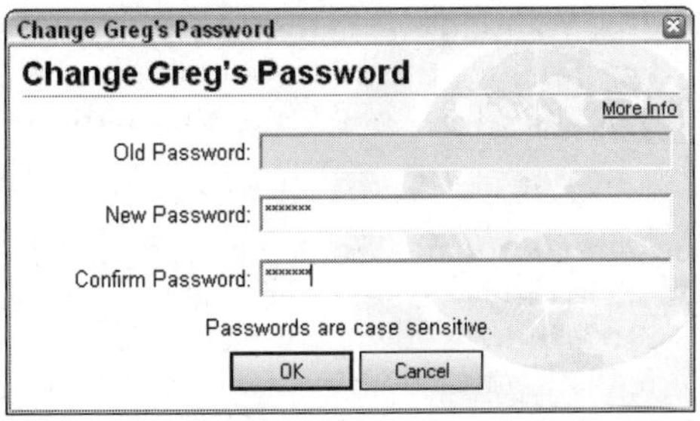

Figure 12-2:
Use this dialog box to assign yourself a password for greater security.

4. **Change the password and then click OK.**

   The Change [*your username*]'s Password dialog box closes and you return to the User Accounts options.

5. **Click Properties.**

   The Account Properties dialog box appears. Optionally, you can use this dialog box to change the account name, password, level of privileges, or make the highlighted account the startup account.

6. **Click OK.**

   The Account Properties dialog box closes and you return to the main NIS window.

The usual "best practices" rules for setting good passwords applies to your Supervisor password: Choose a password that has at least 6 to 9 characters, that is not a recognizable word in the dictionary, and that uses a mixture of letters and numerals.

Working with the Not Logged On account

The second default account, Not Logged On, becomes active when no one is currently logged on to the computer. When you have multiple user accounts present and you log off, Not Logged On is the current account until someone else logs on. This prevents anyone who doesn't have a user account from accessing the Internet because the Not Logged On account blocks all Internet access.

NIS accounts versus Windows accounts

There's an argument to be made for making the NIS accounts the same as the accounts you currently have in place on your Windows computer. The reason is simplicity. If you have, for example, four or five accounts in place for Windows users and you create four or five different NIS accounts with different usernames and passwords, you have to keep track of eight to ten separate usernames and passwords. Your kids have to remember not one but two passwords. They're likely to write down the information on a piece of paper that a sibling or friend (or someone who is not a friend) can discover and use to get on the Internet.

On the other hand, if you assign your usual Windows accounts to corresponding NIS accounts, you have only one set of usernames and passwords to manage. When you log on to Windows using your Windows account name and password, you automatically log in to Norton Internet Security with the same account name. Conversely, when you log off of Windows you log off of NIS, too.

Note: The ability to assign Windows accounts to your NIS accounts presupposes that you have created separate Windows usernames and passwords for each of your family members or each person in your office. If you haven't done so yet, you should create such accounts, for the same security reasons that apply to NIS.

To assign Windows accounts to NIS accounts, follow these steps:

1. **Open the User Accounts options as described in the steps in the preceding section, "Protecting the Supervisor account."**

   The User Accounts options appear.

2. **Click Parental Control Wizard or Productivity Control Wizard, depending on which version of Norton Internet Security you have installed.**

   This example uses the Parental Control Wizard; I discuss the Productivity Control Wizard later in this chapter.

   The Choose Account Manager screen appears (see Figure 12-3).

3. **Make sure Use Existing Windows Accounts is selected, and click Next.**

   After a few seconds, the Choose Account Level screen appears with all of your current Windows accounts listed.

4. **Select an account level from the drop-down list next to each account name.**

   NIS makes four default accounts available to you: Supervisor, Adult, Teenager, and Child.

5. **Click Next, then Finish when the Finished screen appears.**

   The Parental Control Wizard closes and you return to the main NIS window.

Figure 12-3:
You can use the same Windows accounts and Norton Internet Security accounts.

Parental Control Wizard

Choose account manager

Norton Internet Security lets parents create accounts containing personalized Internet security settings. You can create accounts for individual users or group accounts containing settings for several users.

If you have multiple Windows accounts on this computer, you can use the existing Windows accounts. If you do not have multiple accounts, you can create Norton Internet Security accounts for each user.

What would you like to do?

○ Use existing Windows accounts.

○ Create Norton Internet Security accounts.

< Back   Next >   Close

If you ever want to separate your Windows accounts from your NIS accounts, you can open the User Accounts options, highlight the account you want to change, click Properties, and change the options for each account.

See Chapter 11 for more on the differences between the access levels of each default user account, and for instructions on how to create a custom account.

The Guest account that is created when Windows is installed is a security risk. It gives hackers a way to gain access to your computer, and if you don't use it, you should disable it.

Creating User Accounts

If one of your children needs your computer to access the Internet, or if you hire a new employee who needs to go online with a machine that is also used by other individuals, you can always create new accounts. You are given the option to create new accounts when you first install Norton Internet Security. But if you skip this step or need to add accounts after installation, you can do so at any time.

Creating accounts at startup

After you complete the installation process, the Summary screen appears (see Figure 12-4), which gives you the opportunity to complete a variety of post-installation tasks. One of those tasks is creating user accounts by running either Parental Control or Productivity Control. Parental Control is intended to restrict Internet access for students whereas Productivity Control is intended for employees in a work environment.

Leave either Parental Control or Productivity Control marked as Selected, click Finish, and follow the instructions in subsequent screens in order to create your accounts immediately.

Creating accounts after startup

If you ever want to add a new account or modify an existing account after startup, you have two options:

- ✔ **Choose the Parental Control Wizard or Productivity Control Wizard.** If you set up one of these access control features, you should use the wizard.

- ✔ **Click User Accounts under the Norton Internet Security heading in the main NIS window.**

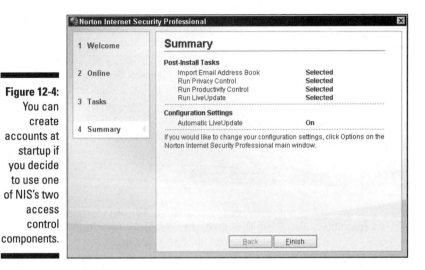

Figure 12-4:
You can
create
accounts at
startup if
you decide
to use one
of NIS's two
access
control
components.

If you choose the wizard, you first create a supervisor account. Then you go to the Create accounts screen, where you are given four "slots" for accounts (see Figure 12-5). Enter a username and choose the type of account you want to create. Then follow the steps shown in subsequent steps of the wizard to finish creating accounts.

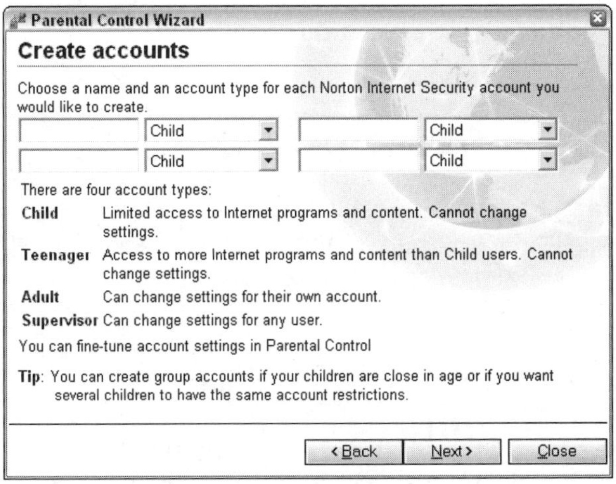

Figure 12-5:
The
Parental
Control or
Productivity
Control
Wizard lets
you create
four user
accounts.

You may ask what to do if you need to create five, six, or more separate accounts for NIS/Windows users. If that's the case, you can create the first four accounts using one of the wizards, and then open the User Accounts window and create new accounts for all users after the first four.

Logging on and off

In order for accounts to work, you need to remember to log off and log on. In Windows, you click Start⇨Log Off. In Norton Internet Security, you right-click the System Tray icon and choose Log Off from the shortcut menu. When a new user attempts to access the Internet, he or she will be prompted to log on with his or her username and password.

Customizing User Accounts

The whole reason for having user accounts is the ability to change access settings and restrictions to meet the needs of each user. For young users, it means specifying Web sites, applications, and newsgroups they cannot access when they go online (or, on the other hand, specifying resources they *can* use). For adults, it means setting AntiSpam options that apply to each user's e-mail account, and privacy control settings that keep out the restrictions that that individual just doesn't want to see. In order to change settings, you first need to log on to the account for the person in question. Then, change the access options as summarized in the sections that follow.

Note: In order to change access settings for each user, you don't need to be aware of that person's username and password. The Parental Control and other dialog boxes allow the supervisor to choose a user by his or her username and then customize settings for that person.

Restricting Internet access

After you create an account for a child, teenager, or co-worker, you gain the ability to restrict the Web sites, programs, or newsgroups that person can access online.

Boosting privacy

Privacy Control restricts the information that a person can send online. You might feel at ease sending your address or phone number to an e-commerce Web site from which you are purchasing a book. But you don't want your young son or daughter to give out such information in a chat room.

You don't need to actually log on with your child's account name and password to change privacy settings. Log on as supervisor, then double-click

Privacy Control to open the Privacy Control window. Select the user's name from the Privacy Control Settings For drop-down list (see Figure 12-6). You can then adjust the private information this person is allowed to release, or move the Privacy Control slider up or down to control whether cookies or other content should be accepted when this user is working.

Blocking ads

You may think all ads shown on the Web should be blocked all the time for all users. But on the other hand, you may want to relax the blocking restrictions for users like yourself. Ad blocking covers both banner ads displayed as static images on Web pages as well as pop-up windows that appear when you connect to some Web sites.

Sometimes, though, the pop-up windows contain useful information and links rather than advertising messages. (I listen to a number of Internet radio stations that use pop-up windows to play their audio streams, for example.) You may want to leave Ad Blocking on and turn off Pop-up Window Blocking for yourself or another user. Double-click Ad Blocking in the main NIS window and deselect the Turn On Pop-up Window Blocking option when the Ad Blocking window appears.

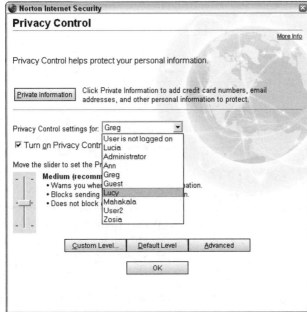

Figure 12-6: Choose one of your account names and then customize privacy control settings for that person.

Blocking spam

Each user on your computer should have his or own inbox and other mail folders as well as distinct passwords. Different AntiSpam settings can be created as well. For your kids, you may want to choose the High spam filtering setting (see Figure 12-7), but for yourself, you may want to choose Medium or Low so there's less likelihood that legitimate e-mail will be filtered out.

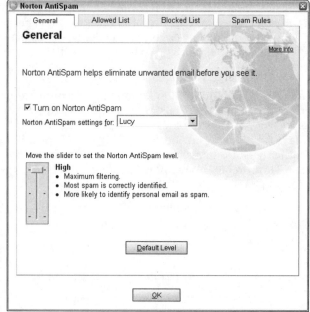

Figure 12-7:
Choose a user's account name and customize his or her level of spam filtering.

Managing Employees with Norton Productivity Control

Productivity Control is the business equivalent of the access control system designed for home users, Parental Control. Productivity Control is only available with Norton Internet Security Professional. If you use NIS in a business environment, it can give you a measure of control over what employees can and can't do online. Productivity Control makes access control less of a personal issue than it would be if you were looking over employees' shoulders and verbally telling them not to visit this or that Web site.

Productivity Control has another benefit. Because many organizations store information on a Web-based internal network called an intranet, accessing company resources is virtually identical to the process of visiting external

Web sites. If you have an intranet or store protected resources on the World Wide Web, you can use Productivity Control to restrict employees from visiting them. You might want to restrict access to financial or personnel information to users with managerial accounts, for example.

Using the Productivity Control Wizard

The process of creating business accounts is virtually the same as creating Parental Control accounts for your children as described in Chapter 13. You create accounts by running the Productivity Control Wizard. You can run the wizard at the end of the installation process, if you don't want to create accounts at installation, or if you want to add accounts at a later date, click User Accounts in the main NIS window, then click Productivity Control Wizard. In either case, the Choose Account Manager screen appears. Choose whether you want your accounts to be the same as your Windows accounts or unique to NIS, and then click Next. The Supervisor screen appears, so you can create a password for yourself (see Figure 12-8).

Click Next, and the Create Accounts Screen appears. The default accounts included in this screen are different than those included in Parental Control. For one thing, there are only three default options:

- ✔ **Supervisor.** You're already familiar with this level of access privileges.

- ✔ **Standard User.** This account holder can change options for his or her account but not for anyone else's. This level of access might be good for managers.

- ✔ **Restricted User.** This account holder cannot change any access restrictions, and is subject to limitations imposed by a Supervisor.

Figure 12-8:
Creating a
Supervisor
account is a
critical step
toward
maintaining
security
in the
workplace.

When no one is logged on to the computer protected by Productivity Control, the User Is Not Logged On account is active. This account, which is created by default, blocks access to the Internet until someone logs on.

As shown in Figure 12-9, the Create Accounts screen only enables you to establish accounts for four individuals, which may not be enough for some offices. You can add more accounts by clicking User Accounts in the main NIS window and then clicking Create.

Click Next, and the Choose Passwords screen appears for each of the users. You then choose the startup account — the account that is active when NIS starts. You then click Finish to exit the wizard. When the wizard closes, you move on to other setup tasks (if you are completing installation) or return to the main NIS Professional window.

Figure 12-9:
You are only
able to
create four
employee
accounts in
this screen
of the
wizard.

When the window first opens, Productivity Control is disabled by default, even if you have just established a group of user accounts (see Figure 12-10). To enable the component, double-click its name; the Productivity Control window opens. Select Turn On Productivity Control, then select a user account name from the drop-down list to set restrictions for each of your employees, as shown in Figure 12-11.

After you activate Productivity Control and select a user whose actions you want to regulate, click Sites to restrict Web sites, Programs to identify applications the user cannot use to go online, and Newsgroups to block access to Usenet discussion forums. The process is identical to that covered in Chapter 13 for Parental Control, so you should refer to that chapter for more details.

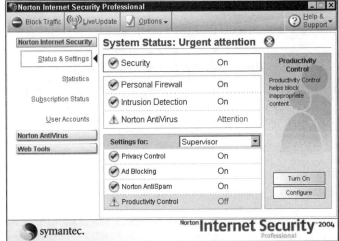

Figure 12-10:
The
Productivity
Control
default
setting.

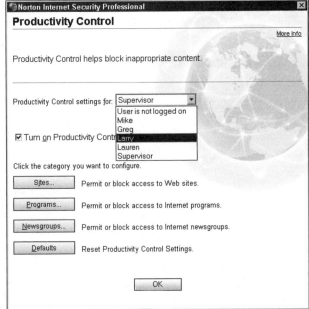

Figure 12-11:
You need to
turn on
Productivity
Control
before you
can start
to set
employee
access
restrictions.

Reviewing user restrictions

Reviewing restrictions for each user rather than just sticking with NIS Professional's default selections is important. By default, Productivity Control specifies:

- ✔ Categories of Web sites that the employee cannot visit from this computer

- ✔ Types of applications that the employee *can* use to access the Internet

- ✔ Parts of newsgroup names that designate groups the employee cannot access (at least, not while in the office)

Productivity Control (like Parental Control) doesn't always restrict by default: It designates types of programs that can be used to go online, for example. Remember, too, that you can change the restrictions at any time: You can designate categories of Web sites that employees can access, for example (although it's up to you to come up with a list of URLs of permitted sites).

Some of the default restrictions, frankly, don't make a lot of sense for employees in an office (see Figure 12-12). An individual who is categorized as a Restricted User, for example, is allowed to connect to the Internet by using Networked Games — a type of application that is probably frowned upon in most corporate environments. On the other hand, Conferencing & Collaboration is not allowed, even though it's a useful business tool.

Figure 12-12:
Be sure to
review and
modify
default
restrictions
to avoid
complaints
and
disputes.

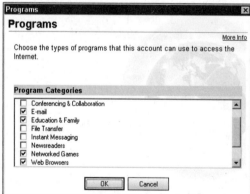

News and Finance Web sites are blocked by default, too, even though these might seem like acceptable choices to many business managers. Be sure to go through the lists of restricted sites/allowed applications to make sure they correspond to your own ideas of allowed and unsuitable content for employees during office hours.

Chapter 13

Issues for Young Users

. . . .

In This Chapter

▶ Configuring Parental Control to limit what your children can do online

▶ Checking the Web sites your kids have visited

▶ Setting passwords to keep computing resources safely "locked away"

▶ Installing software that helps young people use the Internet safely

. . . .

For many children, the Internet is a part of everyday life — a source of information and entertainment and a way to stay connected with their friends. They think nothing of turning to the Internet for information to help them with homework, for games they can play, for instant messages they can send, or any number of wonderful activities that didn't exist when they were born.

The things that make the Internet such a life-enriching resource for young people are the same things that can threaten their privacy and safety. Your children can view X-rated material or gory, frightening images on the Internet; they can exchange casual messages with people who seem to be harmless but who turn out to be criminals or child molesters; they can learn to use profanities and to discuss matters in chat rooms that you would find unsuitable if you were overhearing the same conversation in your presence.

Norton Internet Security includes an optional feature, Parental Control, that enables parents to take some measure of control over the sites their children can visit and the information they give out online. While no software solution can monitor kids all the time, you can at least keep tabs on what your children do online while they are using your computer, by using Parental Control and the other tools and approaches described in this chapter.

Using Norton Parental Control

The single best thing you can do to keep your children safe on the Internet is something that doesn't involve firewalls or other software: It involves spending time with your kids while they're online, explaining how the Internet works. If you can steer them to sites you want them to visit and explain the kinds of dangers they can face online, you'll do more than any software program ever could.

Norton Parental Control, a component of Norton Internet Security, is intended to help when you can't be present at your home computer. You can't be standing behind your son's or daughter's shoulder all the time when they're at the computer, after all. Your kids won't appreciate that, either. Parental Control takes some of the responsibility off your shoulders and defuses the process of telling kids what they can't do online. It lets you identify sites they cannot visit, so you don't have to spell it out for kids all the time. It blocks access to selected Web sites, software applications, and newsgroups so there isn't any question of whether your kids can use them or not; when a site or application is blocked, the kids will hopefully move on to other, more suitable resources.

Your kids' school should be able to help you when it comes to teaching them how to use the Internet and suggest good sites they can visit when they're working on their homework or just having fun. My daughters' school puts out lists of sites it recommends for homework and other activities. Ask your child's teachers if such a list exists.

Enabling Parental Control

By default, Parental Control isn't enabled when you first install Norton Internet Security. Disabling the component conserves computer resources for the many users who don't have children. To start using Parental Control, you first need to enable it. Follow these steps:

1. **Open the main NIS window, and double-click Parental Control.**

    The Parental Control window opens (see Figure 13-1).

2. **Check the box next to Turn On Parental Control.**

    A dialog box bearing the message "Loading Parental Control list, please wait" appears. After a few seconds, the dialog box closes and you return to the Parental Control window.

When Parental Control is enabled, you use the same window to identify users whose access you want to restrict, and identify Web sites you want to restrict. As you might expect, if you ever want to disable Parental Control (for example, if you get a new computer for your children), you uncheck the box next to Turn On Parental Control.

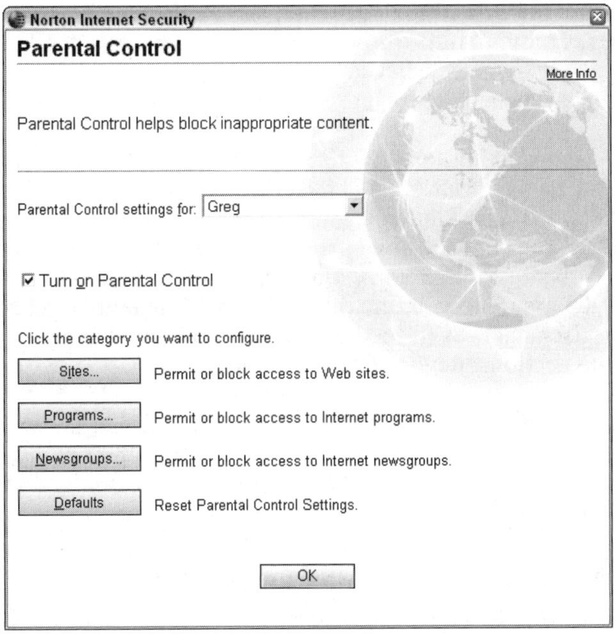

Figure 13-1:
You use this
window to
enable or
disable
Parental
Control.

Identifying users

Parental Control uses lists of restricted Web sites, newsgroups, and resources that are linked to user accounts. Those accounts are set up by you, the program supervisor. Chances are you set up those accounts when you first installed Norton Internet Security.

Note: You were at least *given* the opportunity to set up accounts for yourself and others who will have access to your computer during the installation process. If you were in a hurry during install, you can always create new accounts or change account preferences, as I describe in Chapter 12.

Observing the user account "must-haves"

When users log on to their accounts, Parental Control uses the settings associated with the accounts until the users log off. In order for Parental Control to provide you with any level of protection, you have to observe two basic principles:

✔ **You need to have accounts in place.** Your children need to be identified with Child or Teenager accounts, and you need to have an Adult or Supervisor account.

✔ **You have to log in and log out when you're done.** If you don't log out, your kids can jump in the Internet using your unrestricted Supervisor account. Only by getting in the habit of logging in and logging out can you require your kids to log in themselves and use their restrictions.

When no one is logged in, Norton Internet Security prevents any access to the Internet until a user logs on. As I describe in Chapter 12, user accounts fall into four categories: Child, Teenager, Adult, and Supervisor. Neither Child nor Teenager users can make any changes to NIS's options, including the lists of restricted Web sites and other resources. Whether a child is designated a Child or Teenager is up to you; the difference is in the amount of restrictions placed on the user's access to the Internet. To get an idea of what the difference is, see the section, "Reviewing the restricted list," later in this chapter.

Logging in and out requires dealing with usernames and passwords; make sure your kids know theirs and keep them secret from their siblings. If your 9-year-old is able to use your teenager's account, for example, they can probably gain access to resources you don't want them to use.

Creating accounts with the Parental Control Wizard

Suppose you rushed through the process of creating user accounts during installation, or you want to create a brand-new account for your 7-year-old, who is just beginning to express an interest in going online. Parental Control streamlines the process by guiding you step by step through a series of screens called the Parental Control Wizard. Follow these steps:

1. **From the main NIS window, click the User Accounts subheading under the main heading Norton Internet Security.**

   The User Accounts options appear.

2. **Click the small highlighted <u>Parental Control Wizard</u> link, which appears just beneath the User Accounts heading.**

   The first screen of the Parental Control Wizard opens.

3. **Click Create Norton Internet Security accounts, and then click Next.**

   The Supervisor screen appears. If you have already created a Supervisor password, enter it in the Password and Confirm Password boxes. If not, create one and enter it in the two boxes. Generic dots appear in the two boxes.

   Note: If you already have Windows user accounts for each member of your family, you can identify each individual as a Child, Teenager, or Adult using those accounts. That way, each person has only one username and password to remember. Otherwise, choose Norton Internet Security accounts.

4. **Click Next.**

   The Create Accounts screen appears (see Figure 13-2).

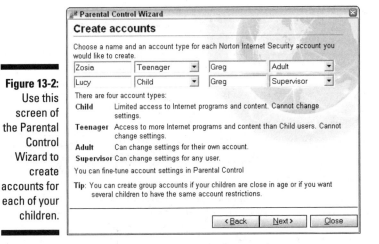

Figure 13-2:
Use this
screen of
the Parental
Control
Wizard to
create
accounts for
each of your
children.

5. **Type the names of each new account you want to create, and select an access level for each from the drop-down list next to each name. Then click Next.**

   The Choose Passwords screen appears.

6. **Type a password for the first of your children and then click Next.**

7. **Repeat Step 6 for each account you want to create and then click Next.**

   The Set Startup Account screen appears.

8. **Click the default account.**

   (You'll probably want to choose your account if you use the account most often, but you can choose Not Logged On, which requires you to log on each time the computer starts up.) The account name is highlighted.

9. **Click Next.**

   The Finished screen appears.

10. **Click Finish to close the wizard and return to the Norton Internet Security main window.**

You may want to encourage your child to suggest a password himself or herself so he or she can remember it more easily. Or select something that your child can figure out easily, such as a nickname, or middle name plus their birth year, or the last two digits of his or her birth year.

Reviewing the restricted list

Parental Control comes with a set of Web sites, newsgroups, and applications already entered on the list of restricted resources. Individuals who are designated with Child accounts won't be able to use those restricted objects. After you create accounts, you can review the list of resources that are restricted. Reviewing the list might give you some ideas for how you can add to it. If you have created different accounts with Child and Teenager access, you can assess the differences between the two and make sure they are suitable choices.

To review the choices, open the Parental Control window, then select one of your children's user account names from the Parental Control Settings For drop-down list. Then click one of the three buttons that list restrictions: Sites (for Web sites), Programs (for applications that let you connect to or use the Internet), or Newsgroups. You may also want to check which sites are blocked for the Supervisor account as well, so your own access is not restricted.

If you click Sites, for example, you may be surprised to see that Parental Control doesn't block access to Web sites by their names but by their contents. By default, a user with Child access has (at this writing; the list may have expanded by the time you read this) 29 categories of sites blocked, ranging from Adult Humor to Weapons. A teenager has 21 categories restricted. Another aspect of the restrictions that may surprise you is that by default, someone with an Adult account has 18 categories restricted. The differences between the three are indicated in Table 13-1. An *X* means that the category is blocked for the corresponding type of user account.

Table 13-1 Default Parental Control Restrictions for User Accounts

Web Site Category	Child	Teenager	Adult
Adult Humor	X	X	X
Alcohol-Tobacco	X	X	X
Anonymous Proxies	X	X	X
Crime	X	X	X
Drugs	X	X	X
Entertainment			
Finance	X		
Gambling	X	X	X
Humor	X		

Web Site Category	Child	Teenager	Adult
Interactive/Chat	X		
Interactive/Mail	X		
Intolerance	X	X	X
Job Search	X		
News	X		
Occult/New Age	X	X	X
Prescription Medicine	X	X	
Real Estate	X	X	
Religion	X	X	
Sex/Sex Education	X	X	X
Travel	X		
Vehicles		X	
Violence	X	X	X
Weapons	X	X	X

It's worth looking at the list for a couple of reasons. Some categories of Web sites are obviously unsuitable for young people, such as Sex/Personals, Intolerance, Weapons, and the like. But some of the categories are very much on the borderline and ones that some people would not consider offensive at all. Do you have a problem with your children viewing real estate sites, for example? Why, you might ask, is the Occult/New Age category blocked, not only for children but also for teenagers and adults?

Creating exceptions

To create exceptions to the list, you can view all the Web sites or other resources in a particular category. As far as I know, you can't view the actual list of Web site URLs or other criteria that Norton Internet Security uses to define one as "humor" and one as "entertainment," for example.

If you know of a Web site that you want to access, however, you can specifically create an exception for that single location. For example, the News category is blocked for children. But if you think it's acceptable to have your son or daughter learn about current events from Yahooligans! News (www.yahooligans.com/content/news), one of several Yahooligans! sites aimed specifically at young people, you can mark it as an exception by following these steps:

1. **Open the Parental Control window as I describe in the section, "Enabling Parental Control," earlier in this chapter.**

2. **Click Sites.**

   The Sites window opens (see Figure 13-3).

Figure 13-3:
Use this
dialog box
to view
blocked
categories
of Web
sites and
make
exceptions
to a
category.

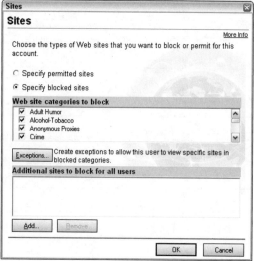

3. **Click Exceptions.**

   The Exceptions dialog box appears. You'll notice right away that the Symantec.com Web site is listed as an exception by default.

4. **Click Add.**

   The Add Web site to Exception List dialog box appears.

5. **Enter the URL of the site you want your kids to see in the Web site Address box (see Figure 13-4).**

   You need only enter a domain name in the Add Web site to Exception List dialog box. A domain name looks like this: `website.edu` or `my company.com`. If you do add a domain name, however, you should be aware that you add every computer that is part of the domain. This could conceivably include computers with names like `computer1.my company.com`, `computer2.mycompany.com`, and so on. If you only want to identify one specific computer as an exception, you can add that computer's fully-qualified domain name: `computer3.mycompany.com`, `www.mycompany.com`, and so on.

Figure 13-4:
Enter the
URL of a
Web site
you want
your kids to
access
in this
dialog box.

Add Web site to Exception List

Add Web site to Exception List

More Info

Web site Address: http://www.yahooligans.com/content/news/

OK   Cancel

6. Click OK three times.

The Add Web Site to Exceptions List, Exceptions, and Sites dialog boxes close and you return to the Parental Control window.

Note: Symantec's own Web site, Symantec.com, is listed as an exception in every category for every type of user account.

Permitting specific Web sites

Parental Control categorizes Web sites by topic. When you add a Web site to the list of restricted sites, it blocks any information from those sites. You can take the opposite approach to controlling the content your kids see online by drawing up a list of sites you specifically want them to access. Drawing up a list of permitted Web sites puts an extra level of responsibility on you — rather than draw from its predetermined list of Web sites to block, Parental Control depends on your list to enable your children to gain access to the Web.

Make sure you're logged in to Norton Internet Security with your supervisor password before you start. Also make sure you choose the child or teenager whose access you want to control in the Parental Control dialog box — not your own user account.

To permit sites, open the Sites window as described in the previous section. Then click Specify Permitted Sites. A dialog box appears, notifying you that the list of blocked sites will not be used, and your children will only be able to connect to the sites you specify. Click OK to close the dialog box.

As you'll notice, the Sites to Permit box, which appears in the Sites dialog box when you click Specify Permitted Sites, is absolutely blank. You need to add the sites one by one, although you can paste a set of URLs you obtain from your children's school or another source, for example. Then click Add, enter the address in the Add Web Site to Permitted List dialog box, and click OK to add each address. When you're done, you'll see a list like the one shown in Figure 13-5.

Figure 13-5:
You can
control your
children's
access
to the
Internet by
specifying
only a few
sites they
can access.

Deciding to permit sites rather than using a restricted set of categories gives
you a greater degree of control over your children's online activities. You can
only limit the number of sites they can see to a select few, for example. But it
makes more work for you because you have to add new sites as they are
identified by you or your kids, and after you approve them.

After you have set up a group of permitted sites, if your son or daughter
attempts to connect to a site that isn't on the list, a message like the one
shown in Figure 13-6 appears.

Figure 13-6:
This
message
lets your
kids know
you have
created
a list of
"accept-
able" sites,
and this site
isn't on
the list.

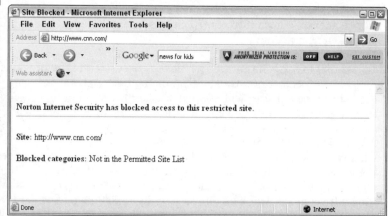

Blocking newsgroups

Newsgroups are blocked in a different way than Web sites. Rather than naming categories of discussion groups that kids cannot access, Parental Control starts with the brief list of words or combinations of words that appear in newsgroups' names. Figure 13-7 shows a brief set of terms.

Figure 13-7: This short list of terms barely begins to cover the thousands of free-wheeling newsgroups on the Internet.

As anyone who has browsed or posted messages on the tens of thousands of newsgroups in Usenet knows, this tiny list of terms barely begins to cover all of the profane, offensive, silly, and inappropriate discussion forums. Most newsgroups are not moderated. Discussions can quickly become profane and confrontational. A far more effective way to control your kids' access to newsgroups is to click Specify Permitted Newsgroups, pick out a few that you want them to access, and add those to the list, rather than relying on Parental Control's meager restricted list.

The concept of permitting rather than restricting applies to newsgroups as well as Web sites.

Blocking applications

Internet applications, like Web sites, are blocked by type rather than specific program names. Instead of preventing your kids from using ICQ or AOL Instant Messenger specifically, you permit or deny access to all instant messaging programs.

Reviewing and adjusting categories

To view and adjust the list of program categories, open the Parental Control window, choose the account you want to review, and then click Programs. The categories in the list are all checked by default, which means they are permitted means of connecting to the Internet for the specified account. By deselecting an option, you block all programs that fall into the selected type.

Table 13-2 shows which types of NIS user accounts can use various Internet applications. The table also provides examples of programs that fall into a particular category. An *X* means the category of applications is permitted for that user account by default.

Table 13-2	Permitted Internet Applications			
Type of Application	Examples	Child	Teenager	Adult
General	Telnet	X	X	X
Chat	ICQ, CU-SeeMe, Net2Phone, Pirch			X
Conferencing & Collaboration	MSN Messenger, Yahoo Messenger, Internet Phone			X
E-mail	Outlook, Eudora, Netscape Messenger	X	X	X
Education & Family	CyberSitter, NetNanny, Eyewitness Children's Encyclopedia	X	X	X
File Transfer	CuteFTP, WS_FTP, Fetch			X
Instant Messaging	ICQ, AOL Instant Messenger, MSN Messenger		X	X
Newsreaders	Agent, Xnews, Outlook Express, Netscape Messenger			X
Networked Games	World Chess, Massive Assault	X	X	X
Web Browsers	Opera, Internet Explorer, Netscape Navigator	X	X	X
User Categories	Any Internet application you designate	X	X	X

NIS's Help files state that users with Child accounts can only use Web browsers, E-mail programs, and General applications by default. But I was surprised to find that Networked Games was allowed by default. You may not want your own children to play violent networked games with other kids online (an activity that uses up a lot of bandwidth); be sure you review what's allowed before you let your Child account user online.

If you don't want your kids to have the ability to send and receive e-mail, be aware that simply deselecting the E-mail category won't do it. Your kids can still use Web-based e-mail interfaces like Hotmail or Yahoo Mail to exchange messages. They can also play many games using their Web browsers.

Adding items to user categories

You can gain a much finer level of control over the applications your children use to connect to the Internet by grouping selected programs into user categories. A user category is a container into which you can place any application you have in your file system. By blocking all of the applications that normally fit into a category, you can select a different application and put it in a user category, thus forcing your kids to use that one instead.

To assign an application to a user category, you need to close Parental Control and open Personal Firewall:

1. **From the main NIS window, double-click Personal Firewall.**

   The Personal Firewall options appear.

2. **Click Programs.**

   The Program Control options jump to the front. Wait a few seconds for your list of available programs to appear in the box at the bottom of the window.

3. **Select a program.**

   The program's name is highlighted in the list of applications.

4. **Single-click the current category for the application, and choose User Category 1 or User Category 2 from the list of categories that pops up (see Figure 13-8).** (These are arbitrary category names; you can add any applications you want to them.)

5. **Click OK.**

   Program Control closes and you return to the main NIS window.

After you assign a program to a user category, it isn't included in the category it was previously in. For example, adding Internet Explorer to a user category takes it out of the Web browser category; you can use this to block all browsers but permit access with Internet Explorer, for example.

Figure 13-8:
Assign an
application
to a user
category
using
Program
Control.

Blocking personal information

After you establish user accounts for your children, it's a good idea to review the personal information that is blocked for each one. Even if you specified the types of information that shouldn't go out on the Internet when you first installed NIS, it doesn't hurt to double-check to make sure your son or daughter doesn't give out a phone number or address when they access one of the Web sites or newsgroups you have permitted them to use. Follow these steps:

1. **Open the main NIS window and double-click Privacy Control.**

   The Privacy Control window opens.

2. **Choose the user whose account you want to adjust.**

   The username appears in the Privacy Control Settings For drop-down list.

3. **Click Private Information.**

   The Private Information dialog box appears.

4. **Review the information that you want to prohibit.**

   Depending on the user, you may want to remove most if not all of the details. Select one of the items and click Remove to remove it from the list. Click Add to add new information to the list.

5. **Click OK.**

   The Private Information dialog box closes and you return to the Privacy Control window.

6. **Repeat Steps 2 through 5 for each of your children's user accounts.**

Adding or removing prohibited private information should serve as a backup to your verbal instructions to your children. Remind your kids to maintain your family's privacy and be selective about what they tell and who they tell it to online.

Symantec updates the list of blocked Web sites regularly. Run LiveUpdate often to ensure that you have the most updated list.

Viewing Web History

The more you're aware of what your children do, the less likely they are to get into trouble. That's a huge generalization, of course, but it's one that holds true when it comes to the Internet — based on my experience, at least. The rules you learned from your parents apply: Don't talk to strangers, don't take candy from a stranger, and so on. If kids know from you what constitutes a suitable or unsuitable online resource and they hear it from you personally, they're more likely, in my opinion, to follow those guidelines when they access the Net at the library, at school, at a friend's house, or another location.

While you do need to trust your kids to behave responsibly online, you can also take a peek behind the scenes and check where they've gone online, as described in the sections that follow.

Spying on surfing activity

After your kids have been at your computer for a while, you can trace their steps (assuming they haven't deleted those traces, of course). It can give you an idea of the sites your kids have viewed online so you can determine whether or not to bring up how they use the Internet and what they do there — or whether you need to add some new sites to your lists of the locations that are specifically blocked.

In Microsoft Internet Explorer, click the History toolbar button and then scan the list of pages that your kids and other computer users have viewed (see Figure 13-9).

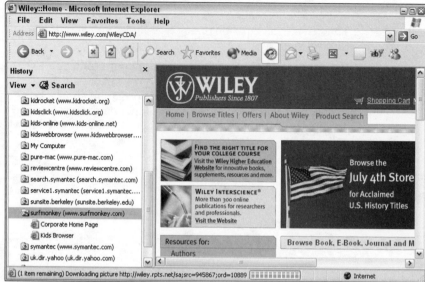

Figure 13-9:
Scan the list
of pages in
the History
pane to see
where your
kids have
been in the
recent past.

In Netscape Navigator, choose Tools⇨History or press Ctrl+H to view the
Web pages visited recently. Another folder, Cache, holds records of recently
viewed Web pages. If the History window can't be used for some reason or is
empty, you can locate the Cache folder in the Internet Options window
(Internet Explorer) or the Preferences window (Netscape Navigator). But it's
difficult to make sense of what you're seeing. First of all, the files stored in
cache don't have names that tell you much. They look like this:

```
02C589D3d01
4D34E101d01
8C808FE2d01
```

You can open a cache file in a browser window, but you'll only see bits of Web
pages — individual images, or ad banners. The cache file might indicate what
type of content was viewed, but there is no indication who viewed it.

Note: Your children have the ability to delete your Web browser's history and
cache files just the way you do; if they take the time to clear out these folders, you won't be able to see where they have been in a particular session. If
you do notice that they have deleted the History or cache files, it may be the
first sign that you need to monitor their online activities more closely.

Monitoring other online activity

Tracing someone's Web surfing activity is relatively easy. When it comes to
e-mail, chat, or newsgroup postings, things are more complicated. Chat and
instant messaging communications leave virtually no trace on your computer

(unless you have installed software that has the ability to record such messages). E-mail stays in an inbox, Sent Items, or Deleted Items folder unless the user empties those folders. If you're seriously concerned about what your kids are doing online, you can install software that literally keeps an eye on them, as though you are looking over their shoulder.

Programs like SpectorPro by Spector Software (`www.spectorsoft.com/products/SpectorPro_Windows/entry.asp`) can almost be classified as spyware because they record your kids' e-mails, chats, and individual keystrokes as well as taking screen images. A program with the intimidating name IamBigBrother (`www.worldvillage.com/follow/bigbrother.html`) can record chat and instant messaging sessions as well as e-mail messages. If you install any of these applications, be sure they are installed so that only the administrator can disable them. Otherwise, your tech-savvy kids will find a way around them.

Be careful when deciding to monitor the online activity of spouses, significant others, roommates, or friends. In states with community property laws, someone could sue you if they find you have been snooping on their Internet activity without their approval.

Password Protection

Another way to supplement your use of filtering, blocking, and "footstep-tracking" software is the use of effective passwords to protect files you don't want your children to see. You can protect individual files or your entire computer.

Password-protecting files and folders

If you use Pretty Good Privacy, a personal encryption application described in Chapter 19, you gain the ability to encrypt virtually any type of application in your file system. But chances are most of the documents you don't want your kids to see are spreadsheets, word processing documents, schedules, business presentations, and the like. If you use Microsoft Office to create those files, you can take advantage of the ability to password-protect documents created by each of the programs:

1. **Open the document that you want to password protect and choose File⇨Save As.**

   The Save As dialog box opens.

2. **Click Tools in the menu bar of the Save As dialog box, and choose General Options.**

   The Save dialog box opens.

3. **Type a password in the Password to Open and Password to Modify boxes (see Figure 13-10).**

4. **Click OK.**

   The Save dialog box closes.

Figure 13-10: You can assign a password to protect Microsoft Office files.

After you password-protect a document, you will be prompted to enter your password whenever you open it or try to save it with a new name.

You can also assign a password to an Office file by choosing Tools⇨Options, clicking Save, and entering the password in the Password to Open or Password to Modify box. Office passwords will only deter casual users; many kids will be able to download and install decryption software that can uncover such passwords.

Password-protecting your computer

It may seem obvious, but many Windows users overlook the need to create a secure password so they log on to their computer with their own account name when the system starts up. Many users choose an obvious password such as Administrator, or use no password at all. The system logon password is not encrypted, but it adds a level of security to your computer and makes it a little bit harder for a hacker (or a young person) to gain unauthorized access.

To create a password or change the one you have currently (it's a good idea to change the password on a regular basis), choose Start⇨Control Panel, double-click User Accounts, and click Create a New Account. Then follow the steps presented in subsequent screens of User Accounts.

Note: The preceding steps assume that you have Administrator-level privileges on your computer or that you have already logged on as the Administrator.

Choosing Kid-Friendly Software

Sometimes, the best way to control what your kids see online is to point them to resources that are designed especially for them. If you can get them in the habit of visiting the Web with the help of Surf Monkey's specially designed Web browser (www.surfmonkey.com), they'll have fun going online and also avoid content you don't want them to see. Some other suggestions for browsers and search engines that can literally point them in the right direction are described in the sections that follow.

Web browsers

For kids as well as adults, Web browsers are the software of choice on the Internet. Restricting Web sites or listing "permitted" Web sites is one way to control what your kids see online. You can achieve an even stronger level of control by making your children use a Web browser that is designed to steer them to authorized Web pages so they cannot stumble onto X-rated or other Web sites.

If you remove your normal Web browser to NIS's list of permitted applications, and add a special kid-friendly Web browser to one of the User Categories (see "Blocking applications," earlier in this chapter), you can force your kids to use your program of choice to go online. AmiWeb (www.midmultimedia.com/Mid_DW/en/home.htm) uses music and colorful graphics to entertain kids as they visit approved educational sites. One of the nicest things about the freeware browser KidRocket (www.kidrocket.org) is a built-in timer that enables you to set a time limit for the length of time your children's Internet session can last.

If you use the Macintosh OS, try KidsBrowser (www.adnx.com/kidsbrowser.html), which is available for $35, or BumperCar (www.freeverse.com/bumpercar/index.html), which is available for $49. Both applications are available in demo versions so you can try them out.

Search engines

Kids often connect to the Internet to look up a fact or download a photo for a homework assignment. They quickly find that search engines provide a convenient gateway to such information. The problem with using many search engines is that results for even the most harmless searches can include links to sites that are "adult" in nature. With a single click, your kids can suddenly be staring at sites (not to mention sights) that you would never want them to see. Some search engines are designed especially for young people. They block links to X-rated or "adult" content. Some of the best-known examples are:

- Yahooligans! (http://yahooligans.yahoo.com)
- Ask Jeeves (www.ajkids.com)
- AOL@School (www.aolatschool.com/elementary/search/browse.adp)
- CyberSleuth Kids (http://cybersleuth-kids.com)
- KidsClick! (http://sunsite.berkeley.edu/KidsClick!)

While some of these search services are run by commercial sites hoping to attract younger users, KidsClick! is operated by librarians working in both New York and Colorado. All of the sites work by maintaining a database of Web sites that are considered appropriate for children, and steering kids to them.

Plenty of search engines cover specific resources rather than the entire Internet. KidsWeb (www.mcpl.lib.mo.us/KidsWeb) and Homework Planet (www.homeworkplanet.com), for instance, specialize in homework resources. You'll find a meta-search engine (a list of search engines and other Web sites) intended specifically for children at www.ivyjoy.com/rayne/kidssearch.html.

Part V
Getting Under the Hood

The 5th Wave   By Rich Tennant

"I'm sure there will be a good job market when I graduate. I created a virus that will go off that year."

In this part . . .

*N*orton Internet Security isn't a simple piece of software. The fact that it consists of a group of separate programs makes it more complex than a single application. You need to keep the software up to date and to adjust configurations to keep up with different networks and new applications you want to use.

This part examines all of the tasks that can be contained under the topic troubleshooting. That includes recovering when the program crashes, when your computer won't function, or when it slows down. But it also covers how to prevent trouble and keep the software and the rest of your computer running smoothly. You find out how to use the program's Help system and how to keep your file system clean, too.

Norton Personal Firewall generates extensive log files that record the traffic that passes through your network gateway. Finally, you discover how to read log files and use them to track attackers or even to prepare reports that you can use in a business environment to help improve security in the workplace.

Chapter 14

Troubleshooting

. . . .

In This Chapter

▶ Restoring connectivity in case you can't access the Internet

▶ Solving problems with starting up or viewing Norton Internet Security

▶ Smoothing out speed bumps with individual components

▶ Uninstalling and reinstalling NIS when all else fails

▶ Finding help within the NIS interface and on the Internet

. . . .

Security programs that perform a single type of function are complex. Even a single standalone firewall application that you download for free and try to use can cause problems. You may have trouble getting reconnected to the Internet; applications may stop working. It's the nature of security programs to be complex because they're configured to react to an ever-changing series of threats. They generate log files, they review rules and signatures, and they store critical information in the Windows registry.

Norton Internet Security users can and do run into problems because the program consists of multiple components that need to work simultaneously, and because those components are configured to perform so many functions automatically. As part of installation, program information is installed in the registry, in your Documents and Settings folder, and in the Windows or WINNT directory. If you do encounter a problem with Norton Internet Security, remember two things:

  ✔ Respond in a systematic way. If Symantec provides instructions directly or on its Web site, or if you're following steps in this book, follow them step by step.

  ✔ Be patient and don't give up. Judging from comments left on various Internet message boards, many users who run into a problem simply uninstall the software and move to a shareware program that's not as full-featured.

The fact that the program is divided into separate components means that you may have problems with one function while others continue to work smoothly. In this chapter, I look first at problems that affect all of NIS's components; then, in separate sections, I examine how to troubleshoot problems with AntiVirus, Personal Firewall, AntiSpam, and other applications.

Unblocking Network Communications

One of the most common problems with firewalls is lack of connectivity — the inability to "see" computers on your local network through Network Neighborhood or My Network Places; the inability to connect to a shared folder on another computer; or sudden loss of connectivity to the Internet. Usually, the reason is that the firewall is too restrictive by treating your local computers as though they are potential attackers rather than trusted hosts. In my experience, Norton Internet Security 2004 is much smarter than earlier versions of the software. It doesn't block connections to other computers and it knows which applications regularly access the Internet. But if you do run into connectivity issues, try the approaches I describe in the following sections.

Another reason exists for loss of connectivity. Some hackers take advantage of Microsoft's own networking protocols in order to access shared network resources: If they can break into one computer on a network, they can use File and Printer Sharing for Microsoft Networks to gain access to other devices. If you don't share a printer with other computers, you should disable File and Print Sharing. If you do, you need to add your other networked computers to your Trusted Zone as described later in this chapter.

You're unable to connect to a Web site

The Web is likely to be the part of the Internet you use most frequently (with e-mail a close second). The inability to connect to the Net at all, or view some of the content on a Web page, after you install Norton Internet Security, can be frustrating. Don't be surprised if the problem shows up on some Web pages but not others. Some sites emphasize the use of Web scripting languages like Java and JavaScript, and Norton Personal Firewall may be blocking them. Some sites require the use of cookies, and Norton Privacy Control may be blocking them. Other sites display ads that AntiSpam may be blocking. The following sections describe some ways to unblock the site's content.

Making sure Internet Connection Firewall is disabled

If you can't connect to the Internet at all, one of the first things to check is the status of Windows' built-in firewall. It's useful for blocking ping sweeps from external computers, but it offers a much less fine-grained level of control.

Most important, it interferes with Norton Internet Security. See Chapter 2 for more about how to verify whether ICF is running and how to disable the program if needed.

Connecting through a proxy server

Another reason your connection to the Internet may be totally blocked is a conflict with a proxy server. A proxy server is software that acts on behalf of your browser, e-mail, or other software and processes requests for information to and from a server. The proxy server receives a request to connect to a mail server or a Web server and rebuilds the information in the individual packets for security reasons. When the packets are forwarded by the proxy server, they bear the IP address of the proxy server rather than the originating computer. The external computer is thus unable to determine the actual IP address of the computer making the request, which provides for a high level of security.

Proxy servers are most common in business networks, where security is at a premium and network administrators are available to perform maintenance and configuration, rather than in home networks. The problem is that, if you have a proxy server processing all of your requests to and from Web sites, e-mail servers, and other servers, it can interfere with NIS's operation. Most of the time, proxy servers don't cause problems. But if you access Web sites only after long delays, you do need to check for proxy server problems and adjust NIS's settings.

First, you need to make sure the proxy server is the source of the trouble. If NIS is forwarding your requests to Web sites through the proxy server, the data you download from the remote site will pass through the firewall. To verify that files are actually downloading, follow these steps:

1. **Open the main NIS window and click Statistics under the Norton Internet Security heading on the left-hand side.**

   The Statistics options appear.

2. **Click Detailed Statistics.**

   The Norton Internet Security Statistics window appears (see Figure 14-1).

3. **Note the TCP Bytes Sent in the Network section.**

   If the number is large, just make note of the last three or four digits.

4. **Switch to your Web browser, and enter a URL in the Address box, then press Enter to connect to a Web site.**

5. **Switch back to Norton Internet Security Statistics (which has its own toolbar).**

   The Statistics window jumps to the front of your screen.

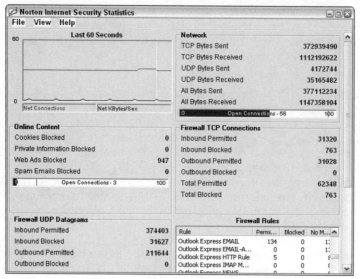

Figure 14-1:
If you think
your proxy
server is
slowing or
blocking
connections,
track the
transfer rate
in this
window.

6. Make note of the TCP Bytes Sent.

> The number should be higher than it was previously. For example, Figure 14-1 shows a TCP Bytes Sent total of 372939490. After connecting to Google's Web site, the number changed to 374694127.

An increase in the number of TCP Bytes Sent means Norton Personal Firewall is processing Web page data through the proxy server correctly. If it remains the same, it means that NIS is not monitoring the correct port — in other words, the port that your proxy server uses to connect to the Web. You need to determine what port is being used, and you do that by using NIS's log files.

I discuss using log files in Chapter 16, and you should look there for details on how to open and interpret the files. But if you open the main window, click Statistics, click View Logs, and click Connections, you should be able to view (in the column labeled Remote Service Port) the port number and IP address of the site you connected to. In Figure 14-2, the Connections log shows a number of current Web page connections using port 8080, a port commonly used by proxy servers.

If you look at your own Connections log files, you are likely to see port 80 listed in the Remote Service Port column. This is the port normally assigned to Web servers that need to connect to remote Web browsers that do not have a proxy server protecting them. Proxy servers use ports such as 8080, 8090, 8105, 8110, 8120, or others in the 8000–8500 range. The Internet Assigned Numbers Authority maintains a list of ports and applications at www.iana.org/assignments/port-numbers.

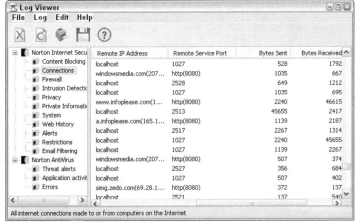

Figure 14-2:
If you
identify the
port being
used to
connect to
your proxy
server, you
can adjust
Personal
Firewall to
work with it.

After you identify the port your proxy is making available to remote Web sites, you need to configure Personal Firewall to work with it:

1. **From the main NIS window, click Options, and select Norton Internet Security from the drop-down list.**

   The Norton Internet Security Options dialog box appears.

2. **Click the Firewall tab.**

   The firewall options appear.

3. **Scan the list of ports in the HTTP port list box (as shown in Figure 14-3.**

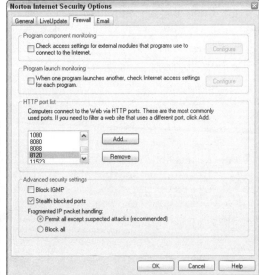

Figure 14-3:
Verify
whether the
port your
computer is
using is on
the list of
HTTP proxy
ports.

4. **Click Add if necessary to add your proxy port.**

   The Norton Internet Security dialog box appears (see Figure 14-4).

5. **Click OK.**

   The dialog box closes and you return to the Options dialog box, where the new port is listed.

6. **Click OK.**

   The Options dialog box closes and you return to the main NIS window.

The ports listed in the HTTP Port List box are the ones that Norton Personal Firewall will allow remote Web sites to use. If your proxy server's port isn't listed, it is being blocked.

Figure 14-4:
Add a proxy
port so
Personal
Firewall can
monitor it for
connections.

Norton Internet Security

Port to monitor:

8120

[OK]   [Cancel]

Changing security settings for a site

Sometimes, Web sites just don't appear in your Web browser window. Either the entire Web page is blank, or part of the page doesn't work. If that's the case, check your Privacy Control settings for that site to see if the site is listed. It may be that Privacy Control is preventing the site from leaving a cookie on your computer, or preventing scripts from being executed on the remote Web page.

Note: Some Web sites require referrer information (the IP address or domain name of the site you visited immediately before visiting their site) to function properly, especially sites that require you to log in. If you're having problems using or viewing all of the content on a site, you may need to configure NIS to allow referrer information to be passed for a domain.

To see whether the problem site has settings that may be blocking some content, double-click Privacy Control in the main NIS window and then click Advanced. The Advanced dialog box opens, where you can view the list of sites under Web Contents options. If your "problem" site is listed, select it by single-clicking its domain name. Check the settings under Global Settings and change them if one of the following situations applies:

✔ If you're unable to view an animated image, check Permit. (You may have to deselect Use Default Settings first; this applies to other options as well.)

✔ If you can't view a Flash animation, select Permit under that setting.

✔ If you can't view any content, it may be that the site cannot determine what type of browser you are using. (The content may be tailored to different browsers.) Select Permit under Information About Your Browser.

With the site still selected, also click the User Settings tab in the Advanced dialog box. This tab allows you to select Permit to permit the site to leave a cookie on your computer or execute a Java applet if needed.

For more information on Privacy Control and the Advanced dialog box settings, see Chapter 10.

Some investment sites use streaming stock tickers to provide real-time investment information. If these features don't function, it may mean that the site's content is subject to content blocking, ad blocking, or intrusion detection. Simply adding a firewall rule for the program may not repair it. Open the Advanced dialog box and check to see whether the site has ads, JavaScript scripts, Java applets, or other content being blocked.

If you cannot connect to a secure Web site

If you are unable to connect to or log on to secure Web sites with Norton Internet Security running, the problem may not be with NIS itself. Such a problem was fixed with an earlier version of NIS. There may be a problem with your Web browser. However, you can still verify that NIS is able to work with secure Web connections:

1. **From the main NIS window, double-click Privacy Control.**

   The Privacy Control window opens.

2. **Click Custom Level.**

   The Customize Privacy Settings dialog box appears.

3. **Make sure the Enable Secure Connections (https) box is checked. Also check the setting under Private Information. If it is set to High, select Medium from the drop-down list.**

4. **Click OK to close the Customize Privacy Settings dialog box, and click OK again to close the Privacy Control window.**

   You return to the main NIS window.

5. **Choose File⇨Exit to close your Web browser if it is open.**

   Your browser closes.

6. **Restart your browser and attempt to connect to the secure site you want to reach.**

If adjusting Privacy Control doesn't work, check your browser's level of encryption. In Internet Explorer, choose Tools⇨Internet Options, click Advanced, and make sure the boxes next to SSL are checked. In Netscape Navigator, choose Edit⇨Preferences, click Privacy & Security, click SSL, and make sure the boxes next to SSL are checked.

A Microsoft Knowledge Base article, `http://support.microsoft.com/ default.aspx?scid=kb;EN-US;q261328`, addresses a problem with the level of encryption in Internet Explorer. This problem may be preventing you from accessing secure Web sites. The cause is that some missing files cause the browser's strength of encryption (called cipher strength) to appear as 0-bit or, essentially, zero. The article shows you how to check your browser's cipher strength and install the missing files.

Problems starting up NIS

You're probably used to having several different options at your disposal for starting up. If the Norton Internet Security and/or Norton AntiVirus icons do not appear in your Windows system tray, or if you are unable to access the NIS configuration options, it can be alarming. Try the approaches I describe in the following sections.

Checking System Configuration

Make sure NIS is set to run when Windows starts up. Choose Start⇨Run, type **msconfig**, and click OK. When the System Configuration Utility window opens, click the Startup tab. Make sure the boxes next to ccApp (which is used by Symantec applications) and UrlLstCk (which is used by Norton Internet Security) are checked. Then click Services, and make sure all of the services needed by NIS — those that begin with Symantec or Norton — are selected. Then click OK to close the System Configuration Utility window, and restart your computer.

Checking the date and time

Make sure your computer is displaying the correct date and time. If your computer's clock is set years in the future by mistake, it can fool NIS into thinking that your subscription has expired. Double-click the time in your system tray and double-check the settings in the Date and Time Properties dialog box.

Configuring NIS to start automatically

Make sure NIS is configured to start automatically, not manually. Choose Start⇨ Control Panel, click Performance and Maintenance, double-click Administrative Tools, and double-click Component Services. When the Component Services window opens, click Services (Local). In the list of services, scan the list for all Symantec services, and make sure the setting under Startup Type is set to Automatic. Restart your computer.

If none of these options works after restart, you have to uninstall and reinstall Norton Internet Security as described in Chapter 15.

Problems with Individual Components

If you encounter problems using AntiVirus, AntiSpam, or Ad Blocking, you may need to change the way the component starts up or operates. You can try one of the approaches described in the sections that follow.

AntiVirus problems

Probably the most basic problem you can have with Norton AntiVirus is failure of the program icon to appear in the Windows system tray. If you don't see the icon present, it means the component is not automatically scanning e-mail messages, word processing documents, and other files for viruses. In other words, you aren't protected from virus infection unless you manually run a virus scan.

The problem may be that Windows does not have AntiVirus configured to run automatically or to start up when the computer starts up. The section "Problems starting up NIS," earlier in this chapter, addresses that issue. Alternatively, AntiVirus may not be configured to run the Auto-Protect feature automatically on system startup. To check this:

1. **From the main NIS window, click Options, and select Norton AntiVirus from the drop-down list.**

   The Norton AntiVirus Options window appears.

2. **Click Auto-Protect in the list of categories on the left-hand side of the Norton AntiVirus Options window, if necessary.**

   The Auto-Protect options appear.

3. **Make sure the three boxes under the heading How to Stay Protected are checked (Enable Auto-Protect, Start Auto-Protect When Windows Starts Up, and Show the Auto-Protect Icon in the Tray).**

4. **Click OK.**

   The Norton AntiVirus Options window closes and you return to the main NIS window.

Another problem occurs when a file keeps infecting your files even after Norton AntiVirus scans your computer. The file may be on a floppy disk or a network share; remove any floppy disks and run a virus scan on any shared network computers to see if that removes the virus.

You can also increase the range of files AntiVirus looks for when it conducts a scan. Open the Norton AntiVirus Options window, as described in the preceding set of steps. Click Manual Scan in the list on the left-hand side of the window. Click Bloodhound to display the Bloodhound virus scanning options. Click the button next to Highest Level of Protection, and click OK. Then run a virus scan and repair any infected files you encounter.

If AntiVirus is unable to repair the viruses it detects, run LiveUpdate to obtain the latest set of virus definitions. It may be that AntiVirus doesn't have a set of definitions that includes the problems you are encountering.

Spam and e-mail weaknesses

If you're unable to receive or send e-mail messages at all, Personal Firewall may be the culprit. Make sure your firewall isn't blocking communications on Post Office Protocol (POP) port 110, or your ISP isn't blocking e-mail because it is coming from Norton Internet Security rather than your computer.

Outgoing mails require port 25, which is assigned to Simple Mail Transfer Protocol (SMTP). Make sure NIS is not blocking it. Review your firewall advanced rules to make sure none are blocking this port. To verify that your computer can use this port (or port 110), you need to obtain the IP address of your outgoing e-mail server. You may have to ask your Internet Service Provider for the IP address, or possibly get the address from your ISP's Web site. When you have the address, follow these steps:

1. **Choose Start⇨Run.**

   The Run dialog box opens.

2. **Type** telnet **in the Open dialog box, then click OK.**

   The Microsoft Telnet window opens, with the prompt Microsoft Telnet>.

3. **Type the IP address of the server followed by > 25 (that's the greater than sign, followed by a blank space, followed by the number 25).**

   For example:

   ```
   207.182.88.23> 25
   ```

4. **Press Enter.**

   If telnet is able to connect to the server, the problem is not with your firewall. If you are unable to connect, disable Norton Internet Security temporarily and try to download your e-mail. If you can download the e-mail when NIS is off but not when it is on, review your firewall logs in detail to see if port 25 is being blocked.

5. **When you're done, type** quit **or the letter** q, **and press Enter.**

The command prompt window closes.

Some ISPs block e-mail that comes from other ISPs on port 25. You may be able to change your SMTP port to 24 instead to circumvent this problem.

Ad blocking problems

On certain Web pages, you may be unable to view advertisements, such as banner ads that appear on the top of a page or along the side. The blocking of ads manifests itself in different ways in Internet Explorer. You might see a completely blank space where the ad would be. Or you see a link that says "click here" (this may appear if the ad was supposed to link to a Web site). If you click that link, it brings you to a page that says "Action canceled. Internet Explorer was unable to link to the Web page you requested."

To see whether Ad Blocking is preventing the ads from appearing (which is likely), open the Advanced dialog box as described in the previous section. Check the list of sites on the left-hand side of the Advanced dialog box for the one that isn't displaying entirely. If you see the site, select it and click Ad Blocking. If Block rather than Permit appears in the Action column (see Figure 14-5), ads are being blocked on the site.

Figure 14-5: If Ad Blocking is preventing you from seeing Web content, you can change that site's ad specification to Permit.

To stop the blocking, click Add to display the Add New HTML String dialog box. Click Permit, then enter all or part of the URL that the site uses for its ad. Then click OK to close the dialog box, and OK to close the Advanced dialog box.

Finding Help

If you encounter a question you can't answer, you can turn to several sources for help. You can always call Symantec's support staff by going to the Symantec Support page (www.symantec.com/techsupp/support_options.html). You can visit the page any time, but visit between 6 a.m. and 5 p.m. PST if you want an immediate response to your call. Click Fee-based Technical Support, choose your version of NIS, and call one of the support numbers provided. The service isn't free by any means. Even though you are a registered user, you have to pay $29.95 per incident. But with the help of this book, NIS's own built-in Help files, and other online resources, you should be able to find the answer you're looking for without having to shell out the big bucks.

Exploring NIS's Help files

One of the most obvious places to turn to for help is NIS's built-in Help system. And the place to turn to access that system is the Help & Support button in the upper-right-hand corner of the main NIS window. When you click the button, a drop-down list appears; select Norton Internet Security Help to open the Symantec Help Center window.

The organization of NIS's Help application resembles that of Windows' own Help system. You can find information by clicking one of three tabs on the left-hand side of the Symantec Help Center window:

- ✔ **Contents.** Drill down through a series of categories and subcategories to find what you want.

- ✔ **Index.** Scroll through an alphabetical index of terms. If you enter a word in the Type In the Keyword to Find box at the top of the Index tab, you'll jump immediately to that part of the list.

- ✔ **Search.** Choose this option when you are looking for a definition or explanation relating to a specific feature or term and you don't see a reference to it in Contents or Index.

The Symantec Help Center window is generally a good source of information. But when you can't find what you want in the Help files, scan the link at the bottom of a Help page; it will take you to a related Help topic. Or click on a link that is highlighted and that has the hyperlink icon next to it (the icon resembles a link in a chain), as shown in Figure 14-6.

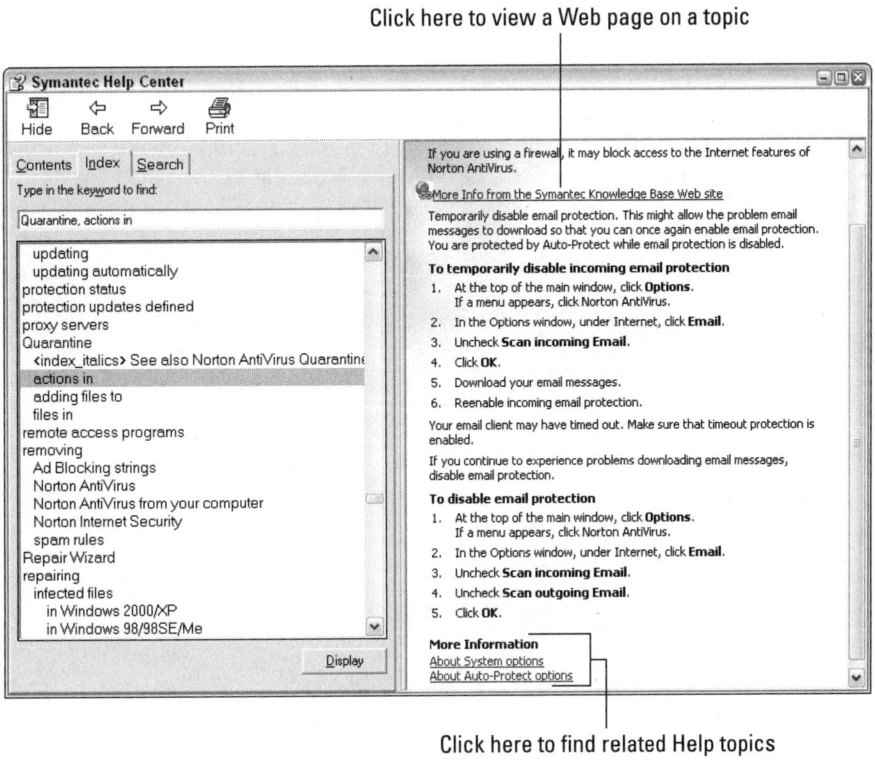

Click here to view a Web page on a topic

Symantec Help Center

Hide Back Forward Print

Contents | Index | Search

Type in the keyword to find:

Quarantine, actions in

updating
updating automatically
protection status
protection updates defined
proxy servers
Quarantine
  <index_italics> See also Norton AntiVirus Quarantine
  actions in
  adding files to
  files in
remote access programs
removing
  Ad Blocking strings
  Norton AntiVirus
  Norton AntiVirus from your computer
  Norton Internet Security
  spam rules
Repair Wizard
repairing
  infected files
    in Windows 2000/XP
    in Windows 98/98SE/Me

Display

If you are using a firewall, it may block access to the Internet features of Norton AntiVirus.

More Info from the Symantec Knowledge Base Web site

Temporarily disable email protection. This might allow the problem email messages to download so that you can once again enable email protection. You are protected by Auto-Protect while email protection is disabled.

To temporarily disable incoming email protection
1. At the top of the main window, click **Options**.
   If a menu appears, click Norton AntiVirus.
2. In the Options window, under Internet, click **Email**.
3. Uncheck **Scan incoming Email**.
4. Click **OK**.
5. Download your email messages.
6. Reenable incoming email protection.

Your email client may have timed out. Make sure that timeout protection is enabled.

If you continue to experience problems downloading email messages, disable email protection.

To disable email protection
1. At the top of the main window, click **Options**.
   If a menu appears, click Norton AntiVirus.
2. In the Options window, under Internet, click **Email**.
3. Uncheck **Scan incoming Email**.
4. Uncheck **Scan outgoing Email**.
5. Click **OK**.

More Information
About System options
About Auto-Protect options

Figure 14-6:
A Help page contains links to related topics, both on the Web and in the Help system itself.

Click here to find related Help topics

After you explore the Help system, take a moment to acquaint yourself with some of the other options under the Help & Support drop-down list. They're easy to overlook in your hurry to open the Help window, yet they can provide assistance in special situations:

✔ **Product Registration.** If you need to change your address, phone number, or other registration information, select this option. The My Profile dialog box opens, where you can choose a product and change your information for it.

✔ **Symantec Help and Support.** Select this option to connect to the opening page of Symantec's support area. You can choose the fee-based telephone option or browse the site's support documents, which are described in the section "Finding answers on the Web," later in this chapter.

✔ **Symantec Response Center.** Select this option and you connect to the Symantec Security Response page, which reports on the latest virus threats and offers repair tools for them.

Trying context-sensitive help

Using Symantec's own Help system is so easy that you may overlook context-sensitive help. When you're looking at an Options window or other dialog box that is part of NIS's interface, and you're scratching your head wondering, "What do I do now?" or "What does *that* mean?" click the tiny More Info link. This link usually appears near the upper-right-hand corner of the window. A Help window opens with information about that specific topic (see Figure 14-7).

Click here to get context–sensitive help

Figure 14-7:
Context-sensitive help opens when you click a Help link in a program window.

Finding answers on the Web

A number of Web sites specialize in answering computer user's questions about troubleshooting and efficiently using their software. The following suggestions list some resources you can visit.

Symantec.com

Symantec's own help resources have been mentioned elsewhere in this book. Frankly, if the Symantec help files were easier to access and use, there wouldn't be a need for books like this. There isn't a hierarchical category list of help files, and no way to limit a search to a specific version of NIS; not only that, you can only access the help documents after having the site detect what version of the software you are using.

1. **Choose Help & Support⇨Symantec Help and Support.**

   The Symantec Support page (`www.symantec.com/techsupp/`) opens in your browser window.

2. **Click Continue under the heading Home and Home Office/Small Business.**

3. **Click Automated Support Assistant under the heading Free Technical Support.**

   The Automated Support Assistant page appears.

   You may see an alert dialog box stating that you need to install and run an application called Symantec Support Utilities. Accept the signed application when prompted to do so. You may also see an alert stating that you have an old version of LiveUpdate even though your version was recently installed. You don't necessarily need to respond to this message.

4. **Click Norton Internet Security.**

   The Automated Support Assistant page appears with a message stating your software version is being detected. Then a page appears stating that Norton Internet Security 2004 has been detected.

5. **Scroll down to the bottom of the page and click the Continue to Free Technical Support button.**

   The support page appears.

6. **Enter a search term in the box that appears beneath the heading Search the Knowledge Base.**

   Then click Search or press Enter.

When the search results appear, you wonder why your software had to be detected: The search results cover virtually all versions of Norton Internet Security, Norton AntiVirus, and Norton Personal Firewall released in the last several years, and there is no way to sort through the results to make them more focused.

 If you want to bypass the preceding steps, go directly to `www.symantec.com/techsupp/nis/nis_2004_tasks.html`. The value of following the steps is that the Automated Support Assistant can detect whether you need a new version of LiveUpdate or other components.

Google Answers

Norton Internet Security occasionally comes up among the answers provided in the Google Answers service (http://answers.google.com). If you want to ask your own question, you have to follow a quirky system: You set the price you are willing to pay for the answer. The advantage of paying is that you don't have to set a very high price, and the incentive of money is likely to attract people who can actually help you.

Before you ask, however, first search the site to see if someone has already received an answer to the same question that's on your fingertips. Enter Norton Internet Security in the box labeled Search Google Answers For, click Google Search, and start exploring the answers to see if one addresses your own question. You'll probably find that there are dozens of answers pertaining to Norton Internet Security already.

Chapter 15

This Old Computer: Housekeeping and Restoration

*N*orton Internet Security's primary goal is to block viruses and intrusions and maintain your privacy. One way you can help is by keeping your computer running smoothly. By blocking ads, unwanted connections, and other harmful software, you ensure that you'll be able to do what you want and work efficiently when you sit down at your keyboard. When you keep NIS running smoothly, you keep your computer running smoothly, too.

Obtaining the Norton Seal of Good Housekeeping

One approach to computer security is keeping unnecessary files off your hard drive. Such files not only consume storage space you need for NIS and other applications, but they provide outsiders with a record of where you have been online and what you've been looking at. By cleaning out your Recycle Bin safely and removing unneeded files that accumulate as you surf the Web, you prevent co-workers, family members, and others from spying on your online activities. Norton Internet Security Professional contains some special housekeeping features that aren't included with the other version of the security suite and that are sure to earn your own seal of approval.

Protecting your Recycle Bin

After you install Norton Internet Security Professional, some new objects appear on your desktop. One is the family green globe, the shortcut icon that enables you to start up the software so you can make configuration changes. Another is your Windows Recycle Bin. You may be surprised to see the new name that appears in Figure 15-1.

What, you ask, is Norton Protected Recycle Bin? It's a Recycle Bin that's protected against accidental deletion of a wide variety of files — even files that are created and deleted automatically by Windows applications. As you probably know already, when you select a file or folder and choose File⇨Delete, or when you drag it atop the Recycle Bin, it isn't deleted immediately. A copy of the object remains in the Recycle Bin until you right-click it and choose Empty Recycle Bin from the shortcut menu.

But some other applications delete files permanently — they bypass the Recycle Bin altogether. These include

- Files that you delete while working in a command prompt window (a window that enables you to enter DOS-style commands).

- Files that are deleted by Windows programs: This is probably the most common way you delete files — you use My Computer or Windows Explorer, or example.

- Files that you modify and overwrite; if you replace the old versions of the files, those previous versions are deleted immediately.

Granted, you don't need such files very often, but in case you do, Norton Protection is there to catch them and put them in your Recycle Bin so you can work with them again.

First, you need to make sure Norton Protection is enabled. Right-click the Recycle Bin and choose Properties from the shortcut menu (see Figure 15-2).

When the Norton Protected Recycle Bin Properties dialog box opens, click the Norton Protection tab and make sure the Enable Protection box is checked. Then click the Recycle Bin tab and select the item you want to have open when you double-click the Recycle Bin icon. You can choose the Recycle Bin, the UnErase Wizard (which I describe in the next section), or all files that have been protected.

Norton Protection reserves disk space for the files it saves. By default, 20MB are set aside. If you are running low on disk space on any of your drives, don't enable Norton Protection for that drive or you may quickly run out of space.

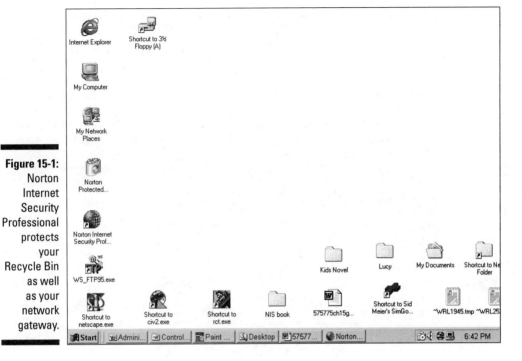

Figure 15-1:
Norton
Internet
Security
Professional
protects
your
Recycle Bin
as well
as your
network
gateway.

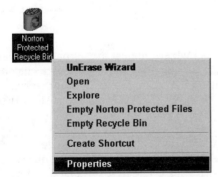

Figure 15-2:
The Recycle
Bin has a
new and
expanded
shortcut
menu
thanks to
Norton
Protection.

Turning back time: The UnErase Wizard

UnErase Wizard is a utility that makes it especially easy for you to recover files you have deleted. Using UnErase Wizard is easier and more powerful than the old system of recovering files by double-clicking the Recycle Bin and searching its contents. It keeps a record of files that were deleted recently and that are protected by Norton Protection. You can open UnErase Wizard in one of two ways:

✔ Configuring UnErase Wizard to open when the Recycle Bin icon is double-clicked, in Norton Protected Recycle Bin Properties.

✔ Clicking Advanced Tools under the Norton AntiVirus heading in the main NIS window, then clicking Start Tool next to UnErase Wizard.

In either case, the UnErase Wizard opens. If you double-click the Recycle Bin, you get a list of any files you have deleted (see Figure 15-3). The benefits of using the tool appear quickly when you view the wizard: It presents you with detailed information about exactly when the file was deleted, its name, size, and original location.

Figure 15-3: UnErase Wizard can help you locate and restore files you have deleted recently.

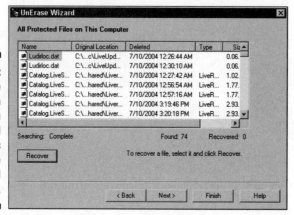

Not all of the files in the UnErase Wizard file list are actually recoverable. To determine whether a file you're looking for can be retrieved, click its name to highlight it. If the Recover button becomes active (in other words, clickable instead of grayed-out), it can be saved. Click Recover to restore the file to its original location.

If you click Start Tool in the Advanced Tools window, you get a different version of the UnErase Wizard: a series of screens that leads you step by step through the process of recovering files. The first screen (see Figure 15-4) gives you the option of finding any recoverable files, or any protected files that have been deleted. What's the difference? Remember that, on Windows 98 and Me, you may be able to recover files that aren't protected by Norton Protection.

The second screen of the UnErase Wizard is the same as the window that appears when you double-click the Recycle Bin; the third screen tells you that the search is finished and gives you the chance to exit the wizard.

In Windows 98 and Me, UnErase Wizard can help restore files whether or not they were protected by Norton Protection. In Windows 2000 and XP, it can only restore files if Norton Protection was activated.

Figure 15-4:
The
UnErase
Wizard
gives you
more
control over
recovering
files than
the version
you access
from the
Recycle Bin.

Saying goodbye forever: Wipe Info

By now, you can see that deleting a file doesn't mean it's gone for good, especially on a Windows computer protected by Norton Internet Security Professional. For security purposes, being able to permanently delete files so they can't be recovered by hackers or other snoopers is important. NIS provides an advanced tool called Wipe Info that can permanently delete (or, in the language of computers, *wipe*) a folder or file.

One advantage of wiping a file, aside from the security benefits, is the fact that Wipe Info attempts to recover the disk space that was consumed by the file's directory entry as well as the file itself. If you use Wipe Info to erase the contents of a folder, all the files in that folder are deleted. When the folder is empty, Wipe Info tries to delete the directory entry or that folder.

Suppose you want to permanently delete a file, and you are absolutely sure you want to do so. Follow these steps to delete it with Wipe Info:

1. **In the main NIS Professional window, click Norton AntiVirus on the left-hand side of the window, then click Advanced Tools.**

   The Advanced Tools window appears (see Figure 15-5).

2. **Click Start Tool next to Wipe Info.**

   The Wipe Info window appears.

3. **Do one of two things to select a file:**

   • If the file is already open and visible in My Computer or Windows Explorer, drag and drop it into the Wipe Info window.

   • Click Browse and choose either Files or Folder from the list that appears (see Figure 15-6).

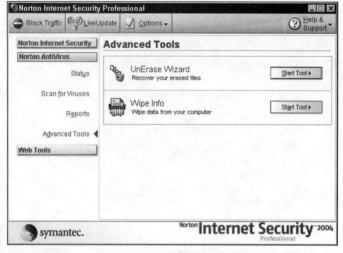

Figure 15-5:
NIS Profes-
sional's
Advanced
Tools either
recover files
or delete
them
completely.

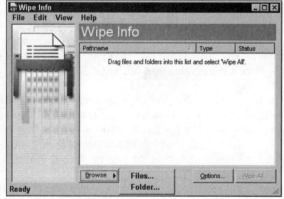

Figure 15-6:
Wipe Info
erases files
by letting
you drag
and drop
them into
the window.

4. **If you clicked Browse and then Files or Folder, in the dialog box that appears, locate the file or folder you want to wipe, click the file, and then click Open.**

   The file appears in the Wipe Info window.

5. **Repeat Steps 3 and 4 for any other files you want to delete, then click the Wipe All button.**

   A warning dialog box appears.

6. **Click Yes.**

   The file is permanently deleted and the Wipe Summary dialog box appears, reporting on how many files were wiped.

7. **Click OK to close the Wipe Summary dialog box and return to the Wipe Info window.**

Note: Even Wipe Info's effects aren't necessarily permanent. If you have the Windows Me and XP feature System Restore enabled, you can restore files, such as Word and Excel files. System Restore keeps backups of files so you can restore your system to a previously functional state in case you encounter serious damage to your operating system.

Using Web Cleanup

One way to keep people from tracing where you've been online is to delete the cache files, cookies, and History records from your hard drive. NIS Professional's Web Cleanup tool streamlines the process of deleting such files, which accumulate naturally as you browse the Internet.

Web Cleanup works in two modes: Quick Clean and Advanced Cleanup. Quick Clean automatically deletes unnecessary files without your inspecting them. Advanced Cleanup lets you inspect the contents of the files before you delete them. Before you begin, exit Internet Explorer to make sure Web Cleanup can delete all of the files you don't need. To get started with Quick Clean, open the main NIS window and click Web Tools. The Web Cleanup window opens (see Figure 15-7).

Figure 15-7: Web Cleanup deletes files that can be used to track your activities online.

The Scan Progress window appears with a summary of the files that were found. Click Cleanup Now! to automatically delete the files that were found (see Figure 15-8).

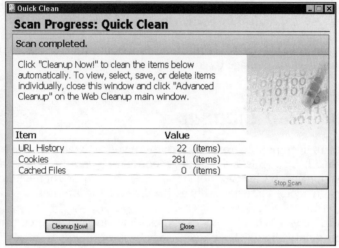

Figure 15-8:
Quick Clean
gives you
a quick
summary of
the number
of files
found
before you
delete them.

If you want to review files before you delete them so you have the opportunity to exclude any you want to save, follow these steps:

1. **Click the <u>Advanced Cleanup</u> link in the bottom-right-hand corner of the Web Cleanup window.**

   The Advanced Cleanup window appears.

2. **Choose View By Date or View By Location to specify how you want the files to be organized.**

3. **Read the Welcome to Web Cleanup message and then click Continue.**

   A dialog box appears, telling you that your drive is being scanned. Then a set of categories appears in the Navigation pane on the left-hand side of the window.

4. **Click the plus sign next to a category to expand it; click the item name beneath the category to view the files in the File List pane (see Figure 15-9).**

5. **Click an item to view detailed information about it in the File Information pane at the bottom of Advanced Cleanup.**

6. **Click Save (which excludes a file from deletion) or click Delete to delete it.**

Note: Web Cleanup only works with files that have been accumulated by Internet Explorer, not with other browsers.

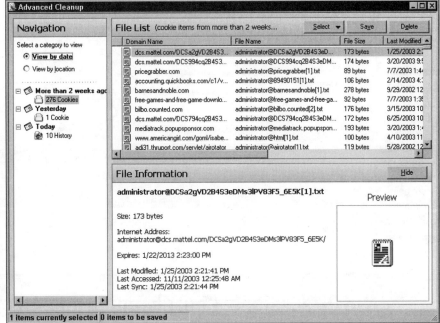

Figure 15-9:
You can save or delete cookies and other files on an item-by-item basis in Advanced Cleanup.

Keeping your connection alive

Norton Internet Security depends on your having a steady and reliable connection to the Internet. If you have a dialup connection (you use a modem to make a phone call connection to a server), you're probably aware that some ISPs automatically break the connection when you're inactive for a period of time (in other words, you aren't surfing the Web or checking your e-mail).

Having your connection go down can be frustrating; for example, it keeps e-mail from arriving in your inbox if you configured your e-mail software to deliver it automatically. NIS Professional includes a utility called Connection Keep Alive that keeps your connection from being broken when you are inactive. In order for the feature to work, you have to have a dialup rather than a direct connection such as a cable modem or DSL line; you also have to enable Connection Keep Alive. Follow these quick steps to start Connection Keep Alive:

1. **From the main NIS window, click Web Tools, then click Connection Keep Alive.**

   The Connection Keep Alive window appears (see Figure 15-10).

2. **Read the Status message, and click Enable if necessary.**

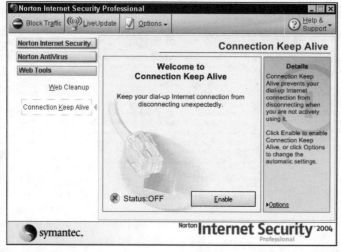

Figure 15-10: Connection Keep Alive prevents a dialup Internet connection from being broken due to inactivity.

NIS Professional housekeeping add-ons

The most obvious difference between the Professional and home versions of Norton Internet Security is that Professional includes Productivity Control instead of Parental Control. But these two access control programs are actually pretty similar. Many of the utilities contained in the professional version of Norton Internet Security are housekeeping utilities that aren't included in the other version of NIS. They include

✔ Transfer settings: This feature allows you to transfer all the firewall rules from earlier versions of Norton Internet Security, Norton Personal Firewall, or Norton AntiVirus to Norton Internet Security Professional 2004. This is a great feature if custom firewall rules already exist and you don't want to recreate the rules.

✔ Stop Web Referral: This feature automatically closes multiple windows that were unintentionally created as a result of continuous referrals and solicitation when you tried to open or exit a Web site.

✔ Web Cleanup: This tool lets you quickly delete unnecessary files from your computer's Internet history, cache, and cookies.

✔ Connection Keep Alive: Prevents your dialup Internet connection from discontinuing unexpectedly or when you are not actively using it. It warns you when your online session is nearing an end, allowing you to choose to remain connected or to disconnect, giving you more online connection control.

Another feature, Install Over Previous and Current Versions, supposedly allows you to install NIS Professional over other versions of Norton Internet Security (NIS), Norton Personal Firewall (NPF), and Norton Internet Security Professional Edition (NIS Pro) without uninstalling the currently installed program. But when I tried it, I had to laboriously remove all traces of the previous version before installing the new one.

You can configure Connection Keep Alive to start up when Windows starts so you don't have to manually enable it; click Options in the main NIS window, select Web Tools from the drop-down list, and click Automatically Start with Windows the Connection Keep Alive tab.

Uninstalling and Reinstalling Norton Internet Security

I hope you never have to resort to completely removing and reinstalling the NIS software in order to solve a serious problem, but it happened to me, and it can happen to you, too. I suggest that you consider this procedure only as a last resort, because it's quite involved and it removes any firewall rules you created. The reinstall won't retain them, either.

The problem with removing NIS is that traces of the software remain throughout your file system. First, try to remove the software using Add/Remove Programs. If that doesn't work, however, you will have to perform the tasks described in the sections that follow to completely remove all traces of the installation.

Removing NIS from the Registry

The Windows Registry stores a lot of detailed and hard-to-understand information that programs use. You should try to edit the Registry only after backing it up and when you have clear instructions to follow. To remove NIS's registry information, Symantec has provided a removal program called RnisUPG. To find this program, go to the Symantec Support area by following the steps described in the "Symantec.com" section in Chapter 14. Search for "RnisUPG.exe", and you should locate the support document that tells you how to download and use the software.

The Symantec support document entitled "Error: The installation encountered an error and was unable to complete . . ." (which has a Document ID of 2003100708194336), explains in detail how to find the registry information you need to remove. It's something you need to do carefully: Choose Start⇨ Run, type **regedit** in the Run dialog box, and press Enter to locate the Registry Editor. You then navigate through registry "keys," which are bits of data stored in the registry. You need to delete two keys completely:

```
HKEY_LOCAL_MACHINE\Software\Symantec
HKEY_CURRENT_USER\Software\Symantec
```

The process is shown in Figure 15-11.

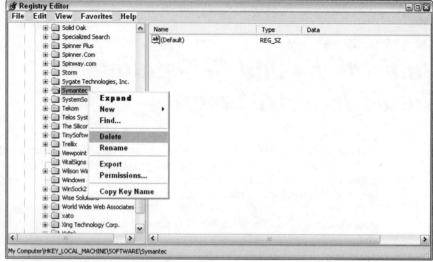

Figure 15-11:
You may
need to
delete
registry
information
to com-
pletely
uninstall
NIS.

After you remove files from the Registry, you need to perform a clean boot of your computer; refer to the Symantec support documents for more information.

Removing Symantec files, folders, and shortcuts

After you clear NIS references from the registry, you need to clear the program references from the folder that holds your system software. This is probably either `C:\WINDOWS` or `C:\WINNT`. Again, the Symantec support documents can point you to the correct files to delete.

Be sure you carefully review the list of files to delete. The Windows system folders contain a good deal of information that is essential to the smooth operation of your computer; you don't want to delete files that are going to cause you problems down the road.

After you remove files from the Windows folders, you need to delete short-cuts to Norton AntiVirus and Norton Internet Security that are contained in your shortcuts folder. On a Windows XP computer, this folder is probably `C:\Documents and Settings\`*your username*`\Application Data\ Symantec`. Throw all references to Symantec products into the Recycle Bin.

Finally, when you have successfully deleted all traces of the security application, you can reinstall that same security application. Put the CD-ROM in your computer's disk drive, start the installation process, and cross your fingers; if you don't see the dreaded error message "Could not complete the installation," you're in business and can start using the application again.

Chapter 16

Working With Log Files
and Advanced Options

· ·

In This Chapter

▶ Reviewing NIS's firewall, connection, and system-related log files

▶ Keeping track of AntiVirus's scans and other activities

▶ Exporting and otherwise manipulating log files

▶ Customizing the way log file data is presented

▶ Tracking user and program activity with NIS's detailed statistics

· ·

A *log file* is a computer document that stores information about all the events that have occurred in connection with a computer program. Web servers, operating systems, and other applications have their own log files. They tend to be techie-looking documents full of numbers and statistics that can be difficult to understand. As you may expect, Norton Internet Security's log files aren't difficult to work with or interpret, and you should get to know them so you can be more security-conscious and solve problems should they arise.

Reviewing and interpreting log files is a part of ongoing firewall administration that isn't glamorous, but it's an important way to understand how well your network is being protected and where your security threats are coming from. By keeping an eye on Norton Internet Security's various logs, you can determine how often virus scans have been performed, understand how the network is being used, and evaluate how well NIS's components are working. If you're using NIS in a small business environment, you can use the log files to prepare usage reports that tell you when the peak times are on your network. In this chapter you'll find out how to understand and configure NIS's different log files in order to maintain your current level of security.

Viewing the Log Files

Log files are an integral part of many applications. The Webmasters assigned to maintain the Web sites you visit every day have to pay close attention to their Web server log files. They need to track who's visiting their sites and what pages are being viewed. Those Webmasters often need to generate reports about what they view. Sometimes, they benefit from user-friendly programs that present the raw log file data in a form that's easy to understand. That's with good reason. Log files aren't pretty: They consist of numbers, dots, addresses, URLs, ports, and lots and lots of bits and bytes. In fact, they're probably everything you *don't* want in a security program. NIS's log files are easy to open, and not overwhelming to inspect. Whenever you want to inspect them, just do the following:

1. **Open the main NIS window and click Statistics under Norton Internet Security.**

   The Statistics options appear.

2. **Click the View Logs button.**

   After a few seconds, the Log Viewer opens. The window is divided into three panes:

   - A list of log files in the left-hand pane

   - Information for the log file you selected in the right-hand pane

   - Detailed information about items selected in the right-hand pane in the bottom pane

   Because no log file has been selected yet, the right-hand pane appears to be empty.

3. **Click Norton Internet Security in the left-hand pane.**

   A list of log file categories appears, along with a brief description of each (see Figure 16-1).

NIS presents you with 14 separate log files. That may seem complicated, but the fact that each log file contains only one type of information makes each one less intimidating; many firewalls present large amounts of complex information in one screen. Having the log files organized in manageable bits makes them easier to absorb and interpret. Some of the interpretations you might make are described below.

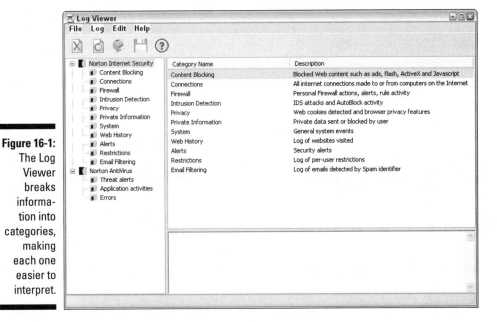

Figure 16-1:
The Log
Viewer
breaks
informa-
tion into
categories,
making
each one
easier to
interpret.

Tracking connections

Any firewall has as one of its fundamental responsibilities the job of tracking attempts to traverse the network gateway. It monitors attempts to connect to the external Internet from the local network, and attempts to access your computer by remote computers. Several of the Log Viewer categories track connection attempts; each monitors a different type of connection, as I describe in the following sections.

Connections

The Connections log gives you a record of all the connections to and from your computer. As you can see in Figure 16-2, the data is very detailed in the sense that every connection your computer makes is recorded — even routine connections to other computers on your network, plus connections your computer makes to itself (these show up as connections to localhost).

You probably won't notice by looking at Connections how small the log file is. If you scroll to the bottom of the log, you'll see that the earliest available listing was only a few hours ago. The default file size of any of the log files is a meager 64K. When the log reaches its maximum, any new entries overwrite the old ones. Check out the section, "Customizing Log Files," later in this chapter, for a broader perspective on increasing the log file size.

Date	User	Local IP Address	Local Service Port	Remote IP Address	Remote Service Port	Bytes Sent	Bytes Rece
→ 7/6/2004 7:53...	Greg	localhost	1027	localhost	3296	321	
← 7/6/2004 7:53...	Greg	PAVILION(208....	3298	www.keepmedia.com(15...	http(80)	536	
← 7/6/2004 7:53...	Greg	localhost	3296	localhost	1027	536	
→ 7/6/2004 7:53...	Greg	localhost	1027	localhost	3293	321	
← 7/6/2004 7:53...	Greg	PAVILION(208....	3294	www.keepmedia.com(15...	http(80)	535	
← 7/6/2004 7:53...	Greg	localhost	3293	localhost	1027	535	
→ 7/6/2004 7:53...	Greg	localhost	1027	localhost	3289	3053	
← 7/6/2004 7:53...	Greg	PAVILION(208....	3291	www.keepmedia.com(15...	http(80)	1933	
← 7/6/2004 7:53...	Greg	localhost	3289	localhost	1027	1933	
→ 7/6/2004 7:53...	Greg	localhost	1027	localhost	3290	4257	
← 7/6/2004 7:53...	Greg	PAVILION(208....	3292	www.keepmedia.com(15...	http(80)	922	
← 7/6/2004 7:53...	Greg	localhost	3290	localhost	1027	922	
→ 7/6/2004 7:53...	Greg	localhost	1027	localhost	3286	321	
← 7/6/2004 7:53...	Greg	PAVILION(208....	3288	www.keepmedia.com(15...	http(80)	484	
← 7/6/2004 7:53...	Greg	localhost	3286	localhost	1027	484	
→ 7/6/2004 7:53...	Greg	localhost	1027	localhost	3285	320	
← 7/6/2004 7:53...	Greg	PAVILION(208....	3287	www.keepmedia.com(15...	http(80)	483	

Details: Connection: localhost: 3296
to localhost: 1027
321 bytes sent
712 bytes received
0.630 elapsed time

All internet connections made to or from computers on the Internet

Figure 16-2:
The Connections log displays routine local traffic as well as external connections.

You can ignore most of the "localhost" traffic shown in the Connections window; the connections that count are the ones your computer makes to external computers on the Internet. When you click one of the listings, a set of details appears in the small pane at the bottom of Log Viewer.

If you have a computer with several gigabytes of storage space available, I suggest you increase the size of each of your log files. Try 128K or 256K for a start.

Firewall

Norton Personal Firewall's log is much different than the log files maintained by most other firewalls. Rather than show you a record of all the rules and connections that the firewall has worked with, the Firewall log maintains a record only of blocked traffic. Every time a firewall rule, whether a default rule or one you created yourself, takes effect and stops a particular kind of connection, a record is kept here (see Figure 16-3).

Because Personal Firewall does not produce alert messages every time traffic is blocked, it's worth checking the Firewall log once in a while, if only to make sure that it is protecting your computer. It tells you what kinds of threats you face most often.

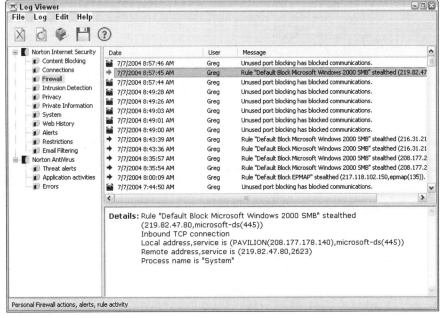

Intrusion Detection

The Intrusion Detection and Firewall logs are similar: They both record attempts to connect to your computer with packets of information that bear the characteristics of known attacks. While Personal Firewall depends on rules that block or permit traffic, Intrusion Detection monitors attack signatures — sets of characteristics that govern not only packets with mal-formed information, but patterns of connection attempts such as ping sweeps and port scans.

Scanning the information shown in the Intrusion Detection log alerts you to any attempts to connect to your computer on a regular basis that match known attack signatures. The events recorded in the log shown in Figure 16-4 included malformed packets and buffer overflows: attempts to overload com-puter memory so that part of memory can no longer block other connection attempts.

Evaluating privacy threats

If you're concerned about the amount of information you or your kids are revealing online, check the two privacy-related logs described below. You may notice that your computer is receiving a large number of cookies you don't want, among other things.

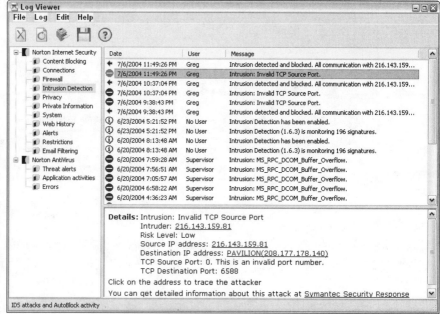

Figure 16-4:
Intrusion
Detection
monitors
connection
attempts
based on
known
attack
signatures.

Privacy

The Privacy log primarily tracks the cookies that you have received, or that have been blocked from Web sites that issue them. In the URL column, you get the exact location of the object you viewed in order to have the cookie issued. You discover that individual images are associated with requests to leave cookies on your computer, for example.

The Privacy log also records attempts to gather "referrer" information from your computer: bits of data contained in the headers of the packets you send to remote Web sites, and that reveal which Web sites you visited before you visited the current site. The references to User Agent that you see in the Privacy log are similar: They reveal to the remote Web site what program (in the case of a Web site, a Web browser) you are using (see Figure 16-5).

Note: An *X* at the far left side of the log details (in other words, the upper right-hand pane) means that the content has been blocked; a green circle means it has been permitted. After you see how many cookies you receive from many different sites, you may want to adjust Privacy Control to block more cookies.

Private Information

The Private Information log is useful if you are tracking the activities of young people who use your computer. The log reveals whether they have attempted to fill out registration or other forms on Web sites that reveal your address, phone number, or other information you have specified as private. If you notice a number of such attempts, you may want to lecture your kids about how to maintain your family's privacy online.

Reviewing blocked content

You think of the Internet as a place to connect to remote servers and gather information that is useful to you. Content providers turn the equation around: They view the Net as a place to provide you with ads and other interactive content that will make their sites more attractive, ensure return visits, and provide marketing information about who visits them. The following logs track content that NIS has prevented you from seeing.

Content Blocking

The Content Blocking log is reassuring: It provides you with a list of the ads that you haven't had to view. When you visit Web logs or commercial Web sites, you see blank rectangles rather than ads. This log lists just how many times the ads have been blocked, when they were blocked, and the URL of the site that contained them. On the other hand, if Ad Blocking is turned off for certain sites or for all sites, you see a green circle to signify that an ad was viewed.

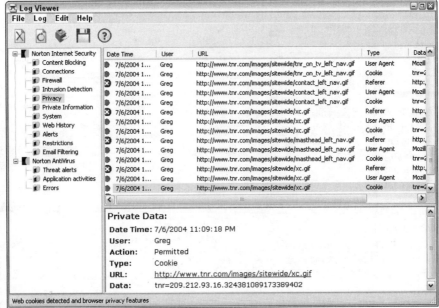

Figure 16-5:
The Privacy log records attempts to leave cookies or get information about your online activities.

E-mail messages

Your e-mail software lets you know whether a message has been sent to the AntiSpam folder or deleted automatically. But in case you need to prepare a report for your business or if you just want a record of all of the messages that have been filtered by AntiSpam, you get a detailed list here.

In the Classification column, Clean means the e-mail message was not considered spam and was sent through to your inbox. Spam means the message was regarded. When you click on a message (either Clean or Spam), the Details pane presents you with a Retrain as Spam button that enables you to tell Norton AntiSpam to filter out such messages in the future (see Figure 16-6).

Alert messages

You're probably familiar with the alert messages that ask you whether or not you want to create a rule for a particular type of connection attempt or that tell you a Trojan horse or other malicious software was blocked from entering your computer. Each time such a message appears, a record is placed in the Alerts log. Listings marked with a blue arrow mean a rule was processed automatically. Listings marked with a gold rectangle mean the user (that's probably you) created a rule to permit or block such attempts in the future.

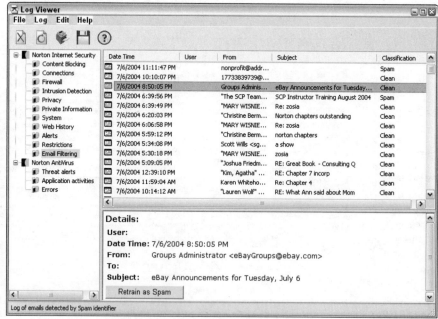

Figure 16-6:
The E-mail Filtering log lets you filter out spam messages that have gone to your inbox by mistake.

The Alert log is particularly useful if you have more than one individual with accounts on your machine, and you're wondering why certain communications have been permitted or blocked; the answer may be that another user created a rule for such attempts.

Restrictions

If you restrict users from accessing certain Web sites or newsgroups or from using some applications, either in Parental Control or in Productivity Control, such restrictions are covered here. Whenever someone tries to access a site that has been blocked or use a program that has been prohibited, a record is placed in the Restrictions log. This record is obviously useful if you are monitoring how others in your family or your small business are accessing the Internet.

Individuals who want to cover their tracks and delete records of where they've been or what they've tried to access online can select Restrictions or other logs and press the Delete button on the Log Viewer toolbar to remove all listings. In other words, there's no guarantee that the logs contain information that is complete.

Keeping records of NIS's activity

Some of the Log Viewer files contain sets of data that, frankly, you're not going to need to look at very often. In rare instances, you may be asked to review the information about Norton Internet Security's activity by a service technician if you're trying to track down a serious problem with the software (and if the solutions suggested in Chapter 14 haven't worked).

The System log keeps meticulous data about each time a user logs in and logs out of Norton Internet Security, every time Intrusion Detection or another feature is enabled or disabled, and each time another component is turned on or off. Again, it may be useful to track when features are disabled if users other than you are at the computer.

The Web History log maintains a detailed record of every Web page or image your Web browser views. If nothing else, you may be surprised at how many entries apply to files that are checked and obtained by Norton Internet Security's own LiveUpdate component.

Using the AntiVirus Activity Log

The three log files at the bottom of the Log Viewer list pertain to Norton AntiVirus. Those files collectively make up the Activity Log, which reports on AntiVirus activity.

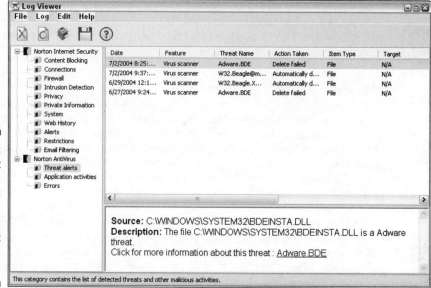

Figure 16-7:
This part
of the
AntiVirus
Activity Log
tracks
viruses that
have been
detected.

✔ The Threat Alert log records any viruses or other threats that have turned up as a result of AntiVirus's virus scans. The log (see Figure 16-7) also records whether each threat was quarantined or deleted, or whether infected files were repaired.

✔ The Application activities log is useful if you're wondering when the last virus scan was conducted: You'll find a list of the recent scans here. The Action Taken column tells you whether the scan was actually completed.

✔ The Errors log provides data about problems that occur when AntiVirus conducts virus scans. Such error system shutdowns, program crashes, or files or folders that can't be accessed for some reason.

You can also view the Activity Log by opening the main NIS window, clicking Norton AntiVirus, clicking Reports, and then clicking Report next to Activity Log.

Working with the Log Files

Just viewing the log files doesn't necessarily make you more secure or help you better understand the threats you face on a daily basis. You can save, refresh, or otherwise manipulate the files so the information they provide is more complete and useful, as I describe in the sections that follow.

Refreshing log files

When you refresh a page or set of content, you tell the software to retrieve the current information from its source. After the Log Viewer remains open for a while, the very latest connection attempts or component activities are no longer included in the logs.

When you move from one log to another, the log files automatically refresh. But in order to refresh the data you have been viewing in a single log, just click the Refresh button in the Log Viewer's toolbar, or choose Log➪Refresh Category.

If you want to refresh all the log files at the same time, do one of two things:

- ✓ Click either Norton Internet Security or Norton AntiVirus in the list of categories in the left-hand pane of the Log Viewer.

- ✓ Right-click Norton Internet Security or Norton AntiVirus and choose Refresh All Categories from the shortcut menu that appears.

If you have increased the size of the log files and they contain an extensive amount of information, it may take a few seconds before all of the log categories are completely refreshed.

Saving log files

As I mention earlier, NIS keeps log files from ballooning to an unwieldy size that can quickly eat up storage space on your computer. NIS keeps files manageable by overwriting older data with newer information when the file is filled. That means log information about a particular time period disappears unless you take steps to save the log file data.

You have two options for saving log files:

- ✓ **Print a file.** Right-click the name of the log category you want to print, and choose Print Category from the shortcut menu.

- ✓ **Save a file.** Right-click the name of the log category you want to save, then choose Export Category As from the shortcut menu. When the Save As dialog box appears, select the location where you want to save the file, and click Save.

When you export a file, it is saved in text-only format so you can view it with a text editor such as Notepad, WordPad, or Microsoft Word. The contents aren't as nicely formatted as in the Log Viewer, but they are readable. You have the advantage of being able to use your text processor's Find function if you need to search for a particular bit of data, such as a type of event, or a Web site IP address.

Disabling log records

Sometimes, log files take up too much space on your hard drive. When they begin to interfere with your productivity, you need to consider cutting back on them. NIS gives you the ability to either disable all log file activity or selectively disable a particular type of logging.

To enable or disable the logging of events, first open the Log Viewer itself, as I describe earlier in this chatper. Then right-click the name of the log category you want to enable or disable, then choose Disable Logging or Enable Logging from the shortcut menu that appears.

Customizing Log Files

Chances are you'll be happy with the way the Log Viewer presents its information. But if you need to prepare a report, make a demonstration of NIS's capabilities, or emphasize one bit of information over another, you can customize the way Log Viewer behaves.

Changing log file size

One of the most useful ways to customize NIS's log files is to increase or decrease their size. As log files go, the default size of 64K to 512K isn't very big. Plenty of firewalls accumulate log files that stretch to several megabytes in size.

By increasing the size, you gain the ability to review data that covers a longer period of time. To change the size of a log category, follow these steps:

1. **Open the Log Viewer, then right-click the name of a log category in the list in the left-hand pane.**

   The name is highlighted.

2. **Choose Log⇨Change Log File Size from the Log Viewer's menu bar.**

   The Log File Size dialog box appears, displaying the log's current maximum size.

3. **Select a new size from the drop-down list (see Figure 16-8), then click OK.**

   The Log File Size dialog box closes and you return to the Log Viewer.

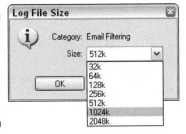

Figure 16-8:
Change the log file size so you can view more information.

Note: When you change the size of a log category, you delete all of the information currently in the log. You may want to export the data before you change the size, as described in the preceding section.

Be selective about the log categories whose size you increase. If you increase all 14 logs to the maximum size of 2,048K, you'll start to consume a significant amount of hard drive storage space.

Adjusting display settings

The time displayed in the log categories is important because it can help you pinpoint events. Many attacks take place within a matter of seconds, while other, more devious intrusion attempts take place slowly. By making sure the log time is accurate or that it's in a format you prefer, you can track it more easily.

Log Viewer enables you to display the date and time of an event using either your local time or Universal Time Coordinated (UTC) format. To change the display settings, open Log Viewer, choose File➪Options, and select the display options you want in the Log Viewer Options dialog box.

The accuracy of log file entries depends on the accuracy of your computer's clock; double-click the time in the system tray to adjust the date and time if needed.

Advanced Options

Most of Norton Internet Security is non-technical, and the interface is friendly in a way that everyday home computer users will appreciate. Not so with the detailed statistics dialog box. It contains a variety of detailed information about your current rate of data transfer: It tells you how many network connections are in place and exactly how many bytes of information are passing through the network gateway — right down to the last byte.

To view detailed statistics, you have to open the Statistics window. Follow these steps:

1. **Open the main NIS window and click Statistics under Norton Internet Security.**

   The Statistics options appear.

2. **Click Detailed Statistics.**

   After several seconds (during which the current information is presumably being gathered), the window shown in Figure 16-9 appears.

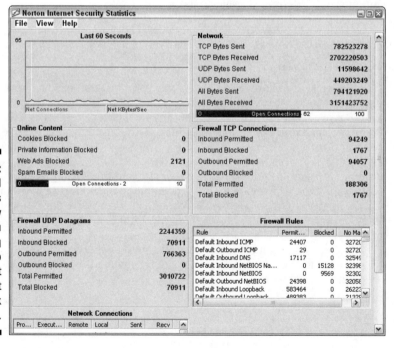

Figure 16-9: The Detailed Statistics window tells you everything you need to know about your current network activity.

Everything you always wanted to know about your firewall

If you ever want to know exactly what Personal Firewall is doing to protect your computer at a given moment, the Detailed Statistics window is the place to turn. Much of the information in this dialog box is more technical in nature than most everyday computer users need; however, if you are wondering what all of the statistics mean, here are some explanations:

✔ **Firewall UDP Datagrams.** UDP, or User Datagram Protocol, is a set of connection methods that govern how information is exchanged by computers on a network. UDP divides a message into numbered segments so it can get from one network location to another more easily. UDP is far less secure than TCP (Transport Control Protocol), which is used on the Internet, because UDP is connectionless: It sends segments without performing error checking or waiting to receive an acknowledgement that the data has actually reached its destination. The data in the Firewall UDP Datagrams area indicates how much of the information going to and from your computer uses UDP.

✔ **Firewall TCP Connections.** While UDP is used primarily by computers on the same network (or by hackers trying to infiltrate a remote computer), TCP is used on the Web, by e-mail, by newsgroups, and by other well-known Internet communications. This part of the Detailed Statistics window lets you know how much information is being exchanged at any given time.

✔ **Firewall Rules.** This section displays how many of Personal Firewall's rules are being used at any one time.

Your firewall should be protecting your computer, and you should be seeing readings in the Blocked column in Firewall Rules. If you don't, check your firewall to make sure it's operating.

Internet Connections

The Net Connections graph in the upper left-hand corner of the detailed statistics window can alert you to network activity that may be taking place without your knowledge. For example, if you aren't using your Web browser or e-mail software and you see a spike in the level of network activity, you may want to check the other areas of the window to see what's going on. Chances are it's an authorized connection being made by LiveUpdate or another program, but it could also be a Trojan horse that AntiVirus hasn't detected yet.

Part VI
The Part of Tens

The 5th Wave   By Rich Tennant

"Do you remember which military web site you downloaded your Bot software from?"

In this part . . .

*I*f you're like me, you've got spare keys scattered around the house and cupboard drawers, as well as passwords written down on scraps of paper and extra locks you can install in case of trouble. There are many different aspects of security, and you can't keep them all in one spot.

This part of the book is called The Part of Tens because it gathers miscellaneous bits of information arranged in groups of ten. You'll find tips, cautions, suggestions, examples, and points related to Internet security in general and Norton Internet Security in particular. You're sure to find information that will help you plan and create a secure computing environment.

Chapter 17

Ten Most Common Attacks

- -

In This Chapter

▶ Attempts to flood your computer or server with too many requests

▶ Malformed packets that attempt to confuse your computer

▶ Attempts to intercept your e-mail or other communications

▶ Worms, Trojan horses, and blended threats: Many points of entry

- -

*N*orton Internet Security performs so many functions automatically that you can easily overlook what it's doing. For example, you may discover after the fact that someone tried to send you a Trojan horse but that NIS blocked it. You'll be a more secure computer user, however, if you have at least a passing knowledge of the kinds of attacks you are likely to confront at some point.

This chapter briefly describes the most common attacks you will face in the course of using the Internet. You'll probably notice some attacks; others usually are launched against large-scale business networks and you're unlikely to encounter them at home. But understanding the major attacks you hear about in the news will make you more security conscious and help you in the workplace as well as at home.

SANS, the well-known security organization, published a Top 10 List of Internet security threats for many years. Recently, SANS felt the need to expand the survey to a Top 20 List and divide it into attacks launched against specific operating systems. You can read the SANS Top 20 Vulnerabilities list at www.sans.org/top20.

Denial of Service Attacks

These mostly affect large-scale networks, but if you work in a small business that's connected to the Net, you are a potential victim as well. And when your system is configured poorly enough to allow a Trojan horse in, you can unwittingly help launch a Denial of Service attack against another Web site.

Traffic into and out of a network is blocked when servers are flooded with malformed packets or other bogus communications. Keep your server OS up to date; log instances of frequent connection attempts against one service.

SYN Floods

A SYN flood is a particular variety of a Denial of Service attack in which a network is overloaded with packets that have the SYN flag set. As you read in Chapter 3, when one computer requests a connection to another over a network that uses Transmission Control Protocol (TCP), it sends a packet that has the SYN control flag set. The SYN flag tells the receiving computer that the originating computer wants to make a connection. A normal TCP connection looks like this:

1. Computer 1 sends Computer 2 a packet with the SYN flag set.

2. Computer 2 responds with a packet that has the SYN and ACK flags set.

3. Computer 1 responds with the SYN and ACK flags.

After the connection is made, Computer 2 responds with the PSH flag, as well as the data that Computer 1 requested. A variety of other packets may be exchanged, but these are the basic ones. Suppose Computer 1, at Step 3, responded not with the ACK flag but the SYN flag only? What if it continued to send SYN packets and no others? The result would be a SYN flood: The server would continually be waiting for an acknowledgement. The resulting half-open session, as a result, uses up server resources and makes it unable to handle any other requests.

Invalid Packets

The SYN flood described in the preceding section is only one kind of an attack that uses invalid or malformed packets. Packets are sent that have invalid ports or an "illegal" combination of flags that a server won't understand. Figure 17-1 shows an alert message for a packet with invalid TCP port information. The packet has a source port of 0, which cannot be used because it is reserved for the operating system kernel.

If you look at NIS's event logs, you might see communications blocked that have a variety of flags set all at the same time (such as the PSH, ACK, and SYN flags) or combinations that make no sense (such as the RST and ACK flags). They are all attempts to confuse the server into a nonresponse. Not knowing how to respond to packets with mixed messages, the server won't respond at all, and will leave the door open for attacks.

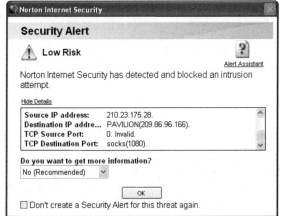

Figure 17-1:
Norton
Internet
Security will
block
attempts to
send illegal
packets.

Port Scans

A port scan takes place when one computer attempts to connect to some, or all of the ports on another computer on the network. Port scans have a legitimate purpose when a network administrator is attempting to verify whether or not a computer is "listening" on certain ports and is thus vulnerable to attack. Hackers also try to see if a computer is listening on a certain port, so they can infiltrate a network by sending packets to it.

Port scans, although not harmful in themselves, have harmful results. They lead to more serious attacks, as I just mentioned. They also consume the resources of the computer and the firewall that protects it. A port scan that continually attempts to connect to all of the 65,000-plus possible TCP ports and the 65,000-plus UDP ports on a computer over and over again may not be a Denial of Service attack, exactly, but it can result in a Reduction of Service because it takes away from the computer and the firewall's ability to perform other functions quickly.

Man-in-the-Middle

Man-in-the-middle attacks (which can be carried out by females as well as males) are among the most insidious around, and you won't likely encounter them often. In such an attack, one computer user attempts to make a secure, encrypted connection to another one by exchanging a long block of encrypted code called a key. In Secure Sockets Layer (SSL) communications that take place with secure Web sites, the browser and server exchange public and private keys and establish a secure connection.

The man-in-the-middle attack occurs when a hacker manages to substitute his or her public key for that of the recipient. The hacker is then able to impersonate the recipient of the encrypted communication, and can potentially read encrypted messages that are exchanged. Because the messages are encrypted, they are likely to contain sensitive information such as credit card numbers.

Covert Channeling

A *channel* is a port or other opening in a computer through which data is allowed to pass. Covert channeling occurs when a hacker is able to gain unauthorized access to a computer or network by sending malformed or infected packets through a channel without the knowledge of the computer's owner or system administrator. After packets are allowed through because the "illegal" configuration within them is one that the computer or its firewall do not recognize, more harmful programs can be sent. For example, a Trojan horse can be sent through a port such as 12345 or 31337 without the knowledge of the computer operator. In addition, any technique that is used to uncover an open port, such as a ping sweep or port scan, constitutes covert channeling.

A *ping sweep* occurs when one computer sends all of the computers on a network a series of ping messages in an attempt to see if any computers can be located. After a computer with a valid IP address is located through a ping sweep, a port scan or other reconnaissance technique might follow in order to locate an open port that can be exploited.

Worms

Worms are probably the most prevalent form of malicious code being distributed on the Internet. Often, worms spread in the form of e-mail attachments that aren't scanned by firewall programs or intrusion detection systems working on their own. Sometimes, a worm's only purpose is to replicate itself, consuming resources on the infected computer. But a few worms that were identified as particularly harmful when this was written could do much more, such as:

> ✔ **W32.Netsky.** Like many worms, this one is configured to e-mail itself to addresses found in the infected computer. But it is fast spreading and has many variants. Worse yet, it opens port 82, which can become a back door for a more serious attack.

✔ **W32.Sasser.** This worm, which began to infect computers in spring 2004, causes significant performance slowdowns on infected computers. It copies information to the folder where the Windows operating system files are located, and to the Windows registry, so that it starts automatically when the computer starts up. Worse, it creates a File Transfer Protocol (FTP) server on port 5554, which is used to send the worm to other computers.

✔ **W32.Beagle.** Like the preceding worms, this one e-mails itself to addresses found on the infected computer, and it opens a potential backdoor port. It comes in an e-mail with a spoofed e-mail address: It is likely to seem to come from someone you actually know.

By the time you read this, new worms will probably be listed among the top threats on the Internet, and Norton AntiVirus will need new definitions for them, which you should download from Symantec's Web site using LiveUpdate (see Chapter 7).

Trojan Horses

As mentioned in Chapter 1 and elsewhere in this book, a Trojan horse is a harmful computer program that appears to be something useful or even welcome. A hacker typically delivers a malicious Trojan horse program through a "back door" of the sort opened up in the preceding section or uncovered through a port scan. Then, the program can perform a variety of harmful functions, such as:

✔ **Trojan.Downloader.xxxx.** The xxxx is a placeholder that stands for a variety of odd virus-type names like Aphex or Swizzor. A Trojan horse with Downloader or Download in the name attempts to download a file from a specific Web site and then execute it on the infected computer. Chances are the application to be executed is not anything helpful to you, but is likely to be adware or malicious code.

✔ **Backdoor.xxxx.** Trojan horses whose names begin with Backdoor enter your computer through an open port. Some are used to conduct Denial of Service attacks on other computers. Others give a hacker remote access to the infected computer.

Families of Trojan horses consist of similar programs that have slightly different code: The code is varied in an attempt to circumvent anti-virus programs, at least until a new definition is created for the latest variety.

Blended Threats

A blended threat is one that uses several different methods in order to spread itself. It can enter through:

- e-mail attachments
- shared file folders
- wireless devices that connect to your network
- Web pages
- laptops
- direct attacks on servers or routers

The blended threat can be a Trojan horse, worm, or other virus. It can hit a network rapidly and spread itself to hundreds or even thousands of computers within minutes. Nimda, for example, had four different ways to propagate itself. Blended threats have the characteristics of two or more kinds of malicious code. They spread without any human intervention, such as clicking on attachments; rather, they can scan the Net continuously for servers to attack. To fully protect yourself against such nasty programs, make sure you not only keep Norton AntiVirus updated, but install all available security patches for Windows and for Microsoft Internet Explorer, too.

Browser Hijackers

A Web browser is hijacked when software that was installed without the operator's knowledge redirects it to other Web sites, slows down operations, and possibly performs more malicious tasks. One of the most notorious and dangerous examples is a piece of spyware called CoolWebSearch.

CoolWebSearch is a name given to a wide range of different browser hijackers. It's put out by a Web site located at www.CoolWebSearch.com. Stay away from this site at all costs. The code that causes the browser to perform specified functions is believed to be downloaded due to a pop-up window that appears when the victim's Web browser connects to a certain Web page. But at this writing, no definite infection agent had even been identified.

The code differs depending on the variants, but all of the hijackers redirect users to coolwebsearch.com and other sites affiliated with its operators. Possibly as many as 80 Web sites affiliated with CoolWebSearch.com are the targets of the redirection.

Removal of the hijack software must be done manually at this writing and can be time-consuming. As of this writing, most anti-spyware programs aren't currently addressing all variants. If you suddenly notice your browser going to a new startup page, detect a new browser menu, or notice strange links in your Windows Start menu directing you to X-rated or other sites, chances are good that you've obtained some browser hijack software.

Web sites like SpywareInfo (`www.spywareinfo.com`) provide you with more information about common hijack programs and instructions on how to remove them.

Chapter 18

Ten More Tools to Boost Your Privacy and Security

- -

In This Chapter

▶ Password management software

▶ Tools for removing spyware and cookies

▶ Patches and updates to prevent recent attack attempts

▶ Personal encryption software for e-mail messages and files

- -

*I*f you put all your security needs in one basket, you're bound for trouble. A single deadbolt lock on your front door won't defend your entire house, for example. In the same way, Norton Internet Security works best if you observe safe computing practices and install some useful security tools as supplements. Depending on NIS for all of your computer security needs because the program covers so many different types of threats is tempting. But the level of protection can be seriously deficient if you don't install software patches, for example.

A number of security programs can enhance your overall computer security. Some of them secure Windows; some duplicate the work of Privacy Control or AntiSpam; still others tackle security tasks from a new angle. All ten software tools will boost your privacy and cover security threats that NIS doesn't manage to catch.

Ad-Aware

This program by Lavasoft (www.lavasoftusa.com) is popular not just because it's free, but because it's an effective tool for detecting spyware: unwanted programs that can record your keystrokes or report on Web pages you visit back to an advertiser's Web site. Norton Privacy Control and AntiVirus aren't able to catch all spyware. For example, when AntiVirus conducted several automatic scans on my computer, a spyware program kept coming up in the results. But AntiVirus wasn't able to repair it. When I ran Ad-Aware, I turned up not only this software but an extensive list of other intrusive programs (see Figure 18-1). I used Ad-Aware to delete them all.

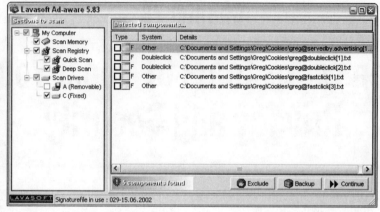

Figure 18-1:
Ad-Aware
scans
your disks
and the
Windows
registry for
spyware.

Windows Update

This program, which starts up automatically each time you start Windows, checks the Windows Update Web site for patches, updates, and add-ons to the current version of your operating system and related software like Internet Explorer and Outlook Express. If updates are available, a window pops up from your system tray to make you aware of it. Click on the window, and your browser connects to the site where the updates are available.

At any time, you can double-click the Windows Update icon in the system tray. When a dialog box called Automatic Updates appears, click Details to view descriptions of the updates that are available. Chances are good that one or more will be security updates designed to prevent attacks that have plagued other computer users. Some examples are shown in Figure 18-2.

Figure 18-2:
Install
security
patches to
keep your
operating
system from
being
attacked.

Pretty Good Privacy

This personal encryption program enables you to encrypt individual files and folders or your e-mail messages. The application uses an algorithm to generate a very large number called a *key*. The key is then used to encrypt information. After you have the key, you can exchange it with others so you can conduct encrypted e-mail correspondence.

Pretty Good Privacy (PGP) is available in two versions: a commercial version that you purchase and a free version available from the MIT Distribution Site for PGP (http://web.mit.edu/network/pgp.html). After you install the version for your operating system and restart your computer, PGP creates your own public and private key pair. You can then view your own PGP key on a "keyring" (see Figure 18-3) by double-clicking the PGPtray icon in the system tray.

Keep in mind that if you use the free version of PGP to encrypt files and then forget your key, you may not be able to decrypt those files. The commercial version of PGP entitles you to key escrow: Your key is saved in a safe location so you can recover it if it is lost.

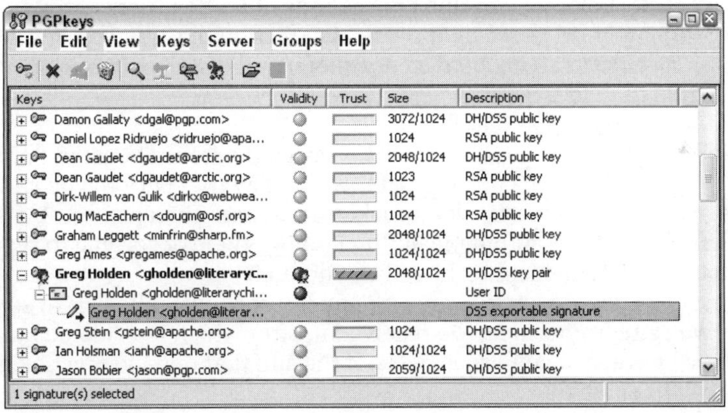

Figure 18-3:
PGP lets
you create
a public-
private key
pair that you
can use to
do your own
encryption.

Keys	Validity	Trust	Size	Description
Damon Gallaty <dgal@pgp.com>	○		3072/1024	DH/DSS public key
Daniel Lopez Ridruejo <ridruejo@apa...	○		1024	RSA public key
Dean Gaudet <dgaudet@arctic.org>	○		2048/1024	DH/DSS public key
Dean Gaudet <dgaudet@arctic.org>	○		1023	RSA public key
Dirk-Willem van Gulik <dirkx@webwea...	○		1024	RSA public key
Doug MacEachern <dougm@osf.org>	○		1024	RSA public key
Graham Leggett <minfrin@sharp.fm>	○		2048/1024	DH/DSS public key
Greg Ames <gregames@apache.org>	○		1024/1024	DH/DSS public key
Greg Holden <gholden@literaryc...	◉	▨▨▨	2048/1024	DH/DSS key pair
Greg Holden <gholden@literarychi...	○			User ID
Greg Holden <gholden@literar...				DSS exportable signature
Greg Stein <gstein@apache.org>	○		1024	DH/DSS public key
Ian Holsman <ianh@apache.org>	○		1024/1024	DH/DSS public key
Jason Bobier <jason@pgp.com>	○		2059/1024	DH/DSS public key

1 signature(s) selected

The commercial version of PGP is available at www.pgp.com. The freeware version provides a high level of security, however, and I suggest that you try it first.

MailWasher Pro

Norton AntiSpam catches most of your spam, but no spam blocker is perfect by itself. You can supplement its activities with MailWasher Pro (www.mailwasher.net), one of several Web-based services that process your e-mail before it gets to you. Such services are configured to recognize spam and remove it before it reaches your inbox — at least, you trust the service to delete the spam rather than any legitimate e-mails, and to keep as much spam as possible from reaching you.

MailWasher Pro is typical of such services, and it has the added pluses of having been around for several years. You can download the software and use it free for 30 days; if you decide to keep MailWasher Pro, you are required to pay $37.

Cookie Crusher

Norton Privacy Control doesn't always clean out all the cookies stored on your computer. (When I scanned my computer with Ad-Aware, the program listed at the beginning of this Part of Tens chapter, it uncovered five cookies.) To completely rid yourself of these bits of code that remote Web sites place on your computer, you need to download and install software specially designed to delete them.

One such program, Cookie Crusher, is available from The Limit Software (www.thelimitsoft.com/cookie). After the 30-day trial period, you can keep the program for a $15 fee. Cookie Crusher does more than just eliminate cookies either manually or automatically. It classifies them according to type and gives you the option of deciding how they should be handled. It also has the ability to make a cookie a session-only object: It lasts only while you're connected to the Web site from which you received it, after which it's deleted automatically. That way you can still use aspects of the site that depend on cookies.

Another cookie-crushing program, Cookie Pal, is available from Kookaburra Software (www.kburra.com/cpal.html). The program costs $15, but you can try it out for 30 days first.

Task Lock

Norton Parental Control has the ability to restrict Internet-related applications such as chat programs so your kids can't use them. But what if you don't want your kids to explore other applications on your computer, or view individual documents? In that case, you need to download a program like Task Lock. This program, by Posum LLC (www.posum.com/tasklock.html), enables you to lock individual folders and files or applications. That way, your kids can be deterred from exploring the family financial records or other documents you'd rather keep private. The program is available for $14.95.

Anonymizer

Anonymizer, a toolbar you install and add on to your Web browser's default set of toolbars, is available from Anonymizer.com (www.anonymizer.com). The program "erases" your computer's IP address as well as records of Web pages you have viewed before you connect to a particular Web site. It slows down your Web surfing somewhat, but it is able to hide information about you and your computer while you surf so remote Web sites can't trace you or follow your "footsteps" online.

Hijack This

This software is frequently recommended by security experts as an advanced diagnostic tool. Use it when you can't seem to remove a virus or other suspicious program with Norton Internet Security. The software scans your machine and produces a detailed list of all the potential spyware, as well as suspicious registry keys and programs that are configured to run when you start up your system. The program is available free from SpyChecker. com (www.spychecker.com/program/hijackthis.html).

The list of programs that Hijack This returns is typically long and very technical in appearance. Be careful about actually deleting something that you see on the list; it can be difficult to determine which items are potentially harmful, and which ones are necessary for your computer's operation. You can copy the list and paste it into a message you present on a newsgroup or an online resource like Google Answers (http://answers.google.com). Individuals who are experienced with computer security can evaluate the list and make you aware of any programs you need to delete — or at least explain what the programs do.

Password Officer

Passwords are difficult to maintain — at least good passwords that are complex and hard to crack. On the one hand, you're told to come up with a password that isn't a recognizable word, and that contains both special characters and numbers. On the other hand, you're told not to write down passwords or keep them on sticky notes affixed to your monitor.

If you want to manage your passwords, create secure passwords, and make sure you have different passwords for all the online services you use, consider a password management program like Password Officer by Compelson Labs (www.compelson.com/pofi.htm). This program creates passwords for you; you assign each password a numeric code. When you need to log in to a Web site, you enter the code (a simple, easy to remember number such as 1, 2, or 3) and tell the program to enter the corresponding password automatically.

ScreenLock Pro

Windows XP has a built-in screen saver password, and you should use it in order to protect your machine from being used without your permission while you're away. But that screen saver password is the same as your Windows password; if someone cracks, guesses, or otherwise obtains your logon password, they can quickly circumvent the screen saver password prompt.

A program called ScreenLock Pro, by iJen Software (www.screenlock.com), is available in a seven-day trial version. After the trial period, should you decide to keep the program, you can pay a $32.95 fee. You don't answer a password; you create a question that only you know the answer to (your mom's maiden name, for example). Whenever your screen is locked, you enter the answer to the original question to unlock it.

In order to make a screen saver password function correctly, you need to disable the optional boot control in your system — the function that enables your computer to boot up from a CD or DVD. Otherwise, someone can get around the screen saver by booting from a CD or DVD.

Right-click the desktop, choose Properties, and click the Screen Saver tab to start creating your Windows screen saver password. Select the box next to On Resume and then click OK. The next time the screen saver appears, you'll be prompted to enter the password, which is the same as your Windows logon password.

Chapter 19

Ten Security Threats NIS Doesn't Cover

Sometimes, all the obvious safety measures in the world can be thwarted by some hidden problem that no one foresaw. The Titanic, for example, was believed to be unsinkable and was equipped with many safety features of its time, but a single design flaw caused it to end up at the bottom of the ocean. Watertight compartments that were supposed to trap sea water were not built high enough; when one compartment flooded, the waters spread to adjacent ones.

Norton Internet Security protects your security and enhances your privacy in many ways. It blocks viruses, stops intrusions, and cuts down on spam. But it, too, can be circumvented by problems you don't see coming — problems you need to be aware of and take steps to prevent. This chapter includes ten examples of security weaknesses that you need to strengthen in order to keep NIS protecting you.

Children Signing Up for Services

My kids are fond of Web sites that offer points or virtual pets for playing games or performing simple tasks. In order to play the games they like, the Web sites require them to sign up for accounts. When my daughter asked for her own account at one online site, I was careful to guide her through the process, just to make sure she wasn't required to give out any information I didn't want her to release, such as our home address (which would probably result in more junk mail than we already receive) or phone number. It's true, Norton Internet Security should block such information from being transmitted to a Web site through its Privacy Control component. But kids should know enough not to give out such details in the first place — or to get permission before they do so.

I wanted to impress upon my kids the importance of guarding their personal contact information and being careful about who receives it. I strongly advise you to do the same. In many households, kids are more at ease with computers and the Web than their parents. They may already be visiting chat rooms and playing online games. Impress upon them the need to keep their personal information private to all but trusted friends, or they can quickly undo the safeguards you worked hard to put into place.

To its credit, the Neopets site my children love (`www.neopets.com`) asks adults to sign a consent form and fax it to their office before they will let the youngsters use it. Children are supposed to be at least 13 years of age in order to participate.

Deceptive E-Mail Messages

By now, you probably know that all of the e-mail messages you receive that ask you to sign up for something, verify your identity, notify you about a breach of security, or otherwise tempt you into clicking a link or an attachment are to be ignored. Even though Norton AntiSpam blocks most of these, some will still get through. And a few will look alarmingly legitimate. The other day, I received one that said my mortgage application had been approved, and I felt a moment's temptation to click the link supplied. Of course, I threw it in the trash when I realized that I hadn't applied for a mortgage lately.

If your kids sign up for online services and obtain their own e-mail accounts, they'll be receiving their own spam e-mail messages, with their own offers. Remember to tell your kids about the need to ignore such e-mail messages from people they don't recognize — not to click on links in the body of the message, and not to open attachments.

Weak or Nonexistent Passwords

Accessing nonsecure passwords is one of the easiest ways for hackers to get into remote systems. In Chapter 2, you found out about Norton Internet Security's capability of setting up separate user accounts for everyone who will be using your computer and accessing the Internet. It's easy to skip this step when you are first setting up the software. You can always create new accounts by clicking User Accounts in the main NIS window, then clicking Yes to run the Parental Control Wizard. You can then create accounts for your children or others who will be using the same machine. When you create passwords, be sure to use at least seven or eight characters, a mixture of letters and numerals, and to avoid recognizable words you can find in the dictionary.

Creating secure passwords is only one part of good password management. The other part is actually *using* passwords. When you're done using the Internet or your computer, log off: Open the main NIS window, click User Accounts, and click Log Off (see Figure 19-1).

Figure 19-1: Don't forget to log off so others can log on with their own security settings.

If you don't log off, your kids can go online with your own security settings, and you'll lose the benefit of any parental controls you have set for them.

Forgetting to Install Patches

Web browsers, as well as operating systems and servers, are continually receiving special software updates called *patches*. A patch is code that the program's developer releases in order to repair a bug or flaw in the program. Many of the most destructive worms, such as Code Red, were able to spread precisely because vulnerable software had not been patched by users.

When you start up your computer, it's easy to ignore the notice from Windows Update that tells you new software is available. The new software may include patches as well as other updates. Take the time to install the new software, and you'll help Norton Internet Security protect your computer that much more effectively.

Although Windows Update automatically checks for system updates on Windows XP and other recent versions of the operating system, you can also install and run a program called HFNetChk, which Microsoft provides. HFNetChk is designed to scan local or remotely networked computers for available patches. You can download this software at `www.microsoft.com/technet/security/tools/hfnetchk.mspx`.

Failing to Encrypt Personal Information

Encryption sounds like something secret agents or security agencies do. But it's something you should do, too, whenever you submit information to a remote Web site. Encryption is the process of using a mathematical formula or other method to render information unreadable to all but the people who are intended to read it.

Although you can obtain software such as Pretty Good Privacy (`www.pgp.com`) that enables you to encrypt e-mail messages and other digital information, you don't have to go to such lengths to make use of encryption. You don't have to learn any complex formulas or even obtain files called digital certificates, which use encryption to certify your identity when you communicate online. It's much simpler than that: Just make sure your Web browser's security icon is in the "locked" or closed position when you submit information to a Web site. Web sites that permit visitors to exchange encrypted data handle the encoding for you by directing your submission to a server that uses Secure Sockets Layer (SSL) security. When you're connected to a secure server, the security icon appears "locked." Both Netscape Navigator and Microsoft Internet Explorer use an icon in the status bar that looks like a padlock to signify that you are connected to a server that uses encryption. When the lock appears to be "closed," as shown in Figure 19-2, you can safely submit information to the remote Web site. Always check this icon and refrain from submitting your information if the lock does not appear or appears "unlocked."

You should also confirm whether your Web browser is configured to use the latest version of Secure Sockets Layer (SSL), the form of encryption used by most Web sites. Follow these steps to check for SSL support for Internet Explorer:

1. **Start up Internet Explorer and, from the Internet Explorer menu bar, choose Tools⇨Internet Options.**

   The Internet Options dialog box opens.

2. **Click Advanced.**

   The Advanced tab jumps to the front.

3. **Scroll down to the Security section.**

   A series of check boxes and security options is displayed (see Figure 19-3).

4. **Make sure the SSL 2.0 and SSL 3.0 boxes are checked, then click OK.**

   The Internet Options dialog box closes and you return to the Internet Explorer window.

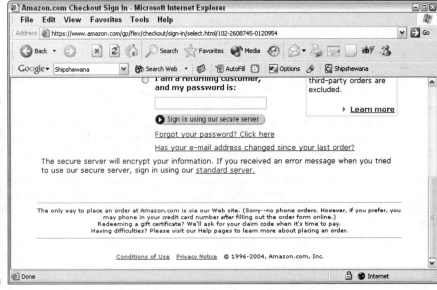

Figure 19-2:
If you don't see the "closed lock" icon, don't fill out a form or submit your personal information online.

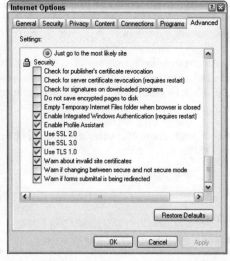

Figure 19-3:
Make sure
your
browser is
configured
to use the
latest
version of
Secure
Sockets
Layer
encryption.

Turning Off the Firewall

With all the protections described in this book, it may seem obvious that
you need to have your firewall turned on while you're connected to the Net
and surfing Web sites. But some legitimate reasons exist for turning off your
firewall:

- ✔ If you're trying to determine why you can't view content on a Web site,
  or why you're having trouble connecting to a Web server or FTP server

- ✔ If a program you want to use to connect to a Web site, such as an audio
  player, isn't working because the firewall is blocking it

Remember that after you conduct your test, enable the firewall again. Right-
click the Norton Internet Security icon in the system tray and choose Enable
to start the firewall up again.

Only users who have Supervisor status can disable Norton Internet Security.
If the currently logged-in user has a child, teenager, or adult account, you
won't be able to turn off the firewall. You'll need to log out and log in again
with your own account.

Forgetting to Opt Out

Virtually every online store or other Web site that conducts commerce online includes a privacy statement for its users. Such a statement spells out how the company plans to collect information from its customers and how it will be used. Some (though not all) statements give customers the chance to "opt out" of promotions or mailings. By opting out, you tell the Web site that they are not to send you junk e-mail or sign you up for newsletters or other promotions you don't want.

Be sure you read such fine print. A friend who signed me up for a "free ticket" movie service neglected to read the privacy policy in detail. It stated that, by agreeing to the privacy policy, the site would have the right to share e-mail addresses with other businesses and send you unsolicited e-mail whenever it liked. Months later, I'm still receiving spam e-mails from this site (which Norton AntiSpam is automatically throwing in its trash folder).

The group PrivacyExchange.org has a particularly good example of a privacy statement at www.privacyexchange.org. The publication *Privacy Journal* provides readers with suggestions about what a strong, consumer-oriented privacy statement should include; find out more at www.privacyjournal.net/newsletter.htm.

Not Being Careful about Where You Shop

All Web-based stores are not created equal. Some meet privacy and consumer safety requirements, and some are interested in supplementing their income from sales by selling their customers' contact information to marketers. In the United States, companies that are committed to consumer-friendly privacy practices are monitored by the Better Business Bureau (BBB). The online arm of this organization, BBB Online (www.bbbonline.org), provides a logo that indicates that a Web site has made a commitment to protect customers' privacy. This logo, the Privacy and Reliability Seal, is a good indication that this is a place where you should shop.

Another organization, TRUSTe (www.truste.org), requires companies that want to display its logo (or *trustmark*) on their Web sites to have a privacy statement and give customers the chance to opt out of marketing efforts. Make an effort to support commercial Web sites that display such logos.

Disgruntled Employees

Who has access to sensitive information about consumers and the ability to access it easily, without having to resort to hacking software? Current or former employees who have a grudge against the company or higher management. As I write this, I'm looking at a ViewSonic computer monitor. In February 2003, the U.S. Department of Justice arrested a former employee of ViewSonic for allegedly hacking into the company computer network, logging into a database server using employee passwords, and erasing an estimated $1 million worth of information.

Employees who have been terminated or who are unhappy over not receiving raises are prime candidates for exacting revenge on the company by stealing computer information. Whenever someone is fired, be sure to delete his or her account information and change any remote access phone numbers or other information the person might use to connect to the network from home. Also make sure, if you are in a work environment, that employees keep their login passwords secret from one another.

Misusing Company Resources

Another security problem that can plague you is the use of office computers for personal purposes. Most companies have rules that govern whether you can send and receive e-mail, surf the Web, or otherwise connect to the Internet from the workplace. Be very careful whether or not you do this: The company has the right to monitor the use of its e-mail servers, for example. If you reveal sensitive information about upcoming projects or financial accounts in e-mail messages, you can face disciplinary action.

You can, of course, get around such restrictions by bringing your own laptop to work and connecting to the Net either wirelessly or by plugging your computer modem into the phone. But this can cause your dismissal and potentially compromise your network as well, especially if you connect your laptop to your computer network, or if you transfer files that have been infected to your work computer. The lesson is to make sure you know what you can and can't do on the office network, make sure your home computer is protected with Norton Internet Security when you use it to connect to the network, and separate home and work cyberactivities as much as possible.

Part VII
Appendixes

The 5th Wave   By Rich Tennant

"Hey Philip! I think we're in. I'm gonna try linking directly to the screen, but gimme a disguise in case it works. I don't want all of New York to know Jerry DeMarco of 14 Queensberry, Bronx NY, hacked into the Times Square video screen."

In this part . . .

Computer security has its own lingo which often bears little resemblance to the language spoken by most people. Terms like *flags* and *signatures* mean something different when it comes to firewalls and intrusion attempts.

This part of the book presents supplementary information that you can refer to as you read the chapters or as you work with Norton Internet Security. You'll find a glossary of terms used in connection with computer security, and a list of security-related Web sites that can make you more aware of the latest threats as well as other security and privacy issues.

Appendix A

Glossary

● ●

Back door: A computer, program, or other resource that can be accessed through an undocumented or unauthorized opening (such as a port).

Buffer overflow: An event that occurs when an application attempts to store more information than the temporary disk storage area that has been assigned to the application can handle. A limited amount of data can be stored by a program or process in a buffer or temporary disk storage area. In a buffer overflow attack, the extra data may contain executable code that is designed to perform unauthorized functions on a victim's computer.

Cache: An area of a hard drive where temporary files are stored (or *cached*). This term also can refer to the act of storing data on a disk for possible later retrieval.

Covert channel: A concealed or invisible communications channel such as a port on a computer or a network connection that enables a hacker to compromise the security of a computer.

Crackers: People who crack or uncover passwords and remove copy protection from software.

Deface: The act of hackers leaving messages on Web sites to announce they've been there.

Destination port: A virtual communications channel where a computer receives data from another computer.

Digital certificate: Public and private keys can be exchanged via this electronic document that is issued by a certification authority and contains information about the certificate holder.

Digital signature: An encryption process is used to generate a series of numbers and characters. The encrypted code, along with other identifying information, creates a digital signature. The signature verifies the identity of its owner, and it can be time-stamped and easily transported.

Distributed Denial of Service (DDoS) attack: An attack in which a Web site server or other computer is flooded with requests from multiple hijacked computers.

DNS spoofing: A hacking technique in which a hacker is able to control a DNS server by causing it to behave as if a domain has a different IP address range than it actually does have.

Domain Name Server (DNS): A server that resolves IP addresses into domain names, and vice versa.

Encryption: The process of making information unreadable to anyone who is not an intended recipient through a process of concealing information.

File Transfer Protocol (FTP): A communications method especially designed for transferring data from one computer to another on a TCP/IP network such as the Internet.

Firewall appliance: A hardware device that has firewall functionality.

Flag: A bit of digital information within a packet sent via Transmission Control Protocol (TCP) that tells the receiving computer what part of a connection is being attempted.

Forensics: An investigatory process used to determine the identity of a hacker when unauthorized access to a system is attempted. Authorities can use data retrieval and analysis from the process to help prosecute a case.

Fragment: One of the packets within a sequence of TCP/IP packets that makes up a whole communication.

Fragmentation: A single IP packet is divided into multiple packets, each of which is a fragment.

Hacker: A computer user or programmer who uses methods such as circum-venting passwords, sending viruses by e-mail, or other attempts to gain access to unauthorized resources on a network.

HTTP Cookie: A short segment of HTML code placed by a server on a visitor's Web browser so the Web server can identify the user when another visit is made.

HyperText Transport Protocol (HTTP): A TCP/IP communications method that, by convention, uses port 80 to transfer data between a Web server and a Web browser.

Internet Control Message Protocol (ICMP): A protocol that functions as a housekeeper for TCP/IP. It is used to "ping" other computers to verify that they are on the network, or to produce alert messages when a network or computer is unreachable.

Intrusion: When an unauthorized attempt is made to gain access to network resources and compromise the integrity and confidentiality of the data contained on the network or the privacy of its owners.

Intrusion Detection: The process of monitoring network traffic so that administrators can be alerted and blocking efforts can be made if unauthorized access to a system or resource is attempted.

IP spoofing: The act of placing a false address into a packet's header that makes it harder to trace the packet back to its source.

Key: A long block of encrypted code that results from a mathematical formula (algorithm) being applied to a text string. The longer the key, the harder it is to crack and the stronger the level of encryption.

Log files: A record of information kept by firewalls and other security applications. The log file is used to identify computers that accessed resources on the server and when access was attempted or blocked.

Man-in-the-middle attack: An attack in which part of a data session is intercepted so a hacker can control the data being exchanged.

Packet analyzer: Software or hardware that monitors traffic going in or out of a network device, capturing information about each TCP/IP packet detected.

Packets: Segments of digital information that are of uniform length, and contain header information and a data payload. Dividing a transmission into packets ensures reliable communication on a computer network.

Ping sweep: A reconnaissance attempt to see if any computers respond when a series of ICMP Echo Request packets are sent in a range of IP addresses.

Port scan: Reconnaissance that attempts to see if any computers are active and listening by connecting to their ports, one after another.

Private key: A block of encoded information that is obtained from an encryption authority and that is not shared with anyone else. The private key is used to generate a public key.

Public key: A public key is created with a private key and given to others in order to conduct secure communications. The public key can be used to verify the authenticity of a message signed with your private key.

Public key cryptography: A form of secure network communications commonly conducted on the World Wide Web and that involves the exchange of public keys that are generated by private keys.

Quarantine: An area of disk storage where viruses and other malicious code or infected files are placed so they can't replicate themselves or damage other files.

Rule base: A set of rules that tells a firewall whether packets should pass through or be dropped.

Script kiddies: Young people who spread malicious scripts (including viruses) and try to find where computer systems are weak.

Server: A computer that provides Web pages, e-mail, or other services to individuals both inside and outside the network being protected.

Signatures: Identifications of a particular type of network traffic (for example, source or destination IP address, protocol, combination of features).

Social engineering: Tricking others into revealing passwords or other sensitive information.

Source port: The port that sends data from one computer to another.

Worm: A virus that occupies disk space by repeatedly copying itself.

Appendix B

Web Resources

• •

*I*ntrusion Detection and network security are all constantly evolving fields these days. In order to keep up with the latest developments in the field, you should visit the Web sites and other resources mentioned in this section. Many of the sites contain information not only about incident response, but they also present white papers, research papers, and other background information on topics like firewalls, packet filtering, authentication, and encryption, among other things.

Viruses and Security Incidents

The following Web sites specialize in information about Intrusion Detection and how to respond to security incidents if they occur. If you encounter an intrusion attempt, a virus, or a worm, go to one of these sites to see if other systems have been affected, and read about countermeasures you should take.

Symantec Security Response

www.securityresponse.symantec.com

This Web site includes information about viruses, Trojan horses, and other malicious code. It also offers an extensive database of viruses that have been reported to Symantec and that have been accounted for in the company's antivirus software. Additional information exists about security incidents, but the focus is protecting against and eliminating viruses and other harmful code.

Whitehats Network Security Resource

www.whitehats.com

Whitehats is a community of network and computer professionals interested in open-source and free software approaches. Recent security incident and news headlines can be found on this home page. There is also an archNIDS database (www.whitehats.com/ids) of Intrusion Detection signatures.

Incidents.org

www.incidents.org

A Web site affiliated with the well-known security organization SANS, the main focus of this site is intrusions, incidents, and security alerts. Information is also included on how to respond. Called the "Internet Storm Center," the site indicates by geographic region types of security breaches that have been reported. There is also data on current attack trends, such as ports that have been attacked most often, and malicious software that has been reported.

Dshield.org

www.dshield.org

Home of the Distributed Intrusion Detection System, network administrators from around the world share firewall and intrusion detection log information in an effort to track attack patterns. The site provides lists of the Top 10 ports that have been attacked recently as well as the Top 10 computers from which attacks have originated.

Security Organizations

The following Web sites provide you with general information about Internet and network security.

SANS Institute

www.sans.org

The mission of the System Administration, Networking and Security (SANS) Institute, a research and education organization, is to convey information about network security. SANS conducts seminars and workshops on security, and provides tests to prepare for important certifications like the CISSP. The SANS Web site includes links to important resources such as a list of the Twenty Most Critical Internet Security Vulnerabilities (`www.sans.org/top20.htm`), and the SANS Security Policy Project (`www.sans.org/resources/policies`), which contains sample security policies plus guidelines for producing them.

The CERT Coordination Center

www.cert.org

The CERT Coordination Center is affiliated with Carnegie-Mellon University. The Web site contains lists of security alerts, incident notes, and vulnerabilities on its home page. CERT also offers tips and articles about aspects of network security plus training courses. The intended audience includes corporate and educational users as well as home users.

FIRST

www.first.org

The Forum of Incident Response and Security Teams (FIRST) is a consortium of security incident response teams working in government, commercial, and academic organizations that seeks to promote rapid reaction to security incidents by coordinating communication and sharing information among its members. If you are part of an incident response team, you should strongly consider joining FIRST and attending periodic technical colloquia. Members discuss their successes and failures by sharing technical data about attacks and experiences with security software and hardware.

Newsletters and Mailing Lists

Remembering to visit sites like Incidents.org to find out about the latest security alerts can be difficult. Sometimes, it's easier to absorb current information if it's sent to your e-mail inbox. Here are a couple of suggested mailing lists and newsletters you can subscribe to in order to keep up with the threats you need to combat.

NTBugtraq

www.ntbugtraq.com

The name refers to Windows NT, but this well known and highly regarded mailing list covers security issues pertaining to Windows 2000 and XP as well. Its mission is to share information about security exploits and bugs that affect Windows systems.

Firewall-Wizards mailing list

http://honor.trusecure.com/mailman/listinfo/firewall-wizards

This closely moderated mailing list deals with security issues, generally, as well as firewall-related issues, in particular. You can subscribe to a regular (one e-mail message at a time) or digest (one consolidated e-mail message per day) version of the list. You can investigate specific topics that have already been discussed on searchable archives.

SecurityFocus HOME mailing lists

http://online.securityfocus.com/archive

SecurityFocus operates a variety of security-related mailing lists on topics ranging from Intrusion Detection to firewalls. You can either investigate specific issues and topics for free or join a list to receive current news and views on a daily basis.

SC Magazine

www.infosecnews.com

This site provides a news service that you can view on the Web or receive as an e-mail newsletter. News items are obtained from around the world.

Index

• *O* •

• *P* •

Notes

FOR DUMMIES®

The easy way to get more done and have more fun

...SONAL FINANCE & BUSINESS

Investing FOR DUMMIES

0-7645-2431 3

Home Buying FOR DUMMIES
2nd Edition

Eric Tyson
A Reference for the Rest of Us!

0-7645-5331-3

Grant Writing FOR DUMMIES

Bev Browning
A Reference for the Rest of Us!

0-7645-5307-0

Also available:

Accounting For Dummies
(0-7645-5314-3)

Business Plans Kit For Dummies
(0-7645-5365-8)

Managing For Dummies
(1-5688-4858-7)

Mutual Funds For Dummies
(0-7645-5329-1)

QuickBooks All-in-One Desk Reference For Dummies
(0-7645-1963-8)

Resumes For Dummies
(0-7645-5471-9)

Small Business Kit For Dummies
(0-7645-5093-4)

Starting an eBay Business For Dummies
(0-7645-1547-0)

Taxes For Dummies 2003
(0-7645-5475-1)

...ME, GARDEN, FOOD & WINE

Feng Shui FOR DUMMIES
A Reference for the Rest of Us!

...7645-5295-3

Gardening FOR DUMMIES
2nd Edition
A Reference for the Rest of Us!

0-7645-5130-2

Cooking FOR DUMMIES
2nd Edition
A Reference for the Rest of Us!

0-7645-5250-3

Also available:

Bartending For Dummies
(0-7645-5051-9)

Christmas Cooking For Dummies
(0-7645-5407-7)

Cookies For Dummies
(0-7645-5390-9)

Diabetes Cookbook For Dummies
(0-7645-5230-9)

Grilling For Dummies
(0-7645-5076-4)

Home Maintenance For Dummies
(0-7645-5215-5)

Slow Cookers For Dummies
(0-7645-5240-6)

Wine For Dummies
(0-7645-5114-0)

...ESS, SPORTS, HOBBIES & PETS

Fitness FOR DUMMIES
2nd Edition
...ference for the Rest of Us!

...7645-5167-1

Golf FOR DUMMIES
2nd Edition

Gary McCord
A Reference for the Rest of Us!

0-7645-5146-9

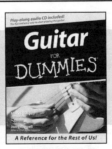

Guitar FOR DUMMIES
Play-along audio CD included!
A Reference for the Rest of Us!

0-7645-5106-X

Also available:

Cats For Dummies
(0-7645-5275-9)

Chess For Dummies
(0-7645-5003-9)

Dog Training For Dummies
(0-7645-5286-4)

Labrador Retrievers For Dummies
(0-7645-5281-3)

Martial Arts For Dummies
(0-7645-5358-5)

Piano For Dummies
(0-7645-5105-1)

Pilates For Dummies
(0-7645-5397-6)

Power Yoga For Dummies
(0-7645-5342-9)

Puppies For Dummies
(0-7645-5255-4)

Quilting For Dummies
(0-7645-5118-3)

Rock Guitar For Dummies
(0-7645-5356-9)

Weight Training For Dummies
(0-7645-5168-X)

...ble wherever books are sold.
www.dummies.com or call 1-877-762-2974 to order direct

WILEY

FOR DUMMIES®

A world of resources to help you grow

TRAVEL

0-7645-5453-0

0-7645-5438-7

0-7645-5444-1

Also available:

America's National Parks For Dummies
(0-7645-6204-5)

Caribbean For Dummies
(0-7645-5445-X)

Cruise Vacations For Dummies 2003
(0-7645-5459-X)

Europe For Dummies
(0-7645-5456-5)

Ireland For Dummies
(0-7645-6199-5)

France For Dummies
(0-7645-6292-4)

Las Vegas For Dummies
(0-7645-5448-4)

London For Dummies
(0-7645-5416-6)

Mexico's Beach Resorts For Dummies
(0-7645-6262-2)

Paris For Dummies
(0-7645-5494-8)

RV Vacations For Dummie
(0-7645-5443-3)

EDUCATION & TEST PREPARATION

0-7645-5194-9

0-7645-5325-9

0-7645-5249-X

Also available:

The ACT For Dummies
(0-7645-5210-4)

Chemistry For Dummies
(0-7645-5430-1)

English Grammar For Dummies
(0-7645-5322-4)

French For Dummies
(0-7645-5193-0)

GMAT For Dummies
(0-7645-5251-1)

Inglés Para Dummies
(0-7645-5427-1)

Italian For Dummies
(0-7645-5196-5)

Research Papers For Dum
(0-7645-5426-3)

SAT I For Dummies
(0-7645-5472-7)

U.S. History For Dummies
(0-7645-5249-X)

World History For Dumm
(0-7645-5242-2)

HEALTH, SELF-HELP & SPIRITUALITY

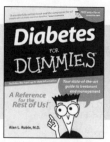

0-7645-5154-X

0-7645-5302-X

0-7645-5418-2

Also available:

The Bible For Dummies
(0-7645-5296-1)

Controlling Cholesterol For Dummies
(0-7645-5440-9)

Dating For Dummies
(0-7645-5072-1)

Dieting For Dummies
(0-7645-5126-4)

High Blood Pressure For Dummies
(0-7645-5424-7)

Judaism For Dummies
(0-7645-5299-6)

Menopause For Dummie
(0-7645-5458-1)

Nutrition For Dummies
(0-7645-5180-9)

Potty Training For Dumr
(0-7645-5417-4)

Pregnancy For Dummie
(0-7645-5074-8)

Rekindling Romance Fo Dummies
(0-7645-5303-8)

Religion For Dummies
(0-7645-5264-3)

Available wherever books are sold. Go to www.dummies.com or call 1-877-762-2974 to order direct